The Next
Three
Futures

The NEXT
THREE
FUTURES

Paradigms of Things to Come

W. WARREN WAGAR

Foreword by Edward Cornish

PRAEGER

New York
Westport, Connecticut
London

Library of Congress Cataloging-in-Publication Data

Wagar, W. Warren.
   The next three futures : paradigms of things to come / W. Warren
Wagar ; foreword by Edward Cornish.
     p. cm.
   Includes bibliographical references and index.
   ISBN 0–275–94049–7 (alk. paper)
    1. Forecasting. 2. Twenty-first century—Forecasts. I. Title.
  II. Title: Next 3 futures.
   CB158.W34   1991
   303.48′2′0905—dc20   91–8277

British Library Cataloguing in Publication Data is available.

A hardcover edition of *The Next Three Futures* is available from the
Greenwood Press imprint of Greenwood Publishing Group, Inc. (Contributions
in Sociology, Number 98; ISBN 0–313–26528–3)

Library of Congress Catalog Card Number: 91–8277
ISBN: 0–275–94049–7

First published in 1991

Praeger Publishers, One Madison Avenue, New York, NY   10010
An imprint of Greenwood Publishing Group, Inc.

Printed in the United States of America

The paper used in this book complies with the
Permanent Paper Standard issued by the National
Information Standards Organization (Z39.48–1984).

10 9 8 7 6 5 4 3 2 1

TO MY GRADUATE TEACHING ASSISTANTS,
who have done most of the work

Contents

Foreword

Edward Cornish
President, World Future Society
Editor, *The Futurist*

The study of the future is, strictly speaking, the study of ideas about the future, because the future itself does not exist. The fact that we can only study ideas rather than concrete objects makes the study of the future seem questionable to many material-minded people. But a moment's reflection reveals the enormous importance of ideas in our lives. It was ideas that brought Columbus to America. Ideas inspired the technological wonders that we see around us. Ideas shaped the United States and other great nations. Quite simply, ideas are the blueprints that we use to create the world of tomorrow and of each succeeding tomorrow.

Ideas about the longer-term future can fill our minds with hope, give us a sense of purpose, and inspire us to work constructively for human betterment. But we must be thoughtful about the ideas that we choose as guides because the wrong ideas can mislead us, perhaps by filling us with unhealthy dread or making us feel that nothing we do is worthwhile. Happily, this book can help readers to be selective about the ideas they hold concerning the future as well as to understand more clearly what the study of the future is all about.

As this book makes clear, we do not study the future so that we can know in advance just what is going to happen, but rather to create a better future for ourselves and for others. The future is not a distant place that we can see if we have a very powerful telescope, but a place that no one can see, no matter how powerful their telescopes, because it does not exist until it is created. Furthermore, we ourselves will do much of the creating, using the resources at our disposal, including especially those resources of knowledge and wisdom and imagination that we carry about in our brains.

Remarkably accurate predictions can be made about many phenomena in the natural world—for example, the exact time of an eclipse of the sun twenty years in the future—and many people think that similarly precise and accurate predictions should be possible for human activities and events. But heavenly bodies do not have minds of their own, and we do. At every moment, we make decisions to do this or not do that, and these choices change not only our own circumstances but even influence in some degree the whole world around us. Thus our future is fundamentally undecided, and therefore unpredictable. And we should all be grateful for that, because a future that could not be changed would hardly be a future at all: We would be nothing but inanimate gears in a mindless clockwork.

Our power as ordinary people to influence the future of the world at large has recently received unexpected support from the mathematicians and computer scientists studying chaos—the random behavior that appears in such things as the movement of water molecules coming through a faucet. The scientists studying chaos talk about the "butterfly effect"—the fact that a tiny action such as the movement of a butterfly's wing can have enormous effects on a complex and apparently random system. This means that when we as individuals make choices we are inevitably making choices for all of the human race. This knowledge should give us all an added sense of responsibility for what we do.

To discharge that responsibility, we need to become more knowledgeable about the choices open to us. We all are likely to make important choices thoughtlessly, doing whatever seems easiest or most immediately beneficial to us. This tendency to make choices for short-term personal pleasure regardless of the longer-term consequences has become accentuated in recent decades because of the decline of the traditional family, community, and religious influences which sought to keep individuals from behaving contrary to their longer-term interests. As the traditional constraints of society have weakened, television has successfully influenced people to focus on satisfying their momentary personal cravings. Television tells us, again and again, "You deserve a treat today" and "Be good to yourself" as if it were only concerned for our happiness, but these insidious messages are, of course, actually motivated by the sponsors' desire to sell goods, and the results are often bad for both ourselves and those around us over the long term.

Short-term thinking aimed at immediate benefits to oneself or one's class has, of course, always been a major obstacle to the creation of a better future world, but perhaps never more so than in today's individualistic, media-filled environment. Still, there are many reasons for hope. People everywhere now are aware that the rapid pace of social and technological change requires that they become more aware of current trends and where they may lead. Moreover, there are impressive efforts underway to require our institutions to consider the longer-term consequences of their actions. For instance, Congress now has an Office of Technology Assessment, which produces an important stream of reports evaluating how various technologies may impact on our lives. Congress then can determine which technologies should be encouraged—and which discouraged—through legislation. In addition, Senator Albert Gore has introduced a bill in Congress to establish an Office of Critical Trends and Analysis in the White House to advise the president on matters related to the longer-term future.

There is a significant movement among enlightened educators to make the study of the future part of the curriculum in colleges and universities. This new book by an outstanding scholar will greatly enhance those efforts because it provides an excellent textbook for courses dealing with the future. The volume is up-to-date, authoritative, and readable, since Professor Wagar brings to the subject deep understanding, long experience in teaching, and a clear and concise literary style.

Acknowledgments

It is a pleasure to thank the people who have mattered most in the writing and publishing of this book. First, a special thanks to all my students at SUNY Binghamton in "History of the Future," "World War III," and "Alternative Futures." Without your stimulus and encouragement, this book would surely not exist. Teaching you has taught me.

Warm appreciation is also owed to the many superb graduate assistants in the Department of History who have eased my burden in these courses. Together, since 1974, they have conducted thousands of weekly discussion meetings, graded thousands of papers and examinations, and made all the difference to our students. Thank you, everybody! I dedicate *The Next Three Futures*, with deep gratitude, to you.

Three futurist friends took valuable time to read this book in manuscript and give me the benefit of their reactions and advice. Many thanks go to Dr. Michael Marien, founder and editor of *Future Survey*; Dr. Lane Jennings, production editor of *Future Survey*; and Edward Cornish, founder and president of the World Future Society, who also very kindly agreed to write the Foreword. None of these good people bears any responsibility for my errors or misjudgments, but I appreciate all their help.

I am grateful, too, for the assistance of Professor Howard F. Didsbury, Jr., who has been my editor on many occasions, and is now the Coordinator of Prep 21, a project of the World Future Society initiated by Dr. Marien. The goal of Prep 21 is to build a worldwide network of secondary and college teachers of futures studies. Interested faculty should write to Professor Didsbury at the World Future Society, 4916 Saint Elmo Avenue, Bethesda, Maryland 20814, U.S.A.

Finally, a word of thanks to Dr. James T. Sabin, executive vice president of Greenwood Publishing Group, for his interest and support from the earliest days of this project.

W. Warren Wagar
Vestal, New York

Prologue: Teaching the Future

In 1973, I had been a college history teacher for nearly sixteen years and had published four books on visions of the human future.[1] I taught a variety of graduate and undergraduate courses in modern European intellectual history. My students were sharp and select, my classes were small, and life was good. Although my research had little to do with my teaching, such is often the case in academe.

Nevertheless, in that year, the fateful thought came to me that it might be possible to combine what I did in the classroom with what I did at the typewriter (in those distant days, a venerable manual machine made of steel). Why not teach a course about the future?

The result, in the spring term of 1974, was "History of the Future," a lightning survey of the last six thousand and a more leisurely exploration of the next two hundred years of world history. We enrolled more than one hundred students, the most I had ever taught in an upper-division course. In the following academic year I was on leave with a research grant, but the second edition of "History of the Future," offered in the fall of 1975, lured an even larger number. The course continued to grow. Eventually I was teaching as many as 450 students with a staff of nine graduate assistants to handle the weekly discussion sections and the grading of essay examinations. "History of the Future" had become a monster.

But a pleasant monster. The fusion of my scholarly and teaching interests had a quickening effect on both. All at once, my research became teachable, and my teaching inspired further research. It was a new—and rejuvenating—experience.

Nor was this the end of the story. I added other futures courses to my repertoire. My undergraduate European intellectual history course became an inquiry into utopian and dystopian images in modern thought. Another offering, taught every few years, was a senior seminar in methods of futures research, reserved for students who had already taken "History of the Future." In the spring of 1983, I also introduced "World War III," a yearly lecture course on the prospects for war and peace. In short order "World War III" (re-dubbed "War and the Future" in 1991) was drawing almost as many registrants as "History of the Future."

It should go without saying (but I will say it anyway) that many American undergraduates enter certain large lecture courses not because they care about the subject matter, but simply because the classes are easy to cut and if one is glib and clever, he or she can acquire at least a passing grade without much work. No doubt I have attracted my share of such enrollees, despite systematic efforts to weed them out. I am also well aware of my limitations as a teacher. I am not a spellbinder, not an evangelist, not even particularly warm or accessible.

No. What makes these courses work, and what brought them such large enrollments in the first place, is their content. A generous fraction of American college students, and of the whole literate population, wants to know what the world is coming to. They want to know what to expect of the time in which they, and their children, and their children's children, will spend the rest of their lives. They want to know if they can help make the future better than it might otherwise be. Most college courses are devoted to examinations of things past and present, which by strict definition we are powerless to affect. Only the future lies open to human enterprise. Only the future can be changed.

Some disciplines represented in the curriculum do study the future. Established programs in environmental studies, peace and war studies, policy studies, macroeconomics, technology assessment, and several other fields investigate future possibilities as a matter of course, as an intrinsic part of their work. But few attempts are made to connect the findings of each field to the findings of the others. Holistic visions of the future are rare in the college classroom, and rarer still in research.

So there is an urgent need, I believe, for a field of inquiry more integrative than any of these. Fortunately, such a field already exists, at least in embryo. Nowadays, we usually call it "futures studies." Drawing liberally on the work of scholars from scores of disciplines, its professed practitioners are still relatively few in number. The latest edition of *The Futures Research Directory* published by the World Future Society lists almost 1,200 individuals from around the world, but many of them would not describe themselves primarily as futurists.[2] Many other scholars who have played a major role in shaping our views of the future—such as Paul Ehrlich, Julian Simon, Richard Falk, and Dennis and Donella Meadows—are not even included. It is a curious "field" of study that relies more on the work of outsiders than on its own would-be disciplinarians.

Yet perhaps this is as it should be. Futures inquiry is still very young.

We are still finding our way. In any case, if our job is more one of synthesis than of original research, it is appropriate and even essential to cast our nets as widely as possible. For better or worse, this is surely what I do in my courses and what I have done in *The Next Three Futures,* a brief summing-up of the progress of futures studies over the past quarter-century and more.

Most products in our enlightened age of consumer protection carry warning labels. Before we get to the first chapter, let me also stick one or two on *The Next Three Futures,* with special reference to the criticisms voiced in an essay published in 1988 in the journal *Change.* The author was Marshall W. Gregory, a professor of English at Butler University. Reviewing a major publication of the World Future Society, he seized the occasion to rake the whole futurist enterprise with scornful fire.[3]

Conceding that futurists were well-intentioned, Gregory also found them wrong-headed, self-deluding, and hopelessly confused. In essence, his critique reduced to three salient points. First, he argued that futures studies proceed from incompatible methodologies. Second, he deplored the claim of futurists to know something that cannot be known—to wit, the future. And third, he warned that too much thinking about the future may unwittingly serve "sinister programs" (like fascism or communism) that devalue the present for the sake of hypothetical future bliss and divert us from addressing the real problems of our own time.

Elaborating on the first point, Gregory observed that futurists employ at least three different ways of reading the future, each strictly at odds with the other. They engage in "everyday planning" of the commonsensical sort that all of us must do; they attempt sophisticated forecasting based on the correlation of statistical data; and they borrow the visionary styles of poetry and religious prophecy.

There is no way, Gregory insisted, to mesh these methods of inquiry. "The fact that professional futurists tend to lump together all these modes of forecasting and call them knowledge—or at least research—may help to explain why so much future studies work seems oddly, if not downright whimsically, dissonant."[4] One might as well toss lettuce and chocolate and cheese into a blender and call the resulting chaos a "dish."

Worse still, futurists imagined that they had actually created a "science,"which produced "knowledge" of things to come. Nothing, said Gregory, could be further from the truth. Not only was the futurists' goulash of methods no basis for a true science, but cognition of what has not yet happened and thus cannot be observed was literally impossible. Gregory concluded by challenging futurists to forget their obsession with imaginary worlds. Take the present seriously, he urged. As Thoreau tended his bean patch, let us tend ours, and refrain from subverting our present with pointless fret and anxiety about hypothetical times to come.

Not a bad case, you might say. Is there really such a thing as the future? Can it be known? And if so, can our study be a science, or at least scientific?

In a subsequent issue of *Change,* four professional futurists wrote letters responding to Gregory's assault.[5] Without trying to recapitulate their arguments, it is enough to say that Gregory was right about the future, and wrong about futurists. Right in pointing to the limitations of futures inquiry. Wrong in supposing that most futures-oriented scholars are unaware of them.

On the question of methodologies, there can be no argument. Let the reader beware! Futurists, as we have just noticed, take their ideas from many sources. They have not so far succeeded in integrating their various methods of study into anything like a coherent whole. Of course futures studies are not alone in this rather wild eclecticism. Historians, for example, engage in narrative story-telling, rigorous quantitative analysis, model-building, close textual criticism, and psychoanalysis of the dead. Some even write works of historical fiction. The *Methodenstreit*, or battle over methods, between humanists and quantifiers in every social science discipline is legendary.

But do futures-oriented scholars, whatever their methods, produce knowledge? Of course not. Gregory's second criticism notwithstanding, few if any serious futurists see the fruits of their research as knowledge. There is a crucial distinction between using some of the methods and findings of science, and claiming that speculation about the future constitutes cognition in itself. Self-respecting futurists do not claim to *know* anything at all about the future. As the Yale sociologist and futurist Wendell Bell commented in his letter to Gregory, speculations about the future and even predictions well grounded in present-day scientific knowledge cannot be defined as knowledge, as long as the events or trends foreseen remain in future time.[6]

What futurists do, rather, is to construct visions of plausible alternative futures: plausible in terms of the best currently obtainable knowledge of nature, earth, and humankind. In the process they may often avail themselves of scientific method. But they cannot tell us what will actually happen in future time, and no one knows it better than they.

Again, however, critics should be careful not to press this point too far. Comparable constraints limit the power of historians to know the past. As a practicing historian, I know that nothing I write about the past is the past itself. The historian devises visions of the past, weaving theories and evidence together into what he or she hopes will be a plausible image. Obviously, the quality of the historian's evidence is far better than the quality of the evidence available to the futurist. By definition, eyewitness accounts of future events are never available. But the products of the two fields of inquiry have much in common. In both instances, we end with a vision: not the thing itself, and not even a faithful replica, but simply a vision.

So please do not conceive of *The Next Three Futures* as a guided tour of the next century. This it cannot be. All it can do is survey the possibilities apparent here and now. Some of these possibilities will very likely come to pass, in one form or another. Others will seem ridiculous in just a few years. The future, like the past, must be continually reexamined and rediscovered.

Nevertheless, when all is said, I find it better to approach the future with at least a few informed notions of what it may bring than simply to tend my bean patch. How, then, should we respond to Gregory's last point, his concern that futurism plays into the hands of those sinister folk who would offer up present generations as a burnt sacrifice to a mythical future? Anyone who has lived through most of the twentieth century knows only too well the kind of people that Gregory has in mind. Stalin, Hitler, Mao, Lyndon Johnson, Pol Pot, Saddam Hussein: the list is long of men obsessed with images of a future felicity, men who were willing to kill and kill again to make a "better" future. Some were no doubt sincere, persuaded of the rightness of their cause, and the loftiness of their plans for humanity. All the same, they readily sacrificed life, the pulsing real life of the present, for a partisan dream of things to come.

Do futurists help form a climate of opinion in which such awful sacrifices become more thinkable, more worthwhile? Certainly not. People who study the future are seldom willing to die for it, and bloodthirsty ideologues need no inspiration from futurists to stoke their appetite for power.

Still, there is Gregory's nagging insistence that to speak of the future as something real, as something we can "enter," is to engage in dangerous fantasizing. We may well ask if the future is real. Or must we always live in the present?

The answer depends on one's choice of perspectives. From an existential perspective, Gregory is right. The present is all we have. Everything exists here and now, in the present. All consciousness takes place in the present. The present is the moment of decision and action. Even all our remembering and anticipating occur in the present.

But from a spectator's perspective, from the perspective of the behavioral or social scientist, human beings are also creatures of past and future. At any considered point in time, the present is an infinitesimal fraction of a human life-span. We may act in the present, but always and only in the context of everything we have been; and until the moment of our death, a steadily dwindling yet initially vast part of our lives is lodged in the future, waiting to be shaped by will and memory and circumstance.

Clearly, a ruthless obsession with the future at all costs may be destructive of humane values. But present-mindedness of the sort Gregory advocates might prove equally dangerous. Living for the present can mean failing to husband non-renewable resources, failing to avert impending economic or environmental disasters, failing to make the long-term sacrifices needed for the systemic redress of social injustice, failing to learn the self-defeating folly of nuclear war. In short, living for the present can mean failing to leave behind a safe and habitable world for our children.

As we look back on the 1980s, when the debate on futures studies appeared in *Change*, it was a decade of presentism par excellence. Under Ronald Reagan, not to mention some of his counterparts in other advanced capitalist countries, the wealth of the very wealthy tripled.[7] The economic condition of the poor and the middle classes deteriorated, and many Second and Third World countries lost even more ground, in part because of their weak position in the world market and in part because for many years they had spent beyond their means in an orgy of presentist hedonism.

At the same time the state of the global environment worsened immeasurably. Every nation, each in its own way, plundered the future for the sake of present pleasures. The greatest offenders of all, ironically, were the centrally planned economies of Eastern Europe and Asia, where attempts to shore up a disintegrating political system took priority over planning for the welfare of future generations. Brainless apparatchiks maimed and raped the earth in a desperate effort to survive.

In the 1990s, the bills have come due. In retrospect, we may decide that Reaganist presentism, the pursuit of wealth and amusement in the here and now at any price, was no less hazardous to humane values than Stalinist futurism. Both attitudes are obsolete.

What must take their place is a time-sensitive humanism that views all life—past, present, and future—as sacred. In the words of Edmund Burke, civil society is a partnership, "a partnership not only between those who are living, but between those who are living, those who are dead, and those who are to be born."[8]

Can futures studies make a contribution, however modest, to the generation of this new world view? There is reason to hope, and believe, that it can.

NOTES

1. They were: *H. G. Wells and the World State* (New Haven: Yale University Press, 1961); *The City of Man: Prophecies of a World Civilization in Twentieth-Century Thought* (Boston: Houghton Mifflin, 1963; and Baltimore: Penguin Books, 1967); *Building the City of Man: Outlines of a World Civilization* (New York: Richard Grossman, 1971); and *Good Tidings: The Belief in Progress from Darwin to Marcuse* (Bloomington, IN: Indiana University Press, 1972).

2. World Future Society, *The Futures Research Directory: Individuals, 1991–92* (Bethesda, MD: World Future Society, 1991).

3. Marshall W. Gregory, "Do Futures Studies Really Help?: 'Futures Research' and Present Troubles," *Change: The Magazine of Higher Learning*, January/February 1988; 50–53. The publication that Gregory reviewed was Michael Marien, ed., with Lane Jennings, *Future Survey Annual 1986: A Guide to the Recent Literature of Trends, Forecasts, and Policy Proposals* (Bethesda, MD: World Future Society, 1987).

4. "Do Futures Studies Really Help?," 50.

5. See the letters by Michael Marien, Wendell Bell, W. Warren Wagar, and Edward Cornish, and the reply by Gregory, in *Change*, July-August 1988; 6–8 and 59–60.

6. Wendell Bell, Letter in *Change*, July/August 1988, 7.

7. See Kevin P. Phillips, "Reagan's America: A Capital Offense," *The New York Times Magazine* (June 17, 1990); 26 ff.; and Phillips, *The Politics of Rich and Poor* (New York: Random House, 1990).

8. Burke, *Reflections on the Revolution in France* [1790] (New York: P. F. Collier, 1909), p. 232.

PART I

FUTURES INQUIRY

Chapter 1 ————————————

The State of the Art

SCOPE

Each year, in my undergraduate course, "History of the Future," students receive an outside reading list that introduces them to futures research. Initially, the list was only two pages long. Over the years it has grown into a smallish book with thousands of entries.

Of course no student, even the most enterprising, will have time to read all these titles, or even a sizeable fraction. The list is distributed primarily to call attention to the vastness of futures inquiry. Although there may be only a few hundred full-time, self-styled futurists in the United States, and a few hundred more elsewhere, they are not the only producers of futures-relevant texts. From time to time the temptation to explore alternative futures has overcome researchers in every academic discipline, as well as journalists and writers of fiction. Indeed, some disciplines (such as economics and meteorology) are deeply involved in forecasting. Together, these occasional futurists, people like the economist Robert Heilbroner, the political scientist Richard Falk, or the novelist Ursula Le Guin, are responsible for much of the best work in our "field."

The reading list for "History of the Future" begins with futures journals and aids to futures research. It continues with surveys of world history, histories of futurist thought, and general works on global and national or regional futures. The heart of the list addresses more specialized topics in a futures context: food and population, resources and the environment, climate, energy, computers and communications, space science, biotechnology, politics, war and security, world law and order, the global economy, work, families and sexes, cities and countrysides, education, health and welfare, and cultural change. A final section suggests novels of the future and critical studies of futurist fiction.

Michael Marien's monthly review of futures literature, *Future Survey*, leaves out fiction, but examines an even broader array of non-fictional materials. Since its founding in 1979, Marien has analyzed well over 10,000 articles and books. The headings he uses are similar to mine, but include topics that I have left out or subsumed under other headings, such as justice, transportation, and public policy planning. Marien said it well in his first *Annual*: "The 20 or so problem areas in this guide can be seen as a 20-ring circus, with action going on in each ring as if it were independent of the others, although we know quite well that, increasingly, everything is connected to everything else."[1]

What do futurists omit? By intention, presumably nothing. As it should be. The future, like the past, will transpire in a single, continuous, synergetic flow. All the activities of humankind will, as always, occur interactively, each in the context of all the others. Do not expect, for example, that the future will consist simply of a growth in world population, *followed* by an impact on resources, *resulting* in a political response, *leading* to new technologies.

Such a cause and effect sequence may occur. So will numberless other sequences running in various other directions. Demographics, the environment, politics, and technology will undergo continuous change and development, in response to one another and to their own internal dynamics, and in response to every activity of humankind everywhere. As Edward Cornish writes in *The Study of the Future*, futures inquiry "picks up where history leaves off."[2] The real future will be just as complex, and ultimately just as unfathomable, as the real past.

But the study of the future, as opposed to the future itself, is even more complex than the study of the past. The past cannot be lived a second time, or improved. It is pointless to investigate how past societies might have done a better job, although few historians can resist the temptation to note their shortcomings.

In futures research, however, since the future has not yet happened and, to some indeterminable extent, lies within the power of living men and women to shape, scholars must grapple not only with probabilities but also with desirabilities. They must confront the question not only of what might happen, but also of what should or could be made to happen.

Thus there are always two kinds of futures research: empirical and normative. The closest analogy here is not with historiography but with political science and political economy, disciplines that on the one hand analyze processes (the empirical function) and on the other prescribe policy (the normative function). Although some futurists try to deal only in probabilities, in practice it is virtually impossible to engage in value-free empirical study of the future. Having analyzed the likeliest outcomes, the most plausible alternatives, the futurist is drawn, willy-nilly, into the business of recommending *which* path we should choose.

There is no harm, and much good, in such recommending. One of the founders of modern futures studies, the late Bertrand de Jouvenel, argued that recommending policies was the whole point, ultimately, of the futurist endeavor. "Man is fortunate," he wrote, "when the desirable and the probable coincide! The case is often otherwise, and thus we find ourselves trying to bend the course of events in a way which will bring the probable closer to the desirable. And this is the real reason why we study the future."[3]

Unfortunately even the futurist's selection of likeliest outcomes may be colored by what he or she would prefer to see happen. Futurist Pollyannas generally anticipate happy futures, in hopes of persuading readers that a given preferred future is in the cards, and should therefore receive all possible support. Futurist Cassandras generally anticipate dire futures, not because they prefer or even necessarily expect them, but in hopes of generating enough terror that policy makers and the public will respond with appropriate remedies.

Either way, when visions of the desirable warp analysis of real world processes, futurists betray their calling. Wishful thinking and apocalyptic hyperbole have no legitimate place in futures research, no matter how lofty the motives of the researcher. In the final showing, the only normative prescriptions worth anything are prescriptions founded in a ruthlessly honest assessment of trends and prospects in the real world.

METHODS

Another way to dichotomize futures studies is to divide them into "hard" and "soft," corresponding to the distinction between the methods and perspectives of the (so-called) exact sciences and those of the humanities. The chasm between these two "cultures," in C.P. Snow's term, was once wider than it is now, thanks to interpenetration and cross-fertilization, but it still exists. One is a culture of quantification, precise measurement, and testing of phenomena and data under controlled conditions; the other is a culture of qualification, relying more on language than on numbers, in the traditions of literary and art criticism, philosophy, and history.

In futures research, not surprisingly, the "hard" approach is favored by scholars who engage in economic and technological forecasting, and the "soft" approach by those primarily interested in cultural and political change. One has only to contrast the articles typically found in two journals that started publication in the 1970s: the hard futurism of *Technological Forecasting and Social Change* and the soft futurism of *Alternatives: Social Transformation and Human Governance*. Hard futurists analyze, for the most part, short-term trends in business, industry, communications, demographics, resources, and other areas that lend themselves well to rigorous quantification. Soft futurists focus on trends, often longer-term, in society, governance, politics, thought, religion, the arts, and other areas more amenable to qualitative analysis.

But not always. Long-term overviews are possible using either approach. Scholars such as Oswald Spengler, Pitirim A. Sorokin, and Arnold J. Toynbee, who sought out the shape of things to come by extrapolating the cycles and spirals of world history, gave us some of our first visions of the global future in this century. But hard futurism has also made its contribution.

In particular, modern futures studies owe much to the techniques of mathematical global modelling pioneered in 1970 by Jay Forrester and made famous (or notorious) by Donella H. Meadows, Dennis L. Meadows, and their associates in *The Limits to Growth*.[4] Such readily quantifiable parameters as population, arable land, non-renewable resource depletion, pollution, energy supplies, and economic growth may be integrated to form a model of the world system. By altering the values of one or more variables, the researcher can create a multiplicity of models and follow the impacts of each alteration into the future for decades or centuries. This is hard futurism par excellence, and yet it can yield images of quite distant futures.

Although most computer-generated models of the world system stress the relationship between resources and economic growth, some even focus on political factors. The best example is the GLOBUS model produced by a team of futurists headquartered in Berlin. The GLOBUS Research Group has developed a model that all but ignores the physical limits to growth and centers instead on such political and economic parameters as market trends, state budgets, rates of taxation, and the vicissitudes of domestic and international politics.[5] The GLOBUS team assumes that the future is driven chiefly by public and corporate policy, rather than by environmental constraints. In its view, realism demands that a computer simulation of the world system pay special attention to social, economic, and political forces, the true engines of change.

Again, the methods employed are those of hard futurism. Even something as intrinsically "soft" as a trend in the fine arts can be subjected to hard methodology if the researcher succeeds in quantifying the relevant data: for example, the rate of increase in female artists exhibited in major metropolitan museums, or the changing ratio of abstract to representational themes in oil painting.

But not everything can be measured and quantified. We need both hard and soft futurism to capture the full range of human possibility. More to the point, we need a synthesis of the two. Although some of the most convincing research in futures inquiry does manage to combine quantitative and qualitative methods, few efforts have been made to construct an overarching theory that would bring all its disparate methods, hard and soft, into a coherent working relationship. Perhaps in view of the incredible diversity of the field, no such overarching theory can be constructed. If the future consists of everything that will ever happen, then futures inquiry is the consideration of everything that can be conjectured about what may (and should) happen, drawing on the wisdom of all sciences, all arts, all humanities. When futurists try to inventory their methods, the result is invariably a long list of ill-assorted techniques borrowed from a wide variety of established disciplines; rarely is thought given to how these techniques connect to one another, or to a unified theory of futures inquiry.

In Edward Cornish's *The Study of the Future*, for example, the list of futures methods includes trend extrapolation, scenarios, mapping techniques (relevance trees, mission-flow diagrams, cross-impact matrices), polling of experts, and simulations (modelling and gaming). Cornish also gives brief consideration to techniques borrowed from military, business, and government planning, such as operations research and technology assessment.[6]

None of these methods, whether hard or soft, is wholly original with futurists, although futurists have added some refinements of their own, such as the Delphi technique, a method of surveying expert opinion, developed in 1953 by Olaf Helmer and Norman Dalkey for the RAND Corporation. In *Looking Forward*, Helmer himself offers a similar array of research methods, with special emphasis on Delphi surveying and cross-impact analysis, which he also helped to develop.[7]

Others, such as David Loye, call attention to the possibility of harnessing paranormal psychic powers in forecasting, and still others limn the future through Spenglerian analyses of the cycles of world history.[8] Hardly anyone mentions what is probably the most overworked method of all: the simple drawing of analogies from past historical experience, as when someone warns of a second Vietnam, a new Hitler, or a Third World War.

Helmer makes the further point that planning and forecasting (especially long-range planning and forecasting) cannot be successful unless they are truly interdisciplinary, taking into account not only the events being anticipated, but also "probable developments in various fields that determine the parameters of the future environment in which the plan needs to prove itself."[9] But his plea for interdisciplinarity is not accompanied by a comprehensive and effective strategy for breaking through disciplinary walls.

How could it be otherwise? If the sciences, arts, and humanities, with all their splendor and tradition, and their millions of practitioners, have not so far succeeded in establishing a common cognitive currency, a way of fusing their methodologies, can a handful of futurists be expected to do the job for them?

And yet the survival and continued growth of futures inquiry may hinge on our ability to perform just such a task, at least with respect to future-oriented research. As Marshall W. Gregory wrote in *Change*, the methodologies in use by futurists are clearly incompatible. Present-day futurism is little more than a rag doll made of scraps from the sewing basket, a

collection of borrowings with no clear identity of its own; and unless all this
changes, there is a good chance that futurism will never make any serious
inroads into the academic world, or fulfill its scholarly promise.

To multiply the confusion, several other radically different approaches to
the study of alternative futures are available that most professional futurists
either dismiss out of hand or do not know. One is science fiction. "From
the point of view of futures studies," Joseph F. Coates and Jennifer Jarratt
write in *What Futurists Believe,* "sci-fi is of little, or no, value. Science-
fiction is usually so barren of plausible psychological, social, or institutional
sophistication as to fall into one of three categories: entertainment, fantasy,
or cautionary tales."[10]

Much of it does fall into one or more of these categories. So does a fair
amount of futurism. But there is also a more durable and serious variety of
science fiction, which consists of detailed anticipations of future worlds in
being, often transformed by new technologies, cultures, or institutions and
ways of thought. Essentially, this science fiction of the literary high road
applies what futurists choose to call "scenario" technique to the investigation
of alternative futures.

The term *scenario* was first used in dramaturgy to mean the synopsis or
outline of a play, and later became synonymous with the script of a motion
picture. In the scenarios of both futurism and science fiction, emphasis falls
on plot; a scenario is always, first and foremost, a story line. The only
difference between the scenarios of professional futurists and the novels and
stories of writers of science fiction is that, in the latter, the story line is more
centered on the lives of imaginary characters, and more fully fleshed out,
with attention to artistic as well as scholarly values. By contrast the scenarios
of futurists are almost threadbare, focused sharply on the projection of a
sequence of hypothetical events, to test (in what Helmer calls, in a slightly
different context, a "pseudo-experiment"[11]) how a given set of premises might
play in a given future world.

But if the writer of science fiction is also a trained natural or social scientist,
humanist, or engineer, which happens more often than the uninitiated might
suppose, he or she can generate images of alternative futures just as well
informed and just as credible as those of the futurist. They may also be
considerably more effective. Plausible stories and characters need plausible
contexts, and the act of imagining a whole future world, including its technology, social structures, ecology, and cultures, demands a synthesizing
intelligence of the highest order.

At the same time, because the writer of fiction enjoys a certain poetic
license, he or she is free to experiment with possibilities that may elude the
plodding futurist. Most of the writer's intuitive leaps lead nowhere. Yet now
and then they hit their mark, as when H. G. Wells, in a science-fiction novel
entitled *The World Set Free* (1914), imagined a war fought with atomic
bombs. At the time he knew little more than Frederick Soddy's work on

radioactive isotopes. But Soddy's ideas were all he needed, together with his own scientific training and imaginative powers, to conceive of nuclear weapons and their use in global war.[12]

Overlapping with science fiction is the literary device of the utopia, or its more recently evolved antithesis, the dystopia: fictional visions of the best (or worst) imaginable society. A certain amount of what passes for science fiction consists of utopian/dystopian speculation, but utopias and dystopias are a very special case. The writer of utopias is essentially a moralist or polemicist, attempting to set goals for humankind, just as the dystopian writer warns us of goals that might be disastrous to pursue. Since in the past hundred years or more, utopian/dystopian visions have usually been set in a hypothetical future, and not in some remote corner of our own present-day world, most modern utopias/dystopias qualify as a form of futures inquiry—with one difference from mainstream science fiction. Unlike most science fiction, utopias/dystopias qualify as experiments only in normative futures, concerned with values rather than expectations, with goals rather than possibilities.

Still, the writer of the well-made utopia, such as William Morris in *News from Nowhere* (1890) or Ernest Callenbach in *Ecotopia* (1975) or Ursula Le Guin in *Always Coming Home* (1985), has in one sense the same task as the writer of serious science fiction. Integrating the knowledge of as many sciences and arts as possible, the utopographer (or dystopographer) must create in his or her imagination a whole world. The common inability of futurists to consider and weigh all the forces interacting to build the human future is surmounted, often in a purely intuitive way, by the writer of utopias/dystopias, just as by the writer of science fiction.

The critical drawback of scenario-building, whether in the work of the professional futurist or in that of the creative writer, is that each scenario necessarily envisages only one future. The whole point is to follow a single set of premises to a plausible conclusion, taking account of how events in history actually occur, one after the other. By contrast a mathematical model can be projected into any number of hypothetical futures, as the values of each characteristic of the model are systematically varied by the researcher. Each run may require only a few minutes of the computer's time, and a day's work can produce literally hundreds of futures.

It follows that the sense of *alternatives*, the awareness that all futures inquiry is speculative and not literally predictive, is less easily lost by the world modeller than by the scenario writer. The more elaborately the scenario is done, the more it runs the risk of seeming fixed and irretrievable, a wager rather than a tool for exploring the unknown. The only remedy for such misperceptions is to produce and encourage the production of many scenarios.[13] The more we have, the wiser we shall be, not only about the future but also about the limitations of the technique.

Yet another approach so far confined to the fringes of futurism is world-system theory, developed by the sociologist Immanuel Wallerstein and others in the 1970s as a way of explaining processes of social change in the post-medieval world. World-system theory blends Marxist and Leninist analysis of capitalist imperialism with the systems approach to modern world history of the late Fernand Braudel. Its most distinguishing feature, apart from this mix of theoretical models, is its insistence on erasing disciplinary boundaries in the social sciences. In its own sphere, it has produced a functional synthesis of history, sociology, economics, anthropology, and political science.[14]

Simply put, world-system theory holds that over the past five centuries the most advanced capitalist countries have created a single global economy with an integrated division of labor. The worldwide expansion of capitalism has been made possible by the continuing existence of a plurality of rival cultures and states, manipulated by the capitalists to their best advantage. Such pluralism stands in sharp contrast with the civilizations of antiquity, when all power tended to be concentrated in vast empires, and entrepreneurs enjoyed little freedom of action. But in modern times, capitalism has germinated and matured, creating a three-zoned world economy (core, periphery, semi-periphery) dominated by the upper strata of the countries in the exploitative core, and characterized by long cycles of economic growth and stagnation and the rise and decline of hegemonic or would-be hegemonic states.

The relevance of world-system theory to futurism may not be immediately obvious. Like Marx himself, not to mention Braudel and the other French historians of the *Annales* school who have strongly influenced Wallerstein and his colleagues, world-system theorists are not given to detailed speculation about things to come. Their forte is macroscopic analysis of the continuities, cycles, and transformations in the life of the capitalist world-system since the Renaissance, illustrated by the three volumes of Wallerstein's still unfinished magnum opus, *The Modern World-System*.[15] In one or more subsequent volumes, Wallerstein plans to carry his investigations, which have so far reached only the middle of the nineteenth century, down to the present day.

One hopes he will also, in his last volume, probe future possibilities, as he has already done briefly in several articles.[16] The traditional aversion of leftist thinkers to futures inquiry (an overreaction to nineteenth-century utopian socialism) does not remove the fact that Marxism in its many varieties is a powerful tool for seeking to understand the global future. It becomes even more powerful when reinforced, as in world-system theory, with broad-gauged historical analysis practiced by scholars like Fernand Braudel.

For the essence of both Marxism (as a social science) and world-system theory is their dynamic view of world history. They take a diachronic, rather than synchronic, approach to social phenomena. They see the world more as a process than as a structure. The world-system exists, but it pulses and changes. If their analysis of the past has merit, it bears all sorts of implications for the future of the capitalist world-system, from new waves of economic growth/stagnation and interstate rivalry to eventual demise as an outcome of the internal contradictions of capitalism analyzed long ago by Marx and Engels. Perhaps world-system theory may even manage, eventually, to furnish futurists with the integrative concepts they need to put their methodological house in order.

Bringing all these techniques—mathematical modelling, scenarios, mapping, trend extrapolation, science fiction, and the rest—into a unified theory of futures research is a task beyond our reach in this book. But, at the risk of betraying my professional bias, I must conclude that a very critical contribution is likely to be made by students and philosophers of world history, whether Marxist or non-Marxist, whether informed by world-system theory or not.

The point is simply that the future and the past (as I noted in the prologue) are fundamentally the same thing. The observer occupies the present moment, like someone floating in the middle of a river. Looking upstream, the observer sees the past; looking downstream, the future. But it is always the same river. The only difference is the position of the observer.

The public time of the human race is such a river. What the trained world historian can offer the futurist enterprise is a sense, first, of the wholeness of the river; and second, of the historicity of its flow. What makes it a river is its motion, the relentless motion of each molecule of its waters from space to space, nanosecond by nanosecond. Events do not happen in a blur or an eternal now. They happen discretely, one after the other in a temporal sequence, which becomes the historian's special task to record, in all its uniqueness and irreversibility. The historian will never get the sequence exactly right, and may not even come close in some instances, but it is surely better to make the effort, and hazard being wrong, than not to try at all.

So it goes with the exploration of future time. The future will consist of a multiplicity of interactive events unfolding in time in a particular temporal order. It will advance along lines already laid down by previous generations, no matter how widely it may eventually diverge from those lines. The force of millennia of past experience will drive it forward. And as each future year transpires, each future year will be joined forever to the past.

These sound like truisms, but they deserve reflection. Obviously the methods and mind-set of the historian have much to contribute to an understanding of *how* the future will happen, even if most of the *what* and the *why* must be left to other disciplines.

Bertrand de Jouvenel expressed somewhat the same thought when he gave his famous definition of *futuribles* in *The Art of Conjecture*. The possible becomes futurible, he wrote, "only if its mode of production from the present state of affairs is plausible and imaginable. . . . A futurible is a descendant of the present, a descendant to which we attach a genealogy."[17] Jouvenel gave as an example the prediction of aviation. In antiquity and long after, aviation remained only a possible. But near the close of the nineteenth century, with advances in science and engineering, powered flight became a futurible, although no airplane had yet flown. In fact it proliferated into many futuribles, as inventors considered all sorts of designs for flying machines, made plausible and imaginable by the progress of technical knowledge.

The key word in Jouvenel's definition is the metaphor of the *genealogy*. A genealogy is a sequence of generation: if you know the great-grandparent, the grandparent, and the parent, you can foresee the child, the grandchild, and the great-grandchild. If you do not, your forecasting will be purely speculative. Even if you are missing just one or two links in the chain of events, you may err badly.

Perhaps such erring can be excused, in this or that special circumstance. The futurist must engage in inspired guesswork from time to time when data are scanty. But the difference between the professional futurist and the casual soothsayer is that the futurist strives always to develop a genealogy of events, a history of the future, moving from point A to point B to point C to point D to point E in a scientifically plausible temporal sequence. Jumping from A to E without at least trying to cover the intervening ground is foolhardy, and—for the serious futurist—impermissible. A thorough grounding in historical method will help the futurist avoid such recklessness.

But the proof of any method is its effectiveness. It is time now to review another kind of history: the history of futures inquiry itself, with particular attention to its successes and failures.

NOTES

1. Michael Marien in Marien, ed., *Future Survey Annual 1979: A Guide to the Recent Literature of Trends, Forecasts, and Policy Proposals* (Washington: World Future Society, 1980), 2.

2. Edward Cornish et al., *The Study of the Future* (Washington: World Future Society, 1977), 103.

3. Bertrand de Jouvenel, *The Art of Conjecture*, tr. Nikita Lary (New York: Basic Books, 1967), 19.

4. *The Limits to Growth* (New York: Universe Books, 1972) was one of several books sponsored by the Club of Rome's Project on the Predicament of Mankind and published in the 1970s. See also Jay W. Forrester, *World Dynamics* (Cambridge, Mass.: Wright-Allen Press, 1971); Barry B. Hughes, *World Modeling* (Lexington, Mass.: Lexington Books, 1980); Donella H. Meadows, et al., *Groping in the Dark: The First Decade of Global Modelling* (New York: Wiley, 1982); and Meadows and J. M. Robinson, *The Electronic Oracle: Computer Models and Social Decisions* (New York: Wiley, 1985).

5. Stuart A. Bremer, ed., *The GLOBUS Model: Computer Simulation of Worldwide Political and Economic Developments* (Boulder: Westview Press, 1987).

6. *The Study of the Future*, 108–126.

7. Olaf Helmer, *Looking Forward: A Guide to Futures Research* (Beverly Hills: Sage, 1983). See especially chs. 5–6.

8. See David Loye, *The Sphinx and the Rainbow: Brain, Mind and Future Vision* (Boulder: Shambhala, 1983); and, for a neo-Spenglerian forecast, David Burnett King, *The Crisis of Our Time: Reflections on the Course of Western Civilization, Past, Present, and Future* (Cranbury, N.J.: Associated University Presses, 1988).

9. Helmer, *Looking Forward*, 23.

10. Joseph F. Coates and Jennifer Jarratt, *What Futurists Believe* (Mt. Airy, Md.: Lomond Publications, 1989), xi.

11. See Helmer, *Looking Forward*, 121–122.

12. The story is told in W. Warren Wagar, "H. G. Wells and the Scientific Imagination," *The Virginia Quarterly Review* 65:3 (Summer 1989): 390–400.

13. An excellent example of multiple scenarios is Paul Hawken, James Ogilvy, and Peter Schwartz, *Seven Tomorrows: Toward a Voluntary History* (New York: Bantam Books, 1982).

14. See Thomas Richard Shannon, *An Introduction to the World-System Perspective* (Boulder: Westview Press, 1989).

15. Immanuel Wallerstein, *The Modern World-System*, 3 vols. (New York and San Diego, Academic Press, 1974–1988).

16. See various articles and passages in Wallerstein, *The Capitalist World-Economy* (Cambridge: Cambridge University Press, 1979); *The Politics of the World-Economy* (Cambridge: Cambridge University Press, 1984); and, especially, "The Capitalist World-Economy: Middle-Run Prospects," *Alternatives: Social Transformation and Humane Governance* 14:3 (July 1989): 279–288. See also Samir Amin, Giovanni Arrighi, André Gunder Frank, and Wallerstein, *The Dynamics of Global Crisis* (New York: Monthly Review Press, 1982).

17. Jouvenel, *The Art of Conjecture*, 18.

2 ―――――――――――――――――――――――――

Past Futures

H. G. WELLS AND THE ORIGINS OF FUTURISM

Like nations, every field of study has its founding mothers and fathers. Figures of legend or history, they help give the oncoming generations a sense of identity. They instill pride, confidence, and purposefulness. They supply standards by which to measure the performance of new practitioners.

Examples spring easily to mind. In modern physics, the great pathbreakers were Galileo and Newton; in economics, Adam Smith and the French physiocrats; in genetics, Mendel and Morgan. But who "founded" the study of alternative futures? Bertrand de Jouvenel? Herman Kahn? Olaf Helmer?

Each made his contribution, but a better candidate is available, born long before any of these noted seers: the English novelist and jack-of-all-intellectual-trades, H. G. Wells. In Wells, most of the tendencies in still earlier futurism coalesced; and his abundant writings furnish models, or at least inspiration, for nearly all that is best in present-day futures inquiry.

The keystone of Wells's futurism is a volume now approaching its one hundredth anniversary. Usually cited as *Anticipations*, its full title is *Anticipations of the Reaction of Mechanical and Scientific Progress upon Human Life and Thought*. I. F. Clarke, who has studied dozens of Wells's immediate forerunners, freely concedes that "*Anticipations* was the first comprehensive and widely read survey of future developments in the short history of predictive writing." Wells's book "represented a peak in human self-awareness."[1]

Anticipations first appeared as a series of articles in an English magazine, *The Fortnightly Review*, in 1901. It was handsomely published as a book the next year by Chapman and Hall in London and by Harper in New York. Hitherto known only as a rising young novelist, Wells now expanded his repertoire to include sociology, in the casual sense in which that term was used at the beginning of the century.

Anticipations ranged widely in its subject matter, from the future of transport to the future of international relations and world order. The first chapters are familiar fare to anyone who has read other books of the same period by journalists puffing the progress they expected from science and technology in the new century. Wells looked ahead to the first aircraft and broad highways teeming with automobiles, buses, and trucks. Suburbia would triumph over city and countryside. In the United States, one vast unbroken sprawl of middle-class life would reach from Boston to Washington. Homes would be prefabricated, and household appliances and chemicals would put an end to the need for servants.

In later chapters, Wells turned from his predictions of miracle dishwashing solvents and tidy electric ranges to something that for him was much more crucial. By the close of the twentieth century, he foresaw the collapse of free-market capitalism and the nation-state system in great mechanized total wars that the tycoons and politicians could not, ultimately, understand or control. Power would slip through their fingers. They would be swiftly replaced by the technically competent, by scientists and engineers and managerial experts, who would learn from their errors and build a world state of peace and plenty.

Taken all in all, *Anticipations* was a tour de force. No brief summary can do it justice. One of its appreciative readers, the future grande dame of British socialism Beatrice Webb, jotted in her diary that it was "the most remarkable book of the year."[2]

The success of *Anticipations* led to an invitation to deliver a lecture at the Royal Institution in 1902. Entitling his remarks "The Discovery of the Future," Wells took a step further and called for the emergence of a whole new science. The time was drawing near, he wrote, when "a systematic exploration of the future" could yield a firm inductive knowledge of the laws of social and political development. A scientifically ordered vision of the future "will be just as certain, just as strictly science, and perhaps just as detailed as the picture that has been built up within the last hundred years of the geological past." Not that geology or any other science gave us absolute and final truth. But a "working knowledge of things in the future" was well within our grasp.[3]

Wells spent most of the rest of his life attempting to fulfill the promises of that early lecture. Despite his call for a strictly scientific futurism, he confined his own work to experiments in what we have termed soft futurism. But in the light of all that he did achieve (and influenced others to achieve), it is not far-fetched to fix January 24, 1902, the day of Wells's Royal Institution lecture, as the day when the modern study of the future was born.

Needless to add, in the history of ideas nothing is born out of nothing. Wells was not the first person to think of studying the future, nor even the first to do so systematically. The future has been a matter of intense curiosity and concern since prehistoric times, above all in the Western world. Wells inherited the wealth of millennia of futurism. Whatever he managed to pass on to his successors, he adapted in good measure from this rich heritage.

The elements of futures study that Wells inherited consist of at least five layers, each "deposited" somewhat earlier than the one above it: divination, revelation, the idea of progress, historicism, and social science. Each of these layers in the archeology of futurism corresponds to a stage in the history of human thought, and each bestowed—in the minds of faithful adherents—knowledge of the future.

The earliest by far is divination, a mode of futurizing perhaps as old as *Homo sapiens* itself. The diviner is either a medium, such as an oracle, who can enter into direct contact with the gods and learn of future events, or a reader of omens, who discerns in the behavior of animals, stars, or other natural phenomena what the gods have in store for their subjects. Divination lingers on today in astrology, palmistry, and the like, but in prehistoric and premodern times, it enjoyed the status, very nearly, of an exact science. States and individuals alike regularly consulted oracles and augurs for guidance in planning their futures.

Pagan divination was overlaid and eventually supplanted in late antiquity by biblical prophecy, construed as a direct revelation from God to humankind through the written words of canonical prophets and apostles. In one sense, there is little difference between divination and the Jewish-Christian-Muslim idea of revelation. Both depend on knowledge gleaned from a supernatural source.

But in both principle and practice they differ sharply. The revelations of sacred books furnish believers with a grand chronological schema of world history, from the Creation to the Last Trump. Although subject to more than one interpretation, biblical prophecy is something relatively fixed. It locates all events, past, present, and future, along a specific time line, in a continuously unfolding drama of trial and judgment ordained by God. In its eschatological visions, its visions of "last things," biblical prophecy finds the whole meaning of history in the end-time, a terrible day of accounting, toward which all nations and all souls inexorably advance.

The contrast, then, between pagan and biblical belief is rather obvious. Although paganism was far from indifferent to the future, in biblical faith history became a linear process, an irreversible march to a great public consummation, from which all temporal events drew their meaning. The future assumed transcendental significance.[4]

The third layer in the heritage of futurism corresponds to the age of the Scientific Revolution and the Enlightenment, roughly the period from the early seventeenth to the late eighteenth centuries, when Judeo-Christian eschatology was in turn supplanted, at least for the intellectual avant-garde, by the idea of the general progress of civilization. In effect, the belief in divine providence and judgment was secularized, yielding to a confidence in the power of humankind to redeem itself by cumulative improvements in knowledge, technique, education, governance, and, in the most full-blown doctrines, social justice, altruism, and even spirituality. A great scholarly literature arose to expound this idea, reaching its apogee in the Marquis de Condorcet's *Sketch for a Historical Picture of the Progress of the Human Mind,* first published in 1795. His final pages glow with the expectation of a golden future for all humanity.[5]

In the nineteenth century, thinkers of every persuasion, including theologians, subscribed to the belief in progress in one form or another. Poets like Tennyson and Whittier sang its splendors, social philosophers formulated elaborate proofs of it, and politicians on the hustings garnered votes by promising more and yet more progress. Even in the fateful half-century before the outbreak of World War I, progress remained the faith of most literate folk, apart from a small and growing elite of antimodernist naysayers.[6]

But the nineteenth century also gave rise to two fresh waves of futurism, on which Wells capitalized. The first of these, historicism, is the more difficult to define, and the less familiar. Springing in good measure from the romantic movement, especially in late eighteenth-century Germany, historicism (or *Historismus*) has never been a formal school of thought or method of reasoning. It is perhaps best seen as a predisposition to explain all things diachronically, in terms of their origins and development in time.

In legal studies, for example, the historicist takes more interest in the history of legal precedent and prescription than in whatever happens to be lawful at the present time, or in whatever is thought to constitute eternally valid law. By the same token, theology becomes a history of religious thought; and nations become ever-changing organisms with roots deep in the folkways of prehistory. Even plants and animals must be viewed as a single great family evolving together through the eons, not simply as an array of contemporary species to be catalogued and classified. In short, historicism argues that things are best defined not by their so-called natures, which are constructs of the human mind, but by their histories.

Chronicled in its earliest manifestations by Friedrich Meinecke,[7] the rise of historicism was a revolution of profound consequences for Western thought. It worked an immediate impact on historical studies themselves, persuading scholars to trace institutions back to their ultimate sources, stressing the uniqueness and interconnectedness of all historical events and the vital importance of temporal and cultural contexts in historical explanation. It encouraged historians to purge their minds of the values and outlook of their own age, and re-enact empathetically the lives of past men and women. It refuted the ancient prejudice that human nature is always the same and that people in past eras, apart from wearing different costumes, must have thought, felt, and behaved more or less as people think, feel, and behave today.

Historicism invaded every branch of art, science, and scholarship. It prompted the writing of great numbers of historical novels, and influenced the rise of science fiction, for which a better name is future fiction. Along with the idea of progress, it persuaded utopists from Louis-Sébastien Mercier onward to set their visions of the ideal society in the future. It transformed nationalism from a simple love of country to a militant racist cult. It permeated the natural and social sciences, as well as linguistics, literary and biblical criticism, psychology, philosophy, and legal studies. The nineteenth and the early twentieth centuries are unimaginable without the fertilizing impulse of historicism. Hegel, Ranke, Comte, Marx, Wagner, Darwin, Freud, Bergson, Jung: all these, and many others, betray its forming influence.

For the futurist, historicism is of critical importance because of its emphasis on temporal process. If everything is defined by its place and sequence in time, then not only does the past become immeasurably more significant; so does the future. Just as a belief in progress glorifies the future by making it the goal or purpose of human effort, so historicism glorifies the future by suggesting that the very essence of all phenomena, both human and natural, is their place in the flow of time.

The last wave of thought crucial to the emergence of futures studies was the arrival of the social sciences as recognized and professionalized disciplines, starting with the "dismal" science of economics and the "scientific" history of Ranke and his disciples early in the nineteenth century. Anthropology, sociology, and political science followed in due course.

The idea of a science of society (or social "physics") was not, of course, new. It had originated early in the Enlightenment, and much pioneering work had been done in all the major fields of social inquiry well before the close of the eighteenth century. But for many years social scientists thought of themselves primarily as philosophers. The full disengagement of the various social sciences from one another and from philosophy, which had taken place in the natural sciences somewhat earlier, did not occur until near the end of the nineteenth century.

The study of the future, as we have already suggested, is in fact a social science in its own right, or at least potentially so. None of the established social sciences directs its whole attention to the future by any means, but each, with the possible exception of historiography, has a predictive component arising from its claims to scientific status. If the social sciences are sciences, akin to the natural sciences, their task is to identify the structure and function of phenomena, their evolution in time, and the laws governing their behavior. Knowing (or claiming to know) all this, they also know (or can hope to know) something about the future of phenomena.

Hence the study of the future may be seen as a project for bringing all the social sciences together into a functional synthesis, fusing the knowledge of each to anticipate the probable development of social phenomena in future time. It may be something more than this, if it also incorporates humanistic learning, but its primary role, one may argue, is to carry forward the mission of the social sciences.

In any event, these are the five layers of futures-relevant thought, from divination and biblical prophecy through the idea of progress to historicism and the social sciences, that made it possible for an H. G. Wells to imagine the "discovery" of the future in his 1902 lecture at the Royal Institution. If knowing the future is of vital importance to humankind, said Wells, scholars should be able to apply their best methods of reasoning and research to unravelling its mysteries, and do so systematically. What past generations have done in their way, we should be able to do in ours.

It may sound like a modest and even obvious proposal. Certainly Wells himself did not shrink from the task he had set. Within his various limitations, he wove most of the strands of earlier futurism into a single body of work, more than one hundred volumes in all, published over a span of fifty years. Until his death in 1946, he was the foremost public advocate of the belief in progress, the foremost popularizer of the social and biological sciences, the foremost writer of science fiction, and the foremost futurist in the English-speaking world.[8]

He even imported eschatology into his futurism, perhaps without realizing it. Time after time, in works both of fiction and non-fiction, he borrowed the biblical paradigm of future days. Like the prophets of the Old and New Testaments, he predicted that an evil season was near at hand, that the nations would wage a spectacular terminal war, and that in the fires of Armageddon would be forged a post-holocaust kingdom of heaven on earth, a veritable New Jerusalem.

Nowadays much of Wells's work is neglected, fairly or unfairly as the case may be. Millions have read some of his early masterpieces of science fiction, such as *The Time Machine* (1895), *The War of the Worlds* (1898), or *The First Men in the Moon* (1901). Many have seen his film, *Things to Come* (1936), the first major science-fiction epic of the talking-picture era. His utopias, such as *A Modern Utopia* (1905) and *Men Like Gods* (1923), are less often delved into, despite their importance in their own day. The same holds for many of his mainstream social novels, like *Tono Bungay* (1909). Of his popularizations of social science, only *The Outline of History* (1920) remains familiar.

Seldom consulted even by specialists are the scores of volumes on social problems and issues that flowed from Well's pen, year after year, throughout his life. Most are now woefully dated. But what stands out, even today, is the single-minded attention that Wells directed in these works to the future of humankind. His obsession with the future is apparent just from the titles he chose: *The Future in America* (1906), *New Worlds for Old* (1908), *The War That Will End War* (1914), *What Is Coming?* (1916), *War and the Future* (1917), *A Year of Prophesying* (1924), and *The Fate of Homo Sapiens* (1939). Most explicit of all is the title of his fictional outline of future history, *The Shape of Things to Come* (1933), a phrase used thousands of times since he coined it, often by people who know nothing of the Wellsian original.

A complete recital of Wells's forecasts would fill a volume in itself. His first published book, *The Time Machine*, gave a terrifying glimpse of a far future England in which unresolved class warfare had caused the separation of humanity into two equally degenerate new species of cannibalistic predators and their pretty but vacuous prey. *When the Sleeper Wakes* (1899) previewed a Brave New World of corporate tyranny and behavioral conditioning, written when Aldous Huxley was still a small boy. Its influence on all subsequent visions of totalitarian polities, including Huxley's, is well documented by Mark R. Hillegas.[9]

As Wells grew into middle age early in the new century, he became more and more convinced of the imminence of global warfare. Some of his luckiest hits as a forecaster—unfortunately!—had to do with the scale and technology of modern war-making. In short stories, novels, and non-fiction, he pictured tanks and warplanes, before either existed. He understood that major wars in the twentieth century would be total wars, fought by nations with all the human and natural resources at their disposal.

The War in the Air (1908) imagined the destruction of civilization by aerial bombardment of cities. *The World Set Free* (1914) foresaw the same, with the further refinement of atomic bombs. In *The Shape of Things to Come*, published six years before the start of World War II, Wells told of the outbreak of a war in 1940, beginning as a conflict between Nazi Germany and Poland and then spreading to the whole world. The real war came only one year sooner than Wells's, and began in the same way. When Hitler invaded the Soviet Union in June 1941, with what seemed like an irresistible host, Wells promptly wrote an article for a London newspaper predicting his defeat. "The war has still to be won," he wrote, "but there is no question that it has been lost by Germany . . . For the first time [Hitler] has thrown himself against something solid through and through."[10]

There is much more. Wells foresaw space flight in 1898, inspiring the American scientist Robert H. Goddard to develop and successfully test-fire the world's first liquid-fuel rocket.[11] He foresaw worldwide television broadcasting and x-rated video cassettes in 1899, lunar landings and moon-earth radio communications in 1901, atomic energy in 1913, a postwar "peace league" in 1914, the failure of the League of Nations in 1921, the downfall of Italian fascism in 1927, a new world order run by multinational corporations in 1928, and intercontinental ballistic missiles in 1932.

In the same piece in which he anticipated ICBMs, Wells renewed his appeal for the professionalization of futures research. He asked why there were so many thousands of professors of history, and "not a single Professor of Foresight in the world." In this era of endless technological surprises "we ought to have not simply one or two Professors of Foresight, but whole Faculties and Departments of Foresight." Wells admitted he was only an amateur. But where were the professionals? When would the human race decide to take its affairs in hand and make a livable world?[12]

Not that Wells was always prescient. In the early days of the First World War, he made the same mistake as almost everyone else, expecting that the war would be over in a few months, with a decisive victory by Britain, France, and Russia. He failed to anticipate the Russian Revolution of 1917. When it came, he had little faith in the power of Lenin and his Bolsheviks to rejuvenate and modernize their shattered nation without massive international aid. Wells also proved fairly unsophisticated as a forecaster of events in the Third World, and, needless to say, his many prophecies of the arrival of world government in the aftermath of a system-wide catastrophe remain unfulfilled.

His most serious shortcoming was one that many of us share: he too often let wishful thinking overshadow his common sense. In his eagerness to "invent" the future, as Dennis Gabor would say,[13] he let himself see events on the horizon that were simply not ready to happen, if ever. Curiously, he made the same mistake in reverse in his last book, *Mind at the End of Its Tether* (1945). Ill, depressed, and clearly not his own man, he now foretold the fast approaching final ruin of civilization. Nothing, he lamented, could save us. Humankind had let its last chances slip away.

All such lapses and losses of nerve notwithstanding, Wells's rightful place as the chief futurist of the first half of the twentieth century cannot be denied him. For decades newspaper and magazine editors automatically turned to Wells if they wanted an article or a comment on the shape of things to come. He was the futurist laureate of the Western world.

But he did not lack rivals. In every category, he had formidable ones. His generation, consisting of men and women born between the early 1850s and late 1870s, contained several great social scientists and popularizers of social science with an abiding interest in the future, such as the British sociologist L. T. Hobhouse. Prominent philosophers often wrote about the future of humankind, including Henri Bergson, John Dewey, Samuel Alexander, and Bertrand Russell. Journalists like Sir Philip Gibbs, utopographers like Edward Bellamy, playwrights like Bernard Shaw, all offered provocative visions of things to come. Wells's science fiction competed with the writings of George Griffith, M. P. Shiel, Jack London, and George Allan England. Wells's generation was also the generation of such great socialist visionaries as G. V. Plekhanov and V. I. Lenin, Leon Trotsky and Karl Kautsky, Eduard Bernstein and Jean Jaurès, all of whom wrote at length about the future and how best to achieve the workers' millennium.

The difference is that none of these many worthies displayed Wells's fecundity and versatility as a futurist or centered his attention so obsessively on things to come or sought to transform the study of the future into a new academic discipline. In this sense, Wells stood alone.

THE POST-WELLSIANS

It also required more than one generation for Wells's initiatives to bear the kind of fruit he had in mind. The first post-Wellsian generation, men and women born in the last quarter of the nineteenth century, carried his work a little further, but without creating an independent science of futures research. They include a similar mix of creative writers, journalists, social scientists, philosophers, and others. Yevgeny Zamyatin and Aldous Huxley produced superior versions of Wells's forecast of the totalitarian state. Olaf Stapledon used the vehicle of science fiction to explore the far future. Sir Julian Huxley, Wells's partner in writing a popular survey of biology, *The Science of Life* (1931), developed a philosophy of the future in a series of essays and books on the theme of evolutionary humanism. His French contemporary, the Jesuit anthropologist Pierre Teilhard de Chardin, who also knew and admired some of Wells's work, espoused a similar philosophy, strangely alloyed in his case with a mystical variant of Catholicism.

Perhaps the most characteristic product of the futurist imagination of the first post-Wellsian generation was the vision of a coming planetary civilization promised by the trends and cycles of world history.[14] Despite Wells's lifelong campaign for world integration and the popularity of *The Outline of History*, the direct influence of Wells among these globalizing prophets, if any, was usually slight. But many resonances may be detected between Wells's futurism and theirs.

The father (or stepfather?) of historical futurism in this sense was the German historian Oswald Spengler, in his only major work, *The Decline of the West (Der Untergang des Abendlandes*, 1918–22). After studying the rise and fall of the major civilizations of the past, Spengler reached the firm conclusion that our own Western culture had exhausted its creative possibilities. The West was now entering its old age, an age of Caesarism, money, and empire, against which all resistance was futile. Although Spengler took no pleasure in his prophecy, and pointedly refused to equate the history of the West with the history of humankind (to him, a meaningless concept), he reawakened serious scholarly interest in comparative world history as a tool for probing the human future.[15]

Spengler's work found a laborious critic and successor in the English historian Arnold J. Toynbee. The twelve volumes of Toynbee's *A Study of History* (1934–1961) offered not only a hugely detailed comparative analysis of the birth and death of dozens of civilizations, but also, scattered throughout, enticing glimpses of the next stage in world history.

For Toynbee, unlike Spengler, the possibility arose of a transcendence of the cyclical pattern of the past. Threading upward through the cycles of history was a movement toward a higher destiny. Instead of the *Untergang* of the West, Toynbee foresaw the sacred union of humankind in a new species of planetary civilization, with a democratic world welfare state sustained spiritually by a universal religious renaissance.[16]

In the same years that Toynbee was publishing his *Study of History*, several other scholars reached comparable conclusions, sometimes under his influence. The Russian-born American sociologist Pitirim A. Sorokin, in the four volumes of his *Social and Cultural Dynamics* (1937–1941), offered Spengler and Toynbee their most strenuous competition. Sorokin also published a comparative critique of historical futurisms, under the title *Social Philosophies of an Age of Crisis* (1950), a work that helped establish the idea of a "school" of historically based studies of the human prospect.

Joining the ranks a few years later were the American humanist Lewis Mumford in *The Condition of Man* (1944) and *The Conduct of Life* (1951), the American philosophers F.S.C. Northrop in *The Meeting of East and West* (1946) and William Ernest Hocking in *The Coming World Civilization* (1956), and the German existentialist Karl Jaspers in *The Origin and Goal of History* (*Vom Ursprung und Ziel der Geschichte*, 1949) and *The Future of Mankind* (*Die Atombombe und die Zukunft des Menschen*, 1958).

All this gave inquiring minds in the 1930s, 1940s, and 1950s much to consider, but very little progress was made toward the acceptance of futures studies as a legitimate field of research. Teilhard, Toynbee, Jaspers, Mumford, and the rest of the post-Wellsians were not seen, and did not see themselves, primarily as futurists. They worked in established traditions of scholarship, and the future was only one of their many concerns.

PROFESSIONALIZING FUTURES

In the 1950s, as the philosophers of world civilization were completing their major works, the second post-Wellsian generation began to make itself heard. Scholars, scientists, and writers born in the first quarter of the century, this second generation included a sprinkling of freelance futurists of the older dispensation. It also produced scores of major writers of science fiction, a genre that came of age at last through the efforts of writers like Arthur C. Clarke, Isaac Asimov, and Robert Heinlein.

Increasingly, however, the study of the future was transformed into a collective effort. Apart from fiction, most of the major work was now done by research institutes, government agencies, corporate planning staffs, teams of scholars financed by grants, and the like. Wells's hope that futures research would someday pass from the hands of "amateurs" like himself to qualified professionals began to materialize, although rarely in pursuit of such Wellsian goals as world socialism or world government.

The shift in emphasis resulted less from decisions consciously taken by futurists than from the changing needs of society itself, reeling under the impact of largely unforeseen shocks to the world-system. These shocks, beginning with the First World War and the worldwide débâcle of the Great Depression, led many governments to seek expert opinion on ways and means of recovering from each new crisis and preventing their recurrence. Herbert Hoover's Research Committee on Social Trends, headed by the eminent sociologist and proto-futurist William F. Ogburn, and Franklin D. Roosevelt's "Brain Trust" of academic advisers were early examples of such collective futurism.

Another was the group of state planners who helped Joseph Stalin devise his Five-Year Plans from 1928 onward. Although much maligned for the harshness with which the dictator implemented them, the Five-Year Plans were also exploits in collective futurism, devised by experts, and crudely successful. Had the Soviet Union not been prepared by state-planned rapid industrialization to wage total war after 1941 against Nazi Germany, Hitler would probably have won the Second World War.

During these same Depression years, growing public demand for a wide range of state-sponsored welfare programs, followed by the mobilization of the full resources of every nation to fight World War II, further increased the need for planning, policy studies, and forecasting of all kinds. The ever-multiplying complexity of scientific research, technology, and industry made its contribution as well.

The wise had always counselled the strong, since the days when Aristotle advised Alexander the Great, but a quantum leap in consultation of experts by governments and corporations occurred in the 1930s, and another, even greater leap in the 1940s and 1950s. Those in power needed to know trends, prospects, synergisms. They needed futures research.

On occasion, an individual scholar might be able to help. But as a rule the problems at hand were too convoluted for futurist lone wolves. People with various degrees and kinds of expertise had to work together, in teams, on a regular basis, to churn out the statistics, projections, and recommendations required.

And so the history of futurism took a new turn. Members of the second post-Wellsian generation founded or joined organizations such the RAND Corporation, a private think tank spun off in 1948 from a U.S. military research project; the Hudson Institute, another think tank created by the former RAND researcher Herman Kahn in 1961; Aurelio Peccei's Club of Rome, organized in 1968 and best known for its sponsorship of a series of reports in the early 1970s on the limits to growth; and the Office of Technology Assessment, created by Congress in 1972 to provide legislators with studies of policy-relevant developments in technology.

Large numbers of futurists were also recruited by the executive branch of governments, undertaking policy studies and futures research for departments of defense, foreign affairs, trade and commerce, education, and many other fields. Futures became a recognized field in France in the 1950s and early 1960s in good part because of its usefulness to economic planning by the French government. A founder of the French futures movement, Pierre Massé, served at one time as high commissioner of the national plan.

Another founder of French futurism, Bertrand de Jouvenel, started his career as an exponent of the state-planned economy, coining the now familiar term *dirigisme* in his first book. In 1960 he helped institutionalize the study of the future by starting the Futuribles project, converted in 1967 at the initiative of his wife Hélène into the Association Internationale Futuribles, a major sponsor of research and clearing house of futurist ideas for France and the world. In 1966 Edward Cornish and his colleagues in Washington founded the World Future Society, which has a similar agenda, although less oriented toward the scholarly community. Futurist societies also formed in Germany, Sweden, Canada, and various other countries.[17]

In these same years, finally heeding Wells's cries for "professors of foresight" and the political scientist Ossip K. Flechtheim's appeal in 1943 for the teaching of "futurology,"[18] faculty at universities began developing courses and even programs in futures inquiry. One of the earliest courses was Alvin Toffler's, given at the New School for Social Research in New York in the fall of 1966. In 1974, the same year that I began teaching "History of the Future" at SUNY-Binghamton, Toffler published a symposium of articles on futures education, with an appendix listing some two hundred courses in futures studies then being offered in North American colleges and universities.[19] Also in 1974, the first graduate degree program in futures opened shop at the University of Houston, Clear Lake.

As futures studies institutionalized and won a toehold in academe, they also generated the array of methods sketched in our previous chapter. Most of the innovative methodological thinking in the futures field occurred in the 1950s and 1960s. Olaf Helmer developed the Delphi technique while employed by the RAND Corporation in 1953, and cross-impact analysis while working with Theodore Gordon in 1966 on a contract for Kaiser Aluminum. One of the first scholars to make effective use of scenario building was Herman Kahn, in his strategic studies on nuclear war for RAND in the 1950s and later the Hudson Institute. Jouvenel's major work as a futurist, *The Art of Conjecture*, with its concept of "futuribles," was published in France in 1964.

By the early or mid–1970s, it appeared that futurism had become airborne at last. University courses proliferated, membership in futurist societies multiplied, and Senator Edward Kennedy promised to create a Department of Futures when he became the next President of the United States. In addition to all the still-blooming efforts of the Kahns and Jouvenels and Helmers, Alvin Toffler wrote the first futurist best-seller, *Future Shock* (1970), which sold six million copies worldwide in five years. Daniel Bell's *The Coming of Post-Industrial Society* (1973) created a considerable stir in academic circles, and his fellow sociologist, Immanuel Wallerstein, published the first volume of *The Modern World-System* in 1974.

The early 1970s were also the seed-time of a new upgrowth of environmentalism, a movement with a strong futures orientation that greatly enlarged the province of futures studies. Spearheaded by scholars and scientists such as Barry Commoner, Paul and Anne Ehrlich, Lester Brown, and Norman Myers, environmentalist futurism reported a dangerously growing gap between resources and population, the degradation of the biosphere, and the possibility of system-wide collapse if concerted measures were not taken promptly.

Global environmentalism is still very much alive and well in the 1990s, but in the early 1970s, it arrived as a revelation. The key document was *The Limits to Growth* (1972), by Donella and Dennis Meadows and their associates, issued as a report to the Club of Rome. As we have already seen, *The Limits to Growth* made extensive use of a computer model of the global economic and environmental system, one of the earliest and certainly the most highly publicized example of computer modelling in futures research to that date.

The findings of the authors were dire. Continued industrial growth along current lines, they foresaw, would result in a collapse of the global economy in the second quarter of the next century, thanks to pollution and the exhaustion of essential resources. All variations of the standard model run, even assuming effective population control, sharp reductions in the emission of pollutants, and a handsome array of technological breakthroughs, led to disaster in the next century, although sometimes later than in the standard run. The only way to prevent a crashing of the curves was to implement a worldwide policy of zero industrial and zero population growth without delay. Postponing such action even for a few decades would prove fatal.

Since, in the popular imagination at least, computers never lie, *The Limits to Growth* terrified many of its millions of readers. The authors recorded all the usual disclaimers. Their model was only a model. The real world was more complex. Nevertheless, from all the smoke generated by their study, the average reader found it hard not to believe that, somewhere underneath the dark billows, a fire was raging. The golden calf of unlimited economic growth, worshipped by generations of capitalists, might well lead all humankind to its doom.

The Limits to Growth provoked plenty of controversy. Most of its conclusions were strongly questioned, as we shall see later. But the success of the book helped encourage other researchers to try computer modelling of the world system, with special reference to the three-cornered relationship between population, economic growth, and the carrying capacity of the environment. By 1985 it was possible for Barry Hughes in his excellent introduction to futures studies, *World Futures: A Critical Analysis of Alternatives*, to leave the impression with his readers that futures studies consisted chiefly of investigations of that relationship undertaken since about 1970, often based on computer models.[20]

In addition to *The Limits to Growth,* Hughes highlights the second Club of Rome report, *Mankind at the Turning Point* (1974) by Mihajlo Mesarovic and Eduard Pestel; *Catastrophe or New Society?* (1976), a reply to *The Limits to Growth* by a team of Latin American world modellers; Herman Kahn and the Hudson Institute's euphoric survey, *The Next Two Hundred Years* (1976); *The Future of the World Economy* (1977) by a UN research team headed by Wassily Leontief; and *The Global 2000 Report to the President* (1981), an elaborate project with pessimistic conclusions prepared by the Council on Environmental Quality, commissioned by outgoing President Carter, and promptly ignored by incoming President Reagan.

Hughes may have given too short shrift to pre–1970s futurism, but his account of the progress of futures studies after 1970 is not entirely misleading. Many futurists, especially those of what we must now call the third and fourth post-Wellsian generations, people born since about 1925, have been and remain preoccupied with the ecological future and its implications for human growth and development. The debate between the "Cornucopians," who set no limits to growth, and the "Malthusians," who advocate a steady-state world in dynamic equilibrium, remains lively. Interest in ecological futures has even quickened in the late 1980s and early 1990s, with the arrival of such relatively new issues as global warming and the apparent end of the East-West Cold War, which frees concerned citizens to be concerned about other things.

But futures studies continue to display more than one dimension. In spite of the rapidly evolving interest in environmental futures since 1970, futurism has advanced along other lines as well, both old and new. In science fiction, younger writers such as Gregory Benford, John Brunner, Kate Wilhelm, and Ursula Le Guin have very nearly achieved the status of grand masters in their profession. Corporations still award contracts to futurist think tanks, and government departments still use futurists to help them formulate policy in all areas. The relentless march of new technologies, including robotics, computers, and space flight, ensure ample business for specialists in technology assessment.

Striking new developments have also taken place in futures inquiry, apart from the rise of eco-futurism. World-system theory, for example, has infected a whole new generation of sociologists. Peace and world order studies, a field with a strong futures component, have grown spectacularly since 1970, although the relaxation of world political tensions since 1989 may well slow their progress through the rest of the 1990s. The futurist credentials of major figures in peace studies such as Kenneth Boulding, Richard Falk, and Rajni Kothari are unimpeachable.

Vast influence has also been wielded in futures studies since 1970 by the New Age movement, with its demand for cultural transformation and spiritual renewal. As promulgated by William Irwin Thompson, Willis Harman, Marilyn Ferguson, Hazel Henderson, and many others, New Age futurism shares few of the methods and values of the futurist mainstream, but its impact has been substantial. We shall have more to say about it in the next chapter.

This hurried history of futurism, for all its inadequacies, demonstrates at least two things. First, curiosity about the future has been a defining characteristic of Western civilization for thousands of years. Each era has developed its own ways of slaking that curiosity, but each era has maintained a lively interest in human destiny. Second, the struggle to professionalize and institutionalize futures studies has occupied most of this century, gaining momentum with each passing generation.

But futurists should know better than to extrapolate mindlessly from the trends of a single century. Whatever its potential, whatever the need for reliable forecasting may be, serious study of alternative futures enjoys no guarantee of success. The groves of academe are littered with the bones of obsolete disciplines. At the moment, for all its progress, the study of the future remains a marginal field, with uncertain prospects and many intrinsic shortcomings. Especially glaring is the poor track record of most futurists in foreseeing critical turns in contemporary world history. They have got things wrong time and time again, most recently in their failure to anticipate the astonishing events in the formerly communist world in the years 1989–90.

Futures is also an endeavor plagued, more than most, by prejudgments rooted in class interests, racial and sexual bias, ideologies, and world views. Before we can begin to discuss in greater depth the achievements of futures studies, we need one more introductory chapter, to explore the role of belief-systems in the day-to-day work of professional futurists.

NOTES

1. I. F. Clarke, *The Pattern of Expectation, 1644–2001* (New York: Basic Books, 1979), 197.

2. Beatrice Webb, *Our Partnership*, ed. Barbara Drake and Margaret I. Cole (London: Longmans, Green, 1948), 226.

3. H. G. Wells, *The Discovery of the Future* [1902] (London: PNL Press, 1989), 25, 27–28.

4. For an appreciation of the role of divination and revelation in the origins of futurist thought, see Bernard Cazes, *Histoire des futurs: Les figures de l'avenir de saint Augustin au XXIe siècle* (Paris: Seghers, 1986), chs. 1–2.

5. R. V. Sampson, *Progress in the Age of Reason* (Cambridge: Harvard University Press, 1956) provides an analysis of the idea of progress in its heyday. See also the relevant chapters of Robert Nisbet, *History of the Idea of Progress* (New York: Basic Books, 1980).

6. The persistence of a faith in progress in the period 1880–1914 is studied in

W. Warren Wagar, *Good Tidings: The Belief in Progress from Darwin to Marcuse* (Bloomington: Indiana University Press, 1972), chs. 3–7.

7. Friedrich Meinecke, *Historism: The Rise of a New Historical Outlook [Die Entstehung des Historismus,* 1936], tr. J. E. Anderson (London: Routledge and Kegan Paul, 1972).

8. For biographies of Wells, see Norman and Jeanne MacKenzie, *H. G. Wells* (New York: Simon and Schuster, 1973), and David C. Smith, *H. G. Wells: Desperately Mortal* (New Haven: Yale University Press, 1986). My own thoughts on Wells are available in W. Warren Wagar, *H. G. Wells and the World State* (New Haven: Yale University Press, 1961). For a recent reappraisal of Wells's thought and writing, consult Patrick Parrinder and Christopher Rolfe, ed., *H. G. Wells under Revision* (Cranbury, N.J.: Associated University Presses, 1990).

9. Mark R. Hillegas, *The Future as Nightmare: H. G. Wells and the Anti-Utopians* (New York: Oxford University Press, 1967).

10. H. G. Wells in the *Sunday Dispatch,* June 29, 1941 reprinted in W. Warren Wagar, ed., *H. G. Wells: Journalism and Prophecy, 1893–1946* (Boston: Houghton Mifflin, 1964), 258.

11. The connection between Goddard and Wells is discussed in my article, "H. G. Wells and the Scientific Imagination," 398–400.

12. H. G. Wells, "Wanted—Professors of Foresight!" (1932), reprinted in *Futures Research Quarterly* 3:1 (Spring 1987): 90. In 1938, another Englishman, A. M. Low, published an article in the short-lived periodical *Tomorrow: The Magazine of the Future* urging the creation of a Ministry of the Future in the British cabinet. Cornish, *The Study of the Future,* 76.

13. Dennis Gabor, *Inventing the Future* (New York: Knopf, 1964).

14. See W. Warren Wagar, *The City of Man: Prophecies of a World Civilization in Twentieth-Century Thought* (Boston: Houghton Mifflin, 1963; and Baltimore, Penguin Books, 1967).

15. For a futurist's evaluation of Spengler, see Bernard Cazes, *Histoire des futurs,* 202–211.

16. See Arnold Toynbee, *A Study of History* (Oxford: Oxford University Press, 1934–1961), and for a recent reassessment of his place in thought, C. T. McIntire and Marvin Perry, ed., *Toynbee: Reappraisals* (Toronto: University of Toronto Press, 1989), especially my chapter, "Toynbee as a Prophet of World Civilization," 127–140. A useful analysis of Toynbee's futurism is also available in Frederik L. Polak, *The Image of the Future,* II:391–401.

17. For the institutionalization of futurism in the United States and France after World War II, see the account in Cazes, *Histoire des futurs,* ch. 9, and also in Cornish, *The Study of the Future,* ch. 6.

18. Ossip K. Flechtheim was a German scholar, living in the United States in exile from the Third Reich, when he wrote his now famous article, "Teaching the Future." His articles on futures research and teaching are collected in *History and Futurology* (Meisenheim am Glan: Anton Hain, 1966).

19. Toffler, ed., *Learning for Tomorrow.*

20. See especially Barry Hughes, *World Futures: A Critical Analysis of Alternatives* (Baltimore: Johns Hopkins University Press, 1985), chs. 1–2. "During the 1970s, there was an explosion of interest in global issues and global futures. More specifically, the interest has been in global issues other than the cold war—issues

such as the rapid acceleration of population growth, the uncertainty of food suffi-
ciency, the degradation of environmental quality, the shortages or crises of resource
(especially energy) availability, and the persistent gap between the global rich and
poor. . . . I have restricted my examination largely to work of the 1970s and early
1980s (simply because of the significant increase in both writing and interest in that
period)." Hughes, *World Futures,* 2 and 12.

3 _____

Paradigms

IDEOLOGY AND THE FUTURE

Two revolutions in thought, the Marxian and the postmodern, assure us that objectivity is an unreachable goal. The Marxian revolution demolished the notion of value-free inquiry, observing that searches for knowledge are always conditioned by class interests. The postmodern revolution in philosophy and criticism, which has occurred in just the past quarter-century, challenges our ability to represent reality through language, or any other symbolic medium. Reality is one thing, and our words are another. We have no way, if the postmodern philosophers are correct, to construct a bridge between the two.

It might be added that the refutation of objectivity by Marxian and postmodern analysis was also the message implicit in historicism. If every moment in time is unique, and each of us is the product of a unique tangle of historical circumstances, then everything we "know" is colored by who, where, and when we are. Empathy cannot literally put us in the shoes, meaning the historical context, of any other human being. We cannot literally set aside our values, feelings, ideas, and interests, even for an instant. We cannot protect our research from contamination by these values, feelings, ideas, and interests, because none of us stands outside history: all scholars, like all people everywhere, are products and prisoners of history.

The relativistic thrust of historicism is not easy for anyone to live with. Few historicists have been willing to follow its logic to an absolute and categorical relativism. Besides, is not the notion of an absolute relativism an oxymoron? How can we be sure that we will never be sure?

In studying the future, considerations such as these become almost overwhelmingly bothersome. For all the reasons already given earlier, the future is a very murky place. There are no eyewitness accounts, no first-hand evidence. Worse still, futures inquiry is always normative as well as empirical. We study the future, as Jouvenel wrote, in hopes of learning how to gain control of it, and make it a better place than it might have been without our intervention.

The joker in the pack is the word "better." Better according to whom? According to you, or according to me? According to Hitler, or according to Stalin? According to the Palestinians, or according to the Israelis? Such questions have no answers. All images of the future, no matter what the methodologies employed, not only fall short of predicting the real future; they are also shaped by the normative preconceptions of the inquirer.

Barry Hughes, in *World Futures,* straightforwardly confronts the issue of subjectivity in futures studies, and in effect has built his whole book around it. He argues that images of the future hinge on the "world view" of the futurist, defining a world view as "a comprehensive set of values, basic assumptions about the way the world works, and derivative 'understandings' of complex events and processes. It implies as well derivative prescriptions with respect to individual, social, and political behavior." Hughes adds that a world view is roughly synonymous with such alternative terms as "paradigm," "prescriptive political theory," and "ideology."[1]

But in other contexts—such as intellectual history—a world view (comparable to the German *Weltanschauung* or *Weltansicht*) is much more than an ideology or prescriptive political theory. Although the phrase can be used loosely to mean almost anything, it usually denotes, as I have written elsewhere, "a conception of the nature of cosmic and human reality that discloses the meaning of life. World views furnish answers to the largest questions that human beings can ask about their condition."[2] One may speak of a Christian or Judaic world view, a rationalist or irrationalist world view, a positivist or romantic world view; but such paradigms go far beyond the ordinary meaning of "ideology." They encompass perspectives in theology, cosmology, ethics, epistemology, and aesthetics, as well as norms or goals for social and political action. Indeed, the same world view can harbor dozens of competing ideologies. The Christian world view, for example, has spawned systems of political thought justifying everything from monarchism to socialism.

There is also the question of whether any thinker, including any futurist, can have more than one world view. Because ideologies are not, in fact, comprehensive belief-systems, it is surely possible to endorse two or more at the same time. Thus, nationalism is not necessarily incompatible with socialism. A classical liberal can also be an environmentalist, an animal rights advocate, and either pro-choice or pro-life on the issue of abortion. That much is clear. But can anyone espouse several world views? I think not.

So one may quarrel with Hughes's choice of the term "world view." But his basic point is well taken. Futurists do subscribe to ideologies—or world views, if you like. And the values held by futurists do structure their images of the future.

Hughes explores futurist values along two axes, a horizontal axis on which he locates various "political economy" world views, and a vertical axis on which he locates, in a phrase of his own coinage, "political ecology" world views. Political economy world views articulate fundamental values in the realm of economics and governance. Political ecology world views express attitudes toward environmental issues, especially in relationship to economic growth. Hughes identifies three basic paradigms on the horizontal axis (radical, internationalist, and classical liberal) and two on the vertical axis (modernist and neotraditionalist).[3] Futurists may adhere to one paradigm on each axis, or occupy the ideological middle ground between any two paradigms on each axis. For example, a futurist can be a "pure" radical or classical liberal on the political economy axis, but take a position midway between the modernist and neotraditionalist world views on the political ecology axis; or vice versa. Almost any combination is imaginable.

Hughes's typology of futurist paradigms is both provocative and useful, at least when studying the ideological perspectives of recent specialists in world futures research. Its strength is the double axis of so-called world views, but the double axis is also its greatest weakness. Although some futurists take stands on political ecology issues apparently unrelated to their positions on issues of political economy, Hughes's typology fails by design to show any organic connection between ideas on these two sets of issues.

My own preference, taught in my course at SUNY Binghamton for more than a decade, is to speak simply of a triad of paradigms, which I define as "technoliberalism," "radicalism," and "counterculturalism," each denoting a range of ideological positions and options for action on futures issues. The three paradigms share some values and do not share others. Their differences and similarities can be represented schematically by drawing three overlapping circles. On some issues, the three circles occupy the same space. On others, adherents of any two paradigms think much alike, but not adherents of the third. Finally, there is a wide variety of issues on which the positions of the three paradigms are mutually exclusive.

Each paradigm, like each of Hughes's "world views," is only an ideal type. In given individual cases, a futurist's values may and often will be eclectic, not corresponding faithfully to the configuration of any single paradigm. But patterns do emerge, as one examines the positions taken by futurists. They do not arrive at their various forecasts and policy recommendations purely or even primarily on the basis of cold, logical, dispassionate research.

LIBERALS AND TECHNOLIBERALS

The first paradigm in my typology, "technoliberalism," is the hardest to label. Encompassing Hughes's modernist, internationalist, and classical liberal world views, it is the paradigm most often chosen by futurists in North America. Some would be surprised to discover that any other choice existed, above all in the wake of the collapse of the communist regimes in the former East bloc.

This first paradigm could just as well be called the "liberal" paradigm, or perhaps even the "conservative" or "neo-conservative" or "capitalist" paradigm. It is embraced by nearly all members of the two major parties in the United States and Canada, by British Tories and Liberals, by Gaullists and Christian Democrats and many other right-wing or centrist parties in Europe and Japan.

But what to call it? The historically correct term is in fact "liberal," well captured in Hughes's phrase "classical liberal." But there are also modern liberals, whose point of view, although not identical, is clearly a lineal descendant of historic liberalism. Unfortunately, the word "liberal" itself has acquired a foul odor in recent decades in American political parlance.

The New Left of the 1960s started the assault by defining liberals as slimy allies of the capitalist ruling class who pretend to love the working people, but in fact care only enough to make their misery a little more bearable, while at the same time staunchly defending the basic structure of the capitalist system and the bourgeois state. Then, in the 1980s, American politicians on the Right began to equate liberalism with socialism. A liberal was a false friend of the free enterprise system, a traitor to liberty, who in reality hoped to bring everyone under the heel of the state.

Both views of liberalism are preposterous and misleading. But to avoid any confusion between these derogatory uses of the term and our first paradigm, let us call the first paradigm "technoliberalism," an ideology that includes abiding faith in the power of technology and managerial technique to solve problems and help preserve liberty.

The technoliberal futurist is foremost a liberal in the original sense. When he or she refers to liberty, it is not an empty term. Liberty encompasses not only political freedoms, such as universal adult suffrage, representative government, and national self-determination, but also economic freedoms, above all freedom of enterprise, and civil freedoms, such as those protected in the American Bill of Rights. At the same time, technoliberalism is a modernizing ideology, favoring growth and development through the resourceful application of knowledge to the satisfaction of human needs.

The technoliberal path to the future in recent generations has really become two paths, heading in similar but not quite identical directions. The liberal road in American political thought forked in the 1930s, and somewhat earlier in other parts of the industrialized world. One group of technoliberals veered somewhat to the right, the other somewhat to the left. We may designate the first group "marketeers" and the other "welfarers."

Marketeers are liberals who cling stubbornly to their faith in the market and appeal for the least possible amount of state regulation of the economy and state-directed redistribution of wealth. Welfarers, by contrast, argue that the capitalist system cannot be saved unless governments intervene to guarantee minimum standards of well-being, both in national economies and in the world economy as a whole. Without state assistance, many of the poor, caught in a socioeconomic whirlpool, will sink further and further into poverty. But with state assistance, poor countries and individuals can be salvaged and in good time make a useful contribution to the world economy.

In recent years comparable differences have opened up between marketeers and welfarers on the subject of the environment. No one argues that the environment should be wrecked, but marketeers in general place more confidence in the market as a device for managing growth. They contend that conservation of scarce or costly resources and pollution control are in the long-term best interests of entrepreneurs, who will act expeditiously whenever resource depletion or harm to the environment endanger profits. Welfarers see continued growth as vitally necessary, but at the same time favor state action to protect the environment from ruthless and short-sighted exploitation. In short, whereas marketeers advocate almost limitless growth, welfarers are quicker to apply the brakes.

The overwhelming majority of leading figures in the futures community can be called technoliberals, and especially those who make their living consulting for corporations and governments. Three well executed assessments of contemporary futures research published in 1977, 1987, and 1989 offered profiles of forty selected individuals, either in their own words or in those of the authors.[4] Of the forty, I would classify at least three-quarters as technoliberals, with several others leaning in that direction. Of the thirty or more technoliberals, most are welfarers.

But classic marketeers have established a clear and forceful presence in futures research. Their greatest spokesman for many years until his untimely death in 1983 was Herman Kahn, the founder of the Hudson Institute. An even clearer exemplar of marketeer technoliberalism is Julian L. Simon, author of *The Ultimate Resource* (1981), and collaborator with Kahn in a volume of essays systematically refuting the findings and policy recommendations of *The Global 2000 Report to the President*.[5]

The welfarers are a mixed bag of futurists, ranging from environmentalists like the authors of *The Global 2000 Report* and Lester R. Brown of the Worldwatch Institute to liberal economists such as John Kenneth Galbraith, Daniel Bell, and Kenneth Boulding to world modellers like Barry Hughes, a one-time disciple of Mihajlo Mesarovic.

Some futurists—examples are Arthur C. Clarke and Gerard K. O'Neill—evince little interest in political or economic systems, but have no fundamental quarrel with capitalism and see a happy future on the way thanks to the galloping progress of science and technology. In general, these futurists, too, are technoliberals, with a heavy emphasis on the first half of the term, and a relatively unsophisticated approach to the issues that separate marketeers from welfarers.

RADICALS

The second of my three paradigms is one that I would characterize, just like Hughes, as the "radical" paradigm, which could almost as readily be termed the "socialist," "social-democratic," or "Marxist" paradigm. For rather obvious reasons, most radicals have had little or nothing to do with the institutionalized futures movement of the last few decades. In the United States at least, they are seldom called upon to work for governments or corporations. They tend to view professional futurists as hirelings of the ruling circles of capitalist countries, co-conspirators at worst, naive flunkeys at best.

Nevertheless, whether they realize it or not, radical social philosophers are futurists almost by definition. The radical view of society and history, especially the view set forth by Marx and Engels and their many followers in the late nineteenth and early twentieth centuries, is simultaneously a forecast of things to come and a project for political action. As Marx and Engels understood their work, they had created a new social science with predictive powers. In Engels's words, with the discovery of the materialistic conception of history and the revelation of the secret of capitalistic production through surplus value, "socialism became a science." As a science, it endowed the workers with the theoretical knowledge they needed to achieve the "universal emancipation" which was their "historical mission."[6] Both Marx and Engels glimpsed, here and there throughout their voluminous works, some of the contours of that dreamed-of emancipation.

To be sure, few Marxists or socialists of any stripe would claim the ability to predict future events in anything like a chronological sequence replete with dates and places. Few late twentieth-century radicals would even argue that the triumph of socialism cannot be prevented. At best it is a "futurible," made plausible by the dynamics of capitalist evolution as analyzed by radical political economists.

But Marxism, and socialism more generally, mean nothing except in the context of a reasoned hope for the future demise of the capitalist world-system with all its festering injustice and its replacement by some form of workers' polity or commonwealth. As in Judaism, Christianity, and Islam, so in the radical paradigm. The promise of a better future is the oxygen of belief. Belief could not survive without it.

Some radicals, of course, have dwelled at greater length on future possibilities than others. In addition to the world-system theory of Immanuel Wallerstein, which is deeply rooted in Marxist analysis, and the non-Marxist technocratic socialism of Wells, futurism owes much to two great German radical philosophers of the first post-Wellsian generation, Ernst Bloch and Herbert Marcuse. Their key texts as futurists are Bloch's *The Hope Principle* (*Das Prinzip Hoffnung*, 1959) and Marcuse's *Eros and Civilization* (1955).[7] Marcuse's futurism, in particular, underlies the vision of a non-repressive society entertained by New Left activists in the 1960s.

Since that time, a number of radicals have made significant contributions to futures theory and research. In the United States, the late Michael Harrington wrote many widely read futures-oriented books and essays on capitalism and democratic socialism, including *The Twilight of Capitalism* (1976). The ecologist Barry Commoner, the economist Robert Heilbroner, the historian Christopher Lasch, and Richard J. Barnet of the Institute for Policy Studies are prominent American radical scholars with futurist credentials. My own *Building the City of Man: Outlines of a World Civilization* (1971) and *A Short History of the Future* (1989) also illustrate the radical paradigm in futures studies.

Radical thinkers whose work is relevant to futurists are relatively more abundant in Europe and Australia, although, once again, few have formal ties with the futures community. The late Raymond Williams and his countryman, the historian E. P. Thompson, have been the senior figures in British futures inquiry. Outstanding radical thinkers in the German-speaking world since Marcuse include André Gunder Frank, Ernest Mandel, and Rudolf Bahro, and in France André Gorz. All have written extensively on the implications of recent political and economic history for the human future. Barry Jones, author of *Sleepers, Wake! Technology and the Future of Work* (1982), is perhaps the best known Australian radical futurist, although he dilutes the radical paradigm with a generous draft of welfarist technoliberalism.[8]

As with technoliberalism itself, the radical stream in futures speculation and research has split into smaller streams that do not flow in just the same direction, or toward the same precise goal. An early split occurred in the middle of the nineteenth century, with the rise of Marxian scientific socialism, which Marx and Engels opposed to the older utopian socialism of Saint-Simon, Owen, and Fourier.

Another split followed the Bolshevik Revolution of 1917, when the socialists (later communists) who formed the Third International broke with the socialists of the Second. Their divorce had been foreshadowed by the debates in pre–1914 Europe over whether or not socialists should serve in non-socialist governments, and whether socialism should take an "evolutionary" or "revolutionary" course. The socialists of the Third International went on to build centrally planned totalitarian societies on the Soviet Russian model. No compromise with capitalism was possible. Because of its inherent rapacity, capitalism could not be constrained to mend its ways, any more than a lion could be taught to graze. The socialists of the Second International by and large evolved into the democratic socialists of contemporary Europe, whose policies, if not their rhetoric, closely resemble the policies of welfarist technoliberals. It is difficult to think of some of them as radicals at all.

Since the 1980s, hard-line revolutionary Marxism has fallen on evil days throughout Europe and North America. Most authentic radicals nowadays take their Marxism in small doses, mingled with many other influences, from a simple populism, to environmentalism, pacifism, feminism, and New Age mysticism. The symbol of radical futurism in the 1980s and early 1990s is the Green party of Germany, whose program is a distinctly post-Marxist mélange of various leftist causes. But eclectic as it may be, the program of the Greens does preserve intact the classical Marxian hope of universal transformation and liberation.

On environmental issues, in particular, the newer radicalism is far less modernist than the old. Radicals throughout most of this century had aligned themselves with the technoliberals on the desirability of rapid economic growth and capital-intensive technology. But a goodly number of the newer radicals lean the other way, toward something approaching Hughes's neo-traditionalism. Some favor selective limits to growth. Most would call themselves environmentalists. Just as the symbol of the new radicalism is the Green party, so its symbolic text is a volume by the former East German Communist dissident Rudolf Bahro with a title that tells all, *From Red to Green* (1984).

Yet a great gulf does separate Red and Green politics, as it separates Red and Green futurism. They are not the same, even now. The radical tradition in Western thought that springs from Marx was committed to modernization and all that modernization implies: reason, science, technology, growth, progress. Although nothing in that commitment forced radicals to embrace a ruthless modernism indifferent to its impact on the environment or the quality of human life, the overriding faith of scientific socialism was in a future made possible by carrying the modernizing process to its logical conclusion, by working *through* capitalism to socialism. Returning to a medieval or bucolic past would only resurrect past scarcities and inequities.

Hence present-day radicals are in something of a quandary. If they recoil too far from their modernist heritage, if they forget the class struggle, the internal contradictions of capitalism, and the promise of socialism as the way to worldwide abundance for all men and women, they lose their identity and perhaps their raison d'être. In effect, they become what Hughes would call neotraditionalists, and what I would prefer to call counterculturalists.

COUNTERCULTURALISTS

Which brings us to the third and last futurist paradigm in our triad. In this instance Hughes and I may actually have identified a world view, and not just an ideology, although it has not yet acquired enough shape and coherence to tell. But for now counterculturalism (or neotraditionalism) is clearly a major futurist paradigm, more attractive to Americans who regard themselves as futurists than the radical paradigm.

As long ago as the mid–1970s, Michael Marien called attention to the emergence of a new direction in futurist thought similar to what Hughes and I have in mind.[9] Marien listed fifteen possible labels for it, including "traditionalist" and "Jeffersonian," but through most of his article referred to the new movement as "decentralist."

He began with the observation that the dominant view of the post-industrial future among both liberal and radical social scientists, crystallized in 1973 by Daniel Bell in *The Coming of Post-Industrial Society*, was that of a centralized and urbanized service state with a highly developed technology. He traced this vision as far back as Herbert Spencer and Thorstein Veblen, but today, he noted, it had become the orthodox view of things to come, the conventional wisdom of the futurist mainstream.

What of decentralism? As early as the writings of Hilaire Belloc and G. K. Chesterton at the turn of the century, Marien found inklings of a diametrically opposed view of the post-industrial future. What if, instead of more urbanization and more centralization of power, humankind chose a different dream, concerned more with the quality of life than with its quantities? What if it turned its back on the frantic quest for abundance, and all the evils that abundance entails, from environmental ruin to technocratic tyranny? Advocates of the decentralizing of governance and the economy, wrote Marien in 1977, had flourished in a sort of intellectual underground ever since, steadily gaining strength from about 1970 onward, as evidenced by the popularity of the works of such decentralist prophets as E. F. Schumacher, Ivan Illich, and Theodore Roszak.

Marien's analysis was focused only on the issues raised by Bell in *The Coming of Post-Industrial Society*. But he had put his finger on a significant shift in loyalties in the futures community. By the late 1970s it was clear that a serious challenge had been mounted to both the technoliberal and radical paradigms.

My term for this third paradigm is counterculturalism, which I have borrowed from Roszak, whose *The Making of a Counter Culture* (1969) captured so effectively the mental climate of the Sixties. In *Where the Wasteland Ends: Politics and Transcendance in Postindustrial Society* (1972) and later books, Roszak was himself instrumental in helping to form an oppositional futurist culture that draws some of its energy from, but has also gone well beyond, the fugitive concerns and enthusiasms of that brief era.

I like the term counterculturalism because it places the emphasis where I think the emphasis belongs, on cultural transformation. Whereas the radical paradigm argues for rejection of an economic and political world-system, the counterculturalist paradigm attacks the core values of modern civilization. Curiously enough, some counterculturalists attack these values without firmly rejecting the economic and political world-system of capitalism, but their program implicitly calls for a clean sweep. At the same time, in many respects, the world they seek to put in place of our own harks back to earlier, simpler, less centralized, more traditional ways of life. They rarely specify *which* traditional model we should try to adopt, nor do they believe in the possibility of literally recreating any given preindustrial society. But Marien's term "decentralist" and Hughes's "neotraditionalist" do help to flesh out our understanding of this vision.

Other descriptors come to mind, such as "New Age" or "transformational." The problem with "New Age" is that it connotes a shallow pop-culture movement identified with dubious Indian gurus, the piano stylings of George Winston, Harmonic Convergence, channeling, and the ruminations of Shirley MacLaine. But there is a more serious side to so-called New Age thought, grounded in both Eastern and Western mysticism and in the work of many of the same social philosophers who have furnished the intellectual foundations of neotraditionalism and decentralism. An early use of the phrase in futures inquiry was by Mark Satin in his *New Age Politics: Healing Self and Society* (1979). There have been many others.

"Transformational" suffers from a certain vagueness, but it too has a considerable following, illustrated by the writings of a prominent convert to counterculturalist futurism, Willis W. Harman. In a memoir of his life in futures studies, Harman speaks of his odyssey from engineering professor, to systems analyst and computer modeller at the Stanford Research Institute, to someone, who, by the early 1970s, saw that the liberal future imagined by Daniel Bell would probably never come to pass. Rising to oppose it were the forces of authoritarian reaction and a "new consciousness" movement, with its "transformational" scenario of a postmodern culture growing from the ruins of a failed industrialism. As he came to understand what was happening in the world, Harman did not hesitate to ally himself with the purveyors of the new consciousness. Today, as he wrote in 1987, he is "totally involved, as best I know how, with the inner and outer transformation that I am now convinced is the only path toward a future that I would feel good about bequeathing to my grandchildren."[10]

Whatever we choose to call them, adherents of the counterculturalist paradigm aspire to be more radical than the radicals. What is wrong with modern man and woman, they say, is not this or that institution or trend, but modernity itself. The rape of the environment is just one example, to which most of us have only recently awakened, of how the values of modernity, so seductive at first blush, are in fact demonic. Thus the great question for late twentieth-century society is not whether to limit growth, as technoliberals imagine, but whether to replace the values of the dominant culture that make us *want* to grow.

The new consciousness referred to by Harman cannot be characterized in one or two easy phrases. It appeals for a revived sense of the sacredness of the person, humankind, and the earth, a sense allegedly torn from us by the exploitative character of modernity. It demands the subordination of science, reason, logic, and technique to the powers of heart and spirit. It rejects the centripetal tendencies in modern social organization toward ever bigger, more complex, and more distant centralized authorities, in favor of local and communal autonomy. It opposes violence and war-making in all its forms, activities that it often associates with a pattern of male domination perfected in the modern world.

In the realm of economics, the new consciousness of counterculturalist futurism argues for a swift transition from heavy reliance on capital-intensive high technology to a mix of technologies in which most of the world's work is done with the help of simpler "intermediate" or "appropriate" labor-intensive technologies. It urges the replacement of non-renewable sources of energy such as oil and coal by renewable sources such as solar and wind power. With its preference for decentralized authority, it would like to see the atrophy of the multinational corporation and the rise of locally based cooperatives. Counterculturalists rarely make a wholesale assault on capitalism, as such, but it is difficult to imagine how capitalism could survive, much less thrive, in a world tailored to their specifications.

Not every adherent of the counterculturalist paradigm would necessarily endorse each of these points. There are at least as many varieties of the paradigm as of any other, with some counterculturalists limiting their inquiries chiefly to cultural concerns, others stressing politics or peace theory, still others the meta-economics and environmentalism of the movement, and so forth. Some are quite radical, expecting a total transformation of civilization no less apocalyptic than the fall of Rome. Others look forward to a gentler and less far-reaching process of graduated reconstruction.

In any case, counterculturalist futurism captured many followers and at least strongly influenced many onlookers in the 1970s and 1980s. It drew much of its earlier inspiration from some of the prophets of a new civilization of the first post-Wellsian generation discussed above, especially Pierre Teilhard de Chardin, Lewis Mumford, and Pitirim Sorokin.[11] Its first major exponent was the late E. F. Schumacher, the German-born British economist who wrote *Small Is Beautiful: Economics As If People Mattered* (1973) and developed the idea of appropriate technology.

Other founders of note, besides Schumacher, Harman, Roszak, and Illich, include the historian and countercultural activist William Irwin Thompson, author of *At the Edge of History: Speculations on the Transformation of Culture* (1971); E. F. Schumacher's British disciple Hazel Henderson, who wrote *The Politics of the Solar Age: Alternatives to Economics* (1981); and the New Age prophetess Marilyn Ferguson, best known for her extraordinarily popular book, *The Aquarian Conspiracy: Personal and Social Transformation in the 1980s* (1980). A fictional evocation of counterculturalist values is Ernest Callenbach's classic novel *Ecotopia* (1975).

Technoliberalism, radicalism, counterculturalism: in my schema, these three are the major paradigms of futurist thought up to now. They furnish moral, spiritual, intellectual, and practical guidance to their adherents, especially in the sphere of normative futures inquiry. It may be presumptuous to call them world views, but they often function as such, in our secularized age. They also largely predetermine how a given futures researcher will conduct his or her research, and what he or she will learn about the shape of things to come.

It remains only to note, as we intimated earlier, that the three paradigms do not disagree on every public issue. They share common ground at various points. They oppose racism in its many versions, together with sexism and religious bigotry and intolerance. They all speak well of democracy, civil liberty, world peace, the rule of law, and the self-determination of peoples. They all, especially nowadays, generate programs to protect the environment, albeit with disparate priorities and methods of proceeding.

The differences between them, however, are obvious and sometimes quite sharp. You may devoutly wish that it were otherwise, but the fact remains that the kind of futurist you will be depends on which paradigm best expresses your idea of the good society, and which you choose to embrace.

NOTES

1. Hughes, *World Futures*, 26.

2. W. Warren Wagar, *World Views: A Study in Comparative History* (New York: Holt, Rinehart and Winston, 1977), 4.

3. Hughes, *World Futures*, ch. 3. See especially Tables 3.1, 3.2, and 3.3 on pp. 34, 42, and 48, respectively.

4. The three surveys are Cornish, *The Study of the Future*, ch. 9; Coates and Jarratt, *What Futurists Believe*; and Michael Marien and Lane Jennings, ed., *What I Have Learned: Thinking about the Future Then and Now* (Westport, Conn.: Greenwood Press, 1987). Curiously, there is not much overlap in the individuals selected. Of the seventeen futurists who contributed to the Marien and Jennings volume, only two (Kenneth E. Boulding and Victor C. Ferkiss) were profiled by Coates and Jarratt. The ninth chapter of *The Study of the Future*, "Futurists and Their Ideas," offered sketches of the life and work of eleven persons, of whom only three appeared in either of the other volumes (Arthur C. Clarke and Daniel Bell in Coates and Jarratt, Willis W. Harman in Marien and Jennings).

5. See Herman Kahn and Julian L. Simon, ed., *The Resourceful Earth: A Response to Global 200* (New York: Blackwell, 1984).

6. Friedrich Engels, *Socialism: Utopian and Scientific*, tr. Edward Aveling [1892] (New York: International Publishers, 1975), 53 and 75.

7. On Bloch and Marcuse as utopians, see Vincent Geoghegan, *Utopianism and Marxism* (London: Methuen, 1987), chs. 6 and 7. Marcuse is also treated as the last exhibit in evidence in Frank E. and Fritzie P. Manuel, *Utopian Thought in the Western World* (Cambridge: Harvard University Press, 1979), 794–800; and similarly in my *Good Tidings: The Belief in Progress from Darwin to Marcuse*, 343–348.

8. Barry Jones, Rudolf Bahro, and André Gorz are centerpieces in Boris Frankel's

study of recent utopian thought, *The Post-Industrial Utopians* (Madison: University of Wisconsin Press, 1987). The fourth featured futurist is none other than Alvin Toffler, not because of his analyses and activities, which, Frankel admits, place him well to the right of radicalism, but because Toffler appears to share many of the same utopian goals as the radical writers in his study. I remain unconvinced.

9. Marien, "The Two Visions of Post-Industrial Society," *Futures: The Journal of Planning and Forecasting*, 9:5 (October, 1977): 415–431. In reviewing the manuscript of this book in January 1991, Marien strongly criticized my assumption that the "decentralist" or "counterculturalist" paradigm remains strong today. He contended that it began to lose significant ground in the early 1980s and has now been largely supplanted by a "Green" or "globalist/environmentalist" paradigm, which shares some of its concerns but not all. In *Future Survey Annual: 1990* he identified three other major ideological orientations in current favor among producers of futures-relevant material: "conservative/libertarian," "progressive/left," and "liberal/moderate." Michael Marien, ed., *Future Survey Annual: 1990* (Bethesda, MD: World Future Society, 1990), p. 180. Although Marien's typology may work better for the late 1980s and early 1990s than the one adopted in this chapter, I still prefer mine as a strategy for surveying the main currents of futurist thought during the past quarter-century.

10. Willis W. Harman, "How I Learned to Love the Future," in Marien and Jennings, ed., *What I Have Learned*, 41. See also Harman, *An Incomplete Guide to the Future* (New York: Norton, 1979), and *Global Mind Change: The Promise of the Last Years of the Twentieth Century* (Indianapolis: Knowledge Systems, 1988).

11. An illustration of this indebtedness is the study of Pitirim Sorokin conducted by Willis W. Harman and his colleagues in the futures research group at the Stanford Research Institute, documented in Harman, "How I Learned to Love the Future," 38. For a sample of Teilhard's influence, see Robert T. Francoeur, "Reproductive Futures: 1964, 1984, and Beyond," in Marien and Jennings, ed., *What I Have Learned*, 62.

PART II

ALTERNATIVE FUTURES

4 ———————————————————————————

The Future of the Earth

THE EARTH AS A SYSTEM

Our task in the next four chapters is to define the issues that command the attention of futurists today, and indicate how subscribers to each of the major paradigms of futures thinking discussed in the previous chapter differ (or agree) on each issue. In the process, depth will be freely sacrificed for the sake of breadth. Our aim is less to construct a synthesis of thinking about the future than to provide a road map for the inquiring traveler. The issues themselves are much too complex to receive anything but cursory treatment in a short book.

Like any good road map, this one will try at least to show all the major roads and the country they traverse. Many futurists who came of professional age in the 1970s and many with a background in the natural sciences give the impression that the study of the future is primarily a study of global environmental crisis. Others, especially if they hold engineering degrees, may convince us that the future will consist largely of a stream of technological marvels. Futurists trained in the social sciences, and many of the technoliberal and radical persuasions, tend to focus on the societal future, probing the future of capitalism and democracy, or war and peace, or education, or the family. Humanists and mages of the futurist counterculture inquire into the future of religion, thought, and art, the latter a subject almost wholly ignored by many others.

Unfortunately for the specialists, all these activities (or whatever may come along to take their place) will continue into the future, and not in isolation from one another. If we do not make a good-faith attempt to consider them all, even the most meticulous investigation of any one or two will probably be in vain.

We begin with the future of the earth, the physical life-support system of our species. The next chapter will focus on political and economic futures, followed by chapters on the prospects for war and peace in the world system and the sociocultural future. But we shall have to do a great deal of shuttling back and forth between these immense topics, to keep track of how they affect one another. The environment, for example, is shaped more and more by the doings of men and women, which in turn are directed by social and cultural configurations over which individual men and women exert little control. Resources, populations, technologies, policies, and values are all dynamically interlinked.

But it makes sense to begin with the future of the earth. Human life is animal life. Human beings need water, air, nutrients, and heat to stay alive. Until we begin colonizing the heavens, all these must be found in the earth. If they cannot be found, whether because of scarcity or contamination or inaccessibility, we must die. The relationship between resources and population is the most basic in all of human experience. So it was in prehistoric times, and so it remains today.

Not too many years ago, the perceived ratio between available resources and the human population was favorable enough that explorers of alternative futures could safely ignore environmental issues. Problems might arise, but they could easily be solved by technological wonder-workers. Since at least 1970, the perception has grown that we can no longer count on a favorable ratio, even with technology operating at wide-open throttle. As the 1990 edition of *State of The World*, issued by the Worldwatch Institute, warns: "Only a monumental effort can reverse the deterioration of the planet."[1]

For some thinkers, especially those wed to the counterculturalist paradigm, the mineral earth and its life forms, including humankind, are actually a single organism, sharing a similar destiny. Since the beginnings of life on earth, they believe, earth and life have co-evolved, each influencing and helping to shape the other in a symbiotic relationship.

I refer to the "Gaia" hypothesis, first put forward in the late 1960s by a British scientist, James Lovelock, and named after the Greek goddess of the earth.[2] In the earliest versions of his theory, Lovelock argued that an environment friendly to living creatures did not develop by accident. Our planet is rich with life because the inorganic earth and its biota may have collaborated, in ways that seem almost purposeful, to maintain optimal conditions for the flourishing of life. We descend from Mother Earth in a quite literal way, and she continues to look after us.

In recent years Lovelock has qualified his thinking, and disputed the mystical conclusions drawn by overzealous counterculturalists. But he has persuaded a variety of scientists to follow his lead on other points. That earth and its living inhabitants have evolved together interactively is no longer considered a wild idea. The rocks, the waters, the gases in the atmosphere, and the biota may form a single self-regulating system that remains always in a rough sort of natural equilibrium. This equilibrium allows life to persist, although from epoch to epoch the earth is more hospitable to certain forms of life than to others, and catastrophes, natural or man-made, can always temporarily upset nature's balance.

A good example of the co-evolution of the mineral and the organic is what happens when the earth's temperature rises steeply. At such a time, lakes and seas lose more than the usual amount of water from evaporation. This increases rainfall, which washes carbon dioxide out of the atmosphere in the form of carbonic acid and erodes or weathers rocks. Pelted by rain rich in carbon, the rocks release bicarbonate ions into the earth's waters, which feed the plankton and help them multiply. As they die or are eaten, the carbon from their microscopic bodies eventually makes its way to the ocean floor and into the earth's crust. The loss of massive quantities of carbon dioxide from the atmosphere reverses the greenhouse effect, causing the atmosphere to cool, which in turn spares many species that had faced extinction in the rising heat.

But this is not the end of the cycle. Eventually, after thousands of years, much of the carbon ingested by the plankton works its way back to the surface of the earth and into the air, helping to initiate a warming trend. From global warming comes global cooling, and the system perseveres, avoiding either catastrophic heat or cold.

Whether this cycle would still occur without the mediation of the plankton or other living things is a subject of furious debate among geologists.[3] But clearly the earth and its creatures affect one another profoundly. A film of life, which ecologists call the biosphere, envelops the earth, altering and being altered in turn by the earth's elements. Futurists increasingly base their environmental forecasts on an understanding of the earth as a single system, subject to all kinds of local variations, but essentially one and whole.

POPULATION AND FOOD

For the future, some would contend (and others would just as vigorously deny) that the single most crucial datum is how many people will be living on this planet in the twenty-first century and beyond. All the other problems, from pollution and dwindling resources to class and international conflict, pale beside the problem of overpopulation.

It is, after all, people who pollute rivers, people who burn oil, people who engage in productive labor, people who need land to raise food, and people who kill one another to acquire land. A world population of 5.3 billion, scattered as all of us are scattered today, is one thing. A world population of 12.3 billion, arranged similarly or differently in the year 2050, would be quite another. In short, supply (air, water, land, food, minerals, energy) is meaningless except in relationship to demand (people).

Sheer numbers do not tell the whole story; much depends also on technological capacity, which can increase or decrease supply, and rates of consumption, the distribution of wealth, and dominant cultural values, which can modify demand. But numbers cannot be ignored. Since the beginnings of agriculture and animal husbandry, the human population has doubled many times, at a generally accelerating pace. Between 1750 and 1850, the early years of the Industrial Revolution, population grew at the rate of .5 percent per year. Between 1850 and 1950, it grew at the rate of .8 percent per year, and between 1950 and 1990, at 1.8 percent per year. The world's total population, which did not reach one billion until the age of Napoleon, stood at two and one-half billion in 1950, three and two-thirds billion in 1970, and five and one-third billion in 1990.

At this phenomenal pace, nearly 100 million births per year as of 1990, the whole current population of the United States could be replaced worldwide in two years and seven months. A great city of three million people, like Chicago or Melbourne, could be replaced, demographically speaking, in just over eleven days. For the species as a whole, our current 1.8 percent growth rate would result in a global population of ten and two-thirds billion by the year 2029.

Of course all this growth does not occur at the same rate in every corner of the world. From the demographer's point of view, there are two large categories of countries: those in which the growth rate averages .5 percent per year, the same rate as in Napoleon's day, and those in which the growth rate averages 2.1 percent per year, more than four times higher. Most rich, industrially developed countries have very low growth rates, and poor countries very high growth rates. Infants in rich countries seldom die, and in 1990 life expectancy at birth was 74 years. In poor countries, infant mortality is high, and life expectancy from ten to fifteen years fewer.

The demographic difference between the two groups of countries is nothing mysterious. In the rich countries and to a lesser extent in the poor, life has been considerably prolonged by modern medicine, hygiene, and better nutrition. But whereas the rich countries have by and large succeeded in dramatically lowering their birth rates, most of the poor countries so far have not.

A good example is India, where a spectacular reduction of the death rate during the 1970s devoured all the gains recorded in a strident national campaign to lower the birth rate. The exhaustive census of 1981 showed that India's total population was now growing at a rate of 2.475 percent per year, as opposed to 2.5 percent per year in 1970. In other words, India made no measurable progress at all toward the goal of reducing her population growth in that decade. By 1990, to be sure, the birth rate had fallen quite a bit further, to 2.1 percent, but even at this more modest rate India's population will double by the year 2023.

The issues that challenge demographers and futurists in the realm of population futures reduce essentially to two: how many people will be alive at various times in the next one or two centuries, and can what Simon and Kahn call the "resourceful earth" feed and house them?

Population forecasting is not quite so risky as weather forecasting, but it has its share of perils. In 1928, Sir George Handley Knibbs calculated that the world's population, at current growth rates, would reach 3.9 billion by the year 2008, and found this figure both "astonishing" and "ominous."[4] In the 1950s, as the postwar baby boom got under way, but before death rates had begun to drop precipitously in the less developed countries, most predictions were also on the low side. Harrison Brown, for example, a pioneer in the field of human ecology, wrote in *The Challenge of Man's Future* (1954) that the planet would house 4.8 billion people in the year 2000 and 6.7 billion in 2050.[5]

By the early 1970s, however, as the evidence mounted of a population explosion in the Third World, some experts foresaw a much steeper rise, to 6.5 or even 7.0 billion by 2000, and twice that many by 2050, if not sooner. Gordon Rattray Taylor, expecting the worst in *The Doomsday Book*, saw "no escape from the fact that, short of plague or nuclear war, we shall have to feed a population of about 7 billion by the year 2000."[6]

Such pessimism was rife for many years. Then demographers discovered that several poor countries were starting to make significant and unexpected progress in fertility control. Forecasters allowed themselves a slightly cheerier outlook. The likeliest scenarios issued by the United Nations and other authorities in the mid-1980s saw about 6.0 billion people on earth by 2000, 9.5 billion by 2050, and an end to growth by 2100, with a total global population of roughly 10.0 billion.[7]

A few years later, however, expectations changed again. As some of the poor countries that had previously recorded gains in fertility control began to backslide, the experts grew a little warier. In 1990 the United Nations looked forward to the stabilization of global population in 2100 at 11.3 billion, rather than the 10.2 billion it had forecast earlier. The Washington-based Population Reference Bureau, which in 1988 had foreseen a world population of 8.0 billion by the year 2020, increased its estimate in 1990 to 8.2 billion, and warned that if replacement level fertility were not reached worldwide until 2080, the earth's population by 2100 would approach 13.5 billion.[8]

All this illustrates a fairly obvious point, that futurists tend to key their forecasts to the latest observable trends. If the world's population is perceived to be rising slowly, they predict modest growth. If it appears to be rising rapidly, they expect mushroom growth. Hardly anyone working in the period from 1930 to 1945 foresaw the postwar population boom, hardly anyone in the 1950s anticipated the sudden decline of Third World mortality, and hardly anyone today looks forward to rapid stabilization. The earlier forecasts were almost ludicrously wrong. Will today's forecasts prove to be just as bad?

We cannot know whether present-day experts will be any luckier than their predecessors, but this is almost universally the case in futures studies, even the "hard" kind. Success depends on variables to which precise values cannot possibly be assigned. In population forecasting, what we need to ascertain are both the future of mortality, or death rates, and the future of fertility, or birth rates, both of which are notoriously difficult to foresee.

Death rates, for example, could increase because of worldwide famines or plagues, such as the AIDS epidemic. Or they could decline sharply because of multiplying prosperity in many Third World countries, or major breakthroughs in prolongevity research. Birth rates could rise because of the collapse or failure of efforts by Third World governments to limit reproduction or because of a general decline in Third World living standards, which would most likely (and paradoxically) entail a regression to high fertility. By the same token, birth rates could drop much further if Third World countries redouble their efforts and if economic progress underwrites public policy. Accurately foreseeing each of these eventualities and calculating the net effect of all of them combined is next to impossible.

Most demographers and futurists do agree on one thing. They concur that in the very long run world population must, should, and can stabilize. But when this happy event will occur, and at what level, remain open questions. Stabilization could occur in 2050, at 8.8 billion; in 2100, at 11.3 billion; or in 2150, at 20.0 billion. No one knows.

The most hopeful indicator is that in every industrially advanced country birth rates have been reduced to near or even below replacement levels. As of 1990, the annual population growth rate of the European countries, excluding the Soviet Union, was .3 percent. Three of these countries reported a negative growth rate. Japan's growth rate was .4 percent, and the United States', Australia's, and New Zealand's was .8 percent.

The reasons for these lower figures are well known. In relatively affluent societies, families understand and freely practice birth control with little need for encouragement from public authorities. The labor of children is not needed, thanks to the high level of mechanization in business, industry, and agriculture. Moreover, children are so expensive to raise and educate that the average husband and wife seldom want more than two. With their affluence, they could easily afford more than two, but affluence breeds other costly tastes and temptations that make short work of all their excess cash.

It follows that as poor countries begin to bridge the gap between poverty and affluence, their birth rates fall correspondingly. As of 1990, prospering South Korea reported a population growth rate less than half that of still impoverished North Korea. At an annual population growth rate of 1.0 percent, South Korea has almost made the demographic transition to replacement level fertility. At an annual rate of 2.1 percent, North Korea remains a typical Third World country.

In some relatively poor countries, progress in limiting births has also been facilitated by government incentive programs, the liberalization of abortion, birth control education, and various other measures. The big demographic story of the late 1970s and 1980s was that many of these countries, such as Egypt, Kenya, Mexico, Brazil, and China had actually begun reducing their birth rates without a corresponding improvement in living standards.

But their continued success is not assured. It may well be that no massive and enduring change in reproductive behavior will take place until every poor country rises to the level of affluence already achieved by countries like France, Germany, and Japan. It may also be true that in countries like the United States, where large numbers of disadvantaged African and Hispanic Americans reproduce faster than their Euro-American fellow citizens, the disparity in growth rates will not be erased until the economic status of the disadvantaged matches that of the privileged.

The question of when and how world population stability will be achieved raises a further question, which transports us from the realm of the empirical to the realm of the normative. Ignoring for the moment the apparent facts of the matter, what is the *optimum* world population? How many people *should* there be?

No one can answer such a question by drawing on the resources of demographics alone. It involves cultural norms, political judgment, social philosophy, economics, ethics, and perhaps even theology. But one empirical consideration does surely come into play; that is, the number of people who can be kept alive by human labor and ingenuity. Even this consideration is highly charged with normative implications, since how much and what kinds of nutrition, clothing, shelter, and other necessities are required to sustain life as it should be lived depend on the values and expectations of whoever decides what constitutes "life as it should be lived."

All the same, certain minimum physical conditions must be met, in the barest of lives. Every human being needs a certain number of calories, vitamins, minerals, molecules of oxygen, and grams of fresh water per day to keep alive. Nor, without adequate clothing, shelter, or both, can a human being survive for long when air temperatures fall well below the freezing point of water.

Determining the future availability of even these minimum necessities of life has divided futurists more fundamentally than the task of forecasting global population growth. At the one extreme, many technoliberal marketeers and even some radicals have argued that the planet can readily support a population much larger than any now predicted. Advances in agriculture, energy technologies, and the like can, they say, make it possible for Mother Earth to extend her hospitality to tens of billions of the yet unborn.

The British economist Colin Clark, for example, astounded readers of the journal *Nature* in 1958 with the observation that population growth was a powerful historic driver of economic progress, and that if agriculture were simply made more efficient, along Dutch lines, the earth's arable land could support a world population of 28 billion. In later writings, he ventured still higher forecasts.[9] In 1976, Herman Kahn and his associates maintained that within two centuries there would be a stable world population of anywhere from 7.5 to 30 billion, fed as well as the average North American is fed today. Food production would climb to meet the increased needs as a result of improvements in conventional agriculture and hydroponics and the development of new technologies capable of transforming what is now inedible into food fit for human consumption.[10] Much more recently, Frank Feather in his super-optimistic *G-Forces* (1989) suggests that if only the whole world emulated the North American corn farmer, "probably enough food could be produced to sustain a world population of up to 48 billion."[11]

At the other end of the spectrum, welfarist technoliberals, most present-day radicals, and counterculturalists insist that such projections are dangerous fantasies. In the 1960s, the loudest tocsins were sounded by William and Paul Paddock in their controversial book *Famine 1975!* (1967) and by Georg Borgstrom in *The Hungry Planet: The Modern World at the Edge of Famine* (1965). Except in parts of central Africa, most of their direst expectations did not materialize. Improvements in the yield of major cereal crops such as rice and wheat, known collectively as the Green Revolution, allowed food production to keep pace with (and even forge slightly ahead of) population growth down through at least 1985.

But pessimists note that recent disturbing developments cast doubt on the possibility of continued progress. United Nations studies show that arable land is turning into desert all over the world at an alarming rate, as a result of overgrazing, erosion, and bad farming. To make matters worse, the new super-crops of the Green Revolution have reached their biological limits and can no longer deliver higher and higher yields. Meanwhile, for poor countries and poor farmers without the resources to purchase the fertilizers and irrigation facilities required for best results, the super-crops cost too much to raise; and the environmental costs involved in diverting so much energy to food production are, in the long run, too high for all of us, even in the rich countries. "As we enter the nineties," Lester R. Brown and John E. Young conclude, "the world has little to celebrate on the food front. . . . Growth in world food output is being slowed by environmental degradation, a worldwide scarcity of cropland and irrigation water, and a diminishing response to the use of additional chemical fertilizer."[12]

Various solutions suggest themselves, depending on one's point of view. For technoliberal welfarers, often the best answer is simply a vigorously renewed effort to reduce population growth, especially in the less developed countries. Those drawn to the radical and counterculturalist paradigms are more likely to contend that the problem can be solved if population control policies are supplemented by more appropriate agricultural methods and technologies, together with reforms in land ownership.

The authors of *Gaia: An Atlas of Planet Management* provide an excellent illustration of radical and counterculturalist strategies. They campaign for a world policy that would combine environmentally sound Western approaches to food production, such as a "Gene Revolution" in plant engineering, with traditional Eastern methods, such as the labor-intensive Chinese system of "ecological agriculture." At the same time, they deplore a variety of Western ways, including high Western consumption of meat, which requires far more land to produce than its nutritional equivalent in plant foods or farm-raised fish, and too much reliance on energy-wasteful agricultural technologies, which not only damage the environment but also widen the gap between rich and poor. With the right policies and support, the farmers of the world can feed us all. "It is merely a matter of getting our priorities right."[13]

ENERGY

Reference to "energy-wasteful technologies" brings up another large category of problems in considering the future of the earth. Given an abundance of cheap and preferably clean energy, many of the difficulties we now experience might well disappear. Cheap energy would accelerate the pace of world trade and raise living standards in the less developed as well as more developed countries. It would, for example, furnish the fertilizer and farm equipment we need to raise more food, help us desalinate ocean water and irrigate the deserts, make the processing of low-grade ores economical, and much more. Above all, the wealth it releases would undoubtedly hasten the demographic transition to replacement-level fertility. Cheap energy could open the gates to an era of almost limitless wealth for all humankind. As Kahn and his colleagues wrote in *The Next 200 Years*, ". . . energy abundance is probably the world's best insurance that the entire human population (even 15–20 billion) can be well cared for, at least physically, for many centuries to come."[14]

Kahn had no doubts that such abundance was just around the corner. For many years after World War II, his view was widely held. The world price of crude oil remained quite low until the Arab oil embargo of 1973, coal was available in almost limitless quantities, and the nuclear power industry was growing like a healthy weed. Taking into account large expected increases in worldwide energy consumption, Harrison Brown estimated in 1954 that the production of fossil fuels would not peak until the middle of the twenty-first century, and then decline as reserves ran low. Toward the end of the twenty-first century, atomic power from uranium and thorium would replace fossil fuels altogether. Hundreds or thousands of years later, atomic power would in turn yield to solar power, as uranium and thorium ores became exhausted.[15]

The arrival of the environmentalist movement in the 1970s, coupled with the jolt to Western complacency supplied by a sharp rise in crude oil prices, led the majority of futurists to envisage a quite different scenario, which lasted well into the 1980s. Fossil fuels were now seen to be in critically short supply, and, along with nuclear energy, toxic to the environment as well. Humankind had to convert, as quickly as possible, to alternative energy sources, preferably renewable energy sources, such as solar, wind, geo-thermal, and tidal power. Meanwhile, energy conservation became the watchword, as families and nations were urged to tighten their belts, use more energy-efficient engines and furnaces, and pare all non-essential uses of energy to the proverbial bone.

In W. Jackson Davis's *The Seventh Year* (1979), a representative futurist text of the period, the first four chapters were devoted largely to the problem of energy. The cover featured a photograph of a windmill facing the sun. David concluded from his research that the U.S. and other oil-importing industrial nations "have an estimated 10–20 years to accomplish the transition from oil to other energy sources. The continuation of industrialism as we have known it therefore depends entirely upon the possibility of employing alternate sources of energy." But when he canvassed the prospects for these sources, including the renewables, he found them inadequate to the task. In fact, he wrote, there is no solution to the energy crisis. By the year 2000, industrial civilization will no longer have enough energy to continue along its historic course. "The citizens of industrial nations and their governments must soon face a new and difficult reality—a future of steadily declining energy."[16]

Davis's solution is basically the solution offered in the counterculturalist paradigm. If industrialism as we know it will soon become impossible, then humankind must undergo a transvaluation of values, and build a new civi-lization that no longer relies on limitless growth, production, and consump-tion, a civilization ruled by "eco-logic" instead of the logic of materialism. Or, to use the image favored by L. S. Stavrianos in *The Promise of the Coming Dark Age*, "if we will but open our eyes we can see the green grass sprouting through the concrete."[17]

But the apocalyptic warnings of W. Jackson Davis soon appeared far-fetched. Since the mid–1980s, interest in energy futures has slipped appre-ciably, except for the question of the relationship between energy use and global warming. Improvements in efficiency and modest conservation efforts helped produce a world oil glut and (until the summer of 1990) a lowering of fuel prices, which in turn lowered levels of anxiety, despite continuing political instability in the Middle East.

But the big issues remain. Are we running out of fossil fuels? Is nuclear power safe and affordable? Will suitable alternatives be ready when and if fossil fuels are finally depleted, or when and if their use is phased out to protect the environment?

The clash of opinion and expectation is similar to the clash on the de-mographic future. Technoliberal marketeers have not been shaken by the news of an energy crisis, and deny there is one. Welfarers are much more concerned, but think the problem can be managed by selective conservation, better engineering, and a gradual changeover in the next century to alternative energy sources. Such sources would include not only solar power and the like, but also the long-awaited perfection of hydrogen fusion power, a source of energy, if practicable, that could furnish humankind with almost unlimited safe energy for millennia.

Radicals, confronting the same issues, hold a variety of views, agreeing only that the root of the problem is the profit motive. Market capitalism leads inevitably, they would insist, to gross inequities in the worldwide distribution of energy, bogus shortages contrived to facilitate price-gouging, manipulation of consumers to maximize sales of energy, and failure to plan ahead for the needs of future generations.

And where do counterculturalists stand? Not all share Davis's assessment of the imminent exhaustion of earth's fossil fuels, but nearly all vigorously condemn reliance on such fuels, as well as on nuclear power. They urge a swift transition to renewable energy sources, and shifts in priorities that would reduce the need for energy, especially in the more developed countries. They are also suspicious of fusion power, a capital-intensive remedy that would duplicate our present-day dependence on continent-wide power grids built and maintained by vast impersonal private or public authorities.

On the empirical side of the energy controversy, we are as far away from a consensus as ever. Are fossil fuels in short supply or not? Most futurists say they are, or soon will be, and produce an array of geological statistics to prove their case. Marketeers say no. They note that reserves have always expanded to meet market demand; once it pays somebody to find more coal, more oil, more gas, more uranium, more will be found. If one fuel does eventually run out, technology will find ways of cheaply converting available fuels into those that are not available. Anti-marketeers reply that just because such things have happened in the past does not mean they will continue to happen. The same arguments, it should be added, routinely turn up whenever futurists talk about the scarcity or non-scarcity of the metals and other minerals essential for future worldwide industrial growth. Marketeers say not to worry. Everyone else worries.

The debate on nuclear energy is equally confusing. Many countries, led by France, Germany, and Japan, depend heavily on nuclear reactors for electricity. Other countries have pulled back, citing environmental hazards, cost overruns, and the high price-tag of reactor maintenance and operation. American futurists, especially, have tended in recent years to foresee the decline and eventual demise of the nuclear power industry. Environmentalists everywhere argue that the threat of meltdowns, the use of nuclear know-how to help Third World countries acquire nuclear weapons, and the dilemma of how safely to dispose of nuclear wastes render such a demise imperative.

Other experts, including a few environmentalists, are having second thoughts. If the alternative to nuclear power is increased dependence on fossil fuels, and in particular coal, the dirtiest of fossil fuels and a major cause of acid rain, why not choose nuclear power as the lesser of two evils? *Our Common Future* (1987), the report of the UN-sponsored World Commission on Environment and Development, reflected the global quandary by hedging on every issue. The Commission cited all the problems and then recommended nothing more drastic than high-priority research to make nuclear energy safer and to find alternative sources of energy.[18]

What of the alternative sources? Writing in 1976, Kahn and his associates estimated that fusion reactors would be on line as early as 1995, and that solar and geothermal power as well as power derived from ocean gradients and conversion of organic wastes would become commercially feasible between 1975 and 2000.[19] Although Kahn's group reported, at the same time, that the estimated potential reserves of fossil fuels alone could meet the world's energy needs for the next two centuries and well beyond, they saw no point in continuing to utilize such fuels, which are also valuable as raw materials for basic chemicals, when other sources would soon be at hand. The transition from fossil fuels would "be largely completed about 75 years from now."[20]

But progress toward alternative sources slowed spectacularly in the oil-rich 1980s. The Czech engineer Petr Beckmann, evaluating that progress for Simon and Kahn's *The Resourceful Earth*, concluded that by the year 2000 "there will be no abundant alternatives to the main sources of energy in the developed countries, nuclear fission, coal, and natural gas." The use of coal and nuclear power would in fact increase. Another contributor to *The Resourceful Earth*, William M. Brown, who had been one of Kahn's co-authors in *The Next 200 Years*, was now much less sanguine about the prospects for alternative energy sources. "During the next one hundred years," he concluded, "a world transition away from increased dependence on petroleum seems likely: however there is still much uncertainty as to if, when, where, or how this transition will occur." The outcome would be "determined largely by economics, technology, geology, and sheer luck."[21]

THE ENVIRONMENT

A complicating factor in speculation about the future of energy is the demonstrable impact of fossil and nuclear fuels on the environment. In the early postwar decades, environmentalism usually meant a concern for the conservation of wilderness areas, wildlife, and scarce resources, along with campaigns to protect the ecosystem from contamination by man-made toxins and wastes. Air and water pollution were special targets of environmentalist activism. Futurists conjured up frightening visions of a world overwhelmed by smog and pesticides, its rivers transformed into sewers, its lakes into cesspools, and its dying oceans laced with mercury and cadmium. An effective compendium of such visions is available in John Brunner's novel of life in a near-future America, *The Sheep Look Up* (1972).

Most of these concerns were addressed by governments and corporations as the years passed. The problems still exist, giving due cause for alarm especially in the Second and Third Worlds, where the race to catch up with the West took priority over environmental action for many years. Ecologists point with special urgency to the spread of desertification in areas like central Africa and the loss of biological diversity associated with the ruthless exploitation by developers of the world's tropical rain forests.

Since about 1970 a new set of environmental issues has risen to the fore, most of them linked to the use of fossil and nuclear fuels. They include a crisis in the disposal of highly toxic nuclear wastes, major accidents in nuclear reactors like those that occurred at Three Mile Island and Chernobyl, acid rain, oil spills along coastlines, and the threat to the earth's climate posed by the greenhouse effect.

All of these problems help feed the agitation by environmentalists to curtail and eventually eliminate the nuclear power and fossil fuel industries. As might be expected, most technoliberals maintain that technological remedies such as emissions control systems can make the offending fuels environmentally safe. But much of the attention of futurists today is centered on just one of these energy-related problems, one that, if it turns out to be genuine, will almost certainly not yield to routine technological solutions. I refer to the greenhouse effect.

By now it is likely that even elementary school children can explain the greenhouse effect. When the atmosphere contains a relatively high proportion of water vapor, carbon dioxide (CO_2), and some rarer gases, these substances act to trap much of the heat radiated from the earth's surface, warming the lower atmosphere. Such warming is normal, permitting life to flourish down below, but excessive amounts of carbon dioxide and the other so-called greenhouse gases lead to excessive warming. A roughly analogous situation occurs in the animal body when there is too much cholesterol in the bloodstream. Some cholesterol is necessary to maintain vital life functions, but too much can clog arteries and cause heart attacks and strokes.

What has happened since the beginnings of industrialism in the nineteenth century is quite simple. The burning of fossil fuels such as coal and oil has liberated enormous quantities of carbon dioxide into the atmosphere. In the middle of the eighteenth century, the estimated amount of carbon dioxide in the atmosphere was about 275 parts per million. Nowadays the figure is 350 parts per million, and rising steadily. Carbon dioxide levels in the atmosphere are also higher because of the wholesale destruction of temperate and tropical forests by humankind since the eighteenth century. Trees are a major consumer of carbon dioxide, which they need for photosynthesis. The fewer trees, the more carbon dioxide in the atmosphere.

Other gases also make a contribution to the acceleration of the greenhouse effect, perhaps as much as carbon dioxide. These too enter the atmosphere largely as the result of human activity. They include methane, one molecule of which can absorb thirty times as much heat as a molecule of carbon dioxide. Methane leaks into the air when we mine coal and transport natural gas. It is also produced by the decomposition of plant matter in rice paddies and by the belching and flatulence of dairy and beef cattle. The atmosphere contains almost twice as much methane as it did at the beginning of the nineteenth century. Another set of greenhouse gases are the chlorofluorocarbons, chemicals used worldwide, which, molecule for molecule, trap far more heat even than methane. Thanks to their use by manufacturers and consumers alike, chlorofluorocarbons are escaping into the atmosphere at a prodigious rate.

The evidence just assembled suggests that human beings in the next century will be living on a hotter planet. This is precisely the prognosis furnished by most earth scientists today. At a conference convened in Toronto by the Canadian government in June of 1988, Irving M. Mintzer of the World Resources Institute presented a series of world climate models projecting trends to the year 2075. Each model assumed a different input of carbon dioxide and other greenhouse gases, from the least likely to the most. He concluded from his models that a rise in world temperatures of somewhere between three and thirty degrees Fahrenheit could be expected in this period. The rise would be as little as three degrees if effective measures were taken immediately, up to thirty if substantial increases occurred in the burning of fossil fuels, and five to fifteen if current trends continued.[22]

What do such figures mean? There is little debate on their seriousness. Even a three to five degree rise, which may sound trivial to the layman, would have profound effects on the ecosystem. A rise of thirty degrees would be unimaginably disastrous, restoring the highest temperatures that prevailed on earth in the age of the dinosaurs. The climatologist Stephen H. Schneider, a reigning expert in the field, reports that despite many uncertainties, there is a "widespread consensus that CO_2 and other trace greenhouse gases are likely to double sometime in the next century." If they do, the best available climate models indicate that a temperature rise of five to ten degrees Fahrenheit would ensue. Anything of this magnitude, if sustained, would represent "a very substantial alteration and unprecedented in the era of human civilization."[23] In a popular, recently published book, Bill McKibben speaks of global warming as "the end of nature," not the end in a literal sense, but the end of nature as humankind has known it for thousands of years.[24]

McKibben may be exaggerating, but not necessarily. If significant global warming does take place in the next century, it will work mischief on a tremendous scale. Weather patterns will be altered in every part of the world, affecting each region somewhat differently. Some areas will experience earlier spring melting of mountain snows, or drier summers, or lower lake levels, or heavier monsoons. Rainfall and water runoff patterns will change dramatically. Storms, floods, and droughts will be far more common. Rich mid-continental farmland may change into desert, and high subarctic plateaux may become arable for the first time in hundreds of years. People will have to make wrenching changes in their ways of life. How easily, for example, can a Kansas wheat-growing family pull up stakes and move to northern Alberta? How do you close down a large city that has run out of water? How can a grape and apple economy, as in upstate New York, be converted expeditiously into a rice and banana economy?

Another major category of impact, besides the disruptive effects of changing weather patterns, will be a steep rise in the world's sea levels, as global warming melts glaciers and polar ice caps. The rise could be as great as three feet. Such an increase would lead to extensive coastal flooding and erosion of beaches in many parts of the world. Large portions of Florida, Indonesia, and Bangladesh, among others, might simply disappear beneath the waves. In many coastal countries, groundwater supplies will be contaminated by seawater and spoiled for human use.

The health of the biota, including *Homo sapiens*, will also be adversely affected by global warming. Relatively sudden climatic change will probably cause the death of large numbers of plants and animals unable to adjust rapidly enough to the change. A temperate forest, for example, cannot be picked up and hauled 500 miles northward to cooler climes if the region where it once flourished becomes subtropical. People and animals will experience more respiratory disease from ozone pollution and more insect-borne diseases, since warmer temperatures increase the formation of lower-atmosphere ozone and the fertility of insects.

In considering what to do about global warming, futurists, environmentalists, and policy-makers alike have no difficulty identifying the most plausible remedies. Obviously, we need to slash carbon dioxide emissions drastically, perhaps in half, which would require a 50 percent reduction in the burning of fossil fuels. We need to phase out the production of chlorofluorocarbons, minimize the escape of methane into the atmosphere, stop burning and cutting down forests, and prepare to defend our shorelines against flooding. But will these things be done, and done in time, especially in view of their almost prohibitive cost?[25]

Many environmentally conscious radicals and technoliberals, and practically all counterculturalists, urge all or most of these actions, and not just to ward off global warming. Nevertheless, on closer analysis, forecasts of what Schneider calls the "Greenhouse Century" are less persuasive than they might at first appear.

One problem is that not all climatologists are convinced that global warming will actually take place. A diametrically opposed view held by many experts in the 1970s, that we are destined for a much colder era, perhaps even an ice age, remains alive and well in some quarters of the scientific community.[26] Climatologists note that the upper atmosphere is filled with untold trillions of particles of smoke, dust, and smog injected there in good part by the doings of men and women, particles that reflect the sun's heat back into outer space and cool the air. Enough cooling by particulate matter could trigger an ice age.

By some accounts global warming may even help *cause* global cooling, as a lower atmosphere warmed by the greenhouse effect interacts with the super-chilled upper atmosphere. Also, global warming enables the air to hold more water vapor, which in turn thickens the earth's cloud cover, which in turn helps to block solar radiation. At the least, some would argue, the two opposing trends may simply cancel one another out.

Other objections are raised by scientists who doubt the usefulness of existing computer models to predict the real future. Such models are too simple, they say, and fail to take into account such factors as the capacity of the oceans to absorb excess heat. Even if global warming does take place, a few reputable scientists contend that, on balance, it may do more good than harm. In particular, global warming may benefit agriculture by extending growing seasons, increasing total arable acreage and the efficiency of plant life, reducing soil erosion, and improving soil fertility.[27]

Whether the models used by climatologists are trustworthy or not, no one can be sure that global warming has actually started to take place in the real world. Given the volume of greenhouse gases pumped into the atmosphere since the late eighteenth century, one would expect the earth's temperature to have already undergone a substantial warming trend.

Has it? The evidence is inconclusive. Since the 1880s, weather statisticians generally agree that the earth has warmed by about one degree Fahrenheit.[28] But even this finding is not accepted by everyone. Nor can those who do accept it prove that the greenhouse effect caused the warming. To add to the confusion, a countervailing cooling trend occurred between 1940 and 1970, not to mention several long-term ups and downs of one or two degrees well before the dawn of the industrial age. Recent reports on weather patterns also fail to clinch the case. On the one hand, the 1980s featured six of the seven hottest years on record, and 1990 was the hottest year of all. On the other hand, data from weather satellites released in March, 1990, detected no trend toward warming or cooling for the planet as a whole during the 1980s.[29]

Despite the wrangling among scientists, however, most futurists and environmentalists who have written about global warming believe that it will happen, will clearly pose a menace to civilization in the twenty-first century, and must be combated at once. A representative statement is Christopher Flavin's in *State of the World 1990*, calling for an immediate response no matter what uncertainties remain. "Societies invest in many programs, such as defense," he noted, "to protect against an uncertain but potentially disastrous threat. Similarly, investing in strategies to slow global warming is a sort of insurance policy—against catastrophes that have far greater odds of occurring than most events for which we buy insurance."[30]

In their ponderous way, governments around the world also began addressing the issue of global warming in the late 1980s and early 1990s, committing themselves to goals for reducing CO_2 emissions that are probably too costly to be implemented. A similar but less ambitious campaign has been mounted, both by environmentalists and governments, to rescue the stratospheric ozone layer, which shields earth from lethal doses of hard solar radiation. In this case, all that is required is a ban on the production of the kinds of chlorofluorocarbons that combine chemically with ozone. More than 90 nations met in London in June 1990, and agreed to phase out their production by the year 2000. So far so good.

But this is not quite the end of the story. Suitable substitutes are still being sought and the likeliest candidates would trap heat almost as effectively as the chlorofluorocarbons already targeted for elimination, compounding the problem of global warming. It is also likely, according to environmentalists, that the chlorofluorocarbons currently in the atmosphere will remain there in a stable state for at least a century, allowing them to migrate to the stratosphere little by little, where they will continue to ravage the ozone layer long after the ban on their production goes into effect.

In worst case scenarios, substantial damage to the ozone layer has already occurred and will actually increase for decades to come, no matter what steps nations take. The result will be damage to crops, increases in skin cancer and cataracts, depressed levels of immunity to disease, and a possible breakdown of the oceanic food chain. A study by Robert C. Worrest has shown that the ultraviolet radiation admitted by a 25 percent decrease in stratospheric ozone would lower the efficiency of photosynthesis in phytoplankton, the lowest link in that vast and vulnerable chain, by one-third.[31]

As we have already indicated, the rank and file of futurists tend to side with environmentalists on issues such as global warming and ozone depletion. But the influence of the paradigms is evident even here. Radicals blame corporate greed for the damage to the environment already reported and still to come. Counterculturalists attack the materialistic value structure of modern industrialism. Technoliberal welfarers lead the parade in seeking solutions through intergovernmental agreements, organized research, and massive spending on environmental action by public authorities. For most of these futurists, the news of global warming and ozone depletion came almost as a godsend, confirming their prejudices and giving them useful causes.

For technoliberal marketeers, the news was far less welcome, and the response has been correspondingly less zealous. Some marketeers doubt that the crises are as bad as rival futurists paint them. Some admit to a sense of urgency. But marketeers have no doubt about one thing. Market forces, timely assistance from governments, and human technological ingenuity, between them, will solve the problems, as they have done so many times before. Humankind will not spend the next century suffocating in Mesozoic heat or cowering in underground shelters to escape ultraviolet rays. To quote Frank Feather, a Toffleresque self-styled "pragmatic businessman" who draws on both wings of technoliberalism and a dash of counterculturalism for inspiration, the earth's carrying capacity "has increased so much that the term no longer has any useful meaning. The world of the future will indeed be less polluted, less vulnerable to resource depletion and more ecologically stable. . . . Remember, destiny is something we create."[32]

Not surprisingly, the destiny that Feather has in mind will include a probable "Super-Boom" starting among the Pacific Rim countries (including North America) in the mid–1990s and extending "well into the 21st Century," as entrepreneurial energy spurs growth and development in all possible ways. Club of Rome doomsayers notwithstanding, the new planetary economy, based on information technologies, will "stabilize in about the year 2050 at 10 billion people, with a gross world product of $300 trillion, and a per capita income worldwide of $30,000 (in 1988 dollars). The end of the 21st Century will likely see worldwide abolition of poverty."[33]

TO GROW OR NOT TO GROW

Feather's euphoria about boundless wealth may cause some futurists to blush with embarrassment. But it does bring us back, conveniently enough, to the old controversy about the limits to economic growth, already discussed in our second chapter. The question of growth is the culminating issue in studies of the future of the earth and its ecosystem. Without people, there is no demand. Without energy, there is no supply. Without a clean and safe environment, both demand and supply are imperilled. But the rate of economic growth determines *how much* demand, *how much* supply, and *how much* peril we may expect in coming years. The question of growth is also the question that most directly links studies of the ecological future to studies of the societal future, since all growth is the result of choices made and implemented by the structures of human society.

Economists specializing in growth and development in the period immediately after World War II seriously projected a more or less infinite worldwide growth in wealth, just like Frank Feather in *G-Forces*. The rich countries were slated to grow steadily richer and the poor countries, through a judicious combination of aid, trade, and self-help, would grow at a still faster rate until no gross inequalities remained anywhere on the planet. The same economists also took cognizance of the theory that capitalism as an economic system cannot survive without growth. How can a system that runs on profits settle into a steady-state, no-growth mode? Apart from "up" the only direction available to the global economy is "down." Boom or bust. Take your choice. So economists argued.

But with the rise of ecology as a major discipline in the life sciences, and the heightened environmental consciousness that emerged in the late Sixties and Seventies, this conventional wisdom came under fierce attack. Unlimited growth, many now said, would result in the exhaustion of resources, the poisoning of the biosphere, famine, misery, and death. Either capitalism would have to learn to survive without growth, or the world would have to learn to live without capitalism.

The first major proclamation of the no-growth gospel came in 1972 with the issuance of *The Limits to Growth*. The model used by the team of futures researchers that produced this book (Donella H. Meadows, Dennis L. Meadows, Jørgen Randers, and William W. Behrens III) viewed the world as a single dynamic system, characterized by the interaction of five parameters: population, food supply, non-renewable natural resources (such as copper and coal), pollution, and per capita industrial output.

On what the team called its "world model standard run," projecting current (1970) trends to the year 2100, the computer generated a series of catastrophically crashing curves. Population, food supply, industrial output, and pollution continued to rise rapidly until the year 2020, while non-renewable resources continued to fall at a corresponding rate. Then, in 2020, although population and pollution went on rising for a few more years, food supplies and industrial output started a precipitous downward slide. By 2050, with famine and disease stalking the planet, the curve representing population also crashed, and industrial output sank to late nineteenth-century levels. In one generation, the proud progress of two centuries was undone.

The researchers then reported a complex series of computer runs in which they varied the quantitative values of their five factors. How might human ingenuity, both technological and societal, save civilization from this terrible crashing of the curves? What if limits were placed on population growth and emission of pollutants? What if new resources were discovered by geologists and prospectors? What if agricultural productivity were greatly increased?

One variation on the standard model, for example, assumed a doubling of the reserves of all natural resources. The results were about the same. Industrial output grew even more rapidly, so did pollution, and the curves crashed between 2040 and 2050. Figure in virtually unlimited resources with the help of virtually unlimited nuclear power; and again, no difference. Too little food and too much pollution force the curves to crash by 2040. Add on pollution controls that eliminate three-quarters of all pollution generated at 1970 levels, and disaster still arrived, although a little less abruptly, and ten to twenty years later.

The team pressed on. They added another variation. They doubled the productivity of land, thereby doubling the food supply, while keeping the unlimited energy, resources, and effective pollution controls. The result was an even greater catastrophe. Industrial output soared, population climbed, but there was still too much pollution to handle because of the greatly increased industrial growth. Food supplies soon fell behind population growth, and the curves crashed even earlier, about 2025. When universal birth control was also added to the model, things went better for a while, but population and output crashed anyway, near the close of the twenty-first century. The cumulative effects of pollution and the failure of resources and food to meet the ever-rising demand for them in a world intoxicated by the promise of universal abundance led in due course to doomsday.

As the authors concluded, "The basic behavior mode of the world system is exponential growth of population and capital, followed by collapse." Given the basic assumption that no limits should be placed on the growth of industrial output, "we have not been able to find a set of policies that avoids the collapse mode of behavior."[34] The lesson for statesmen was unambiguous. No more growth, either of population or of industrial output. Make do with less, and start now. Even waiting no longer than the year 2000 to implement no-growth policies would make it impossible to sustain a state of global equilibrium, and the curves would still fall, less steeply, before the end of the next century.

The Limits to Growth inspired a second report to the Club of Rome, *Mankind at the Turning Point* by Mihajlo Mesarovic and Eduard Pestel, which used much the same basic technique. Again, unlimited growth of industrial output and population was seen as the chief villain in the human drama. But by dividing their model of the world into ten regions, Mesarovic and Pestel were able to project a much more detailed future, in which allowances could be made for selective growth in some industries and regions to help reduce the gap between rich and poor countries in the world system.

The Limits to Growth and its sequel provoked intense criticism. The Science Policy Research Unit at the University of Sussex in England led the way with *Models of Doom: A Critique of The Limits to Growth* (1973). Christopher Freeman, an economist and director of the research unit, made the telling point that behind the mathematical model of the world system utilized by Donella and Dennis Meadows and their colleagues lurked a "mental model," the economic theories of Thomas Malthus, who held nearly two centuries ago that all population growth occurs in a finite world and must sooner or later reach its limits and fall backward. What seemed to be the objective and dispassionate finding of a machine was actually programmed into the machine by the world view of the researchers, according to the formula "Malthus in, Malthus out." Hence, *The Limits to Growth* revealed not so much the limits to growth as the limits to imagination imposed by a neo-Malthusian ideology.[35]

But most of the criticism of *The Limits to Growth* and *Mankind at the Turning Point* issued from followers of other ideologies, who had other axes to grind. Technoliberal marketeers to the last man and woman, and a fair number of technoliberal welfarers, have found all manner of fault with the first two reports to the Club of Rome. Much of the Hudson Institute's motivation in publishing *The Next 200 Years*, by Kahn, Brown, and Martel, was an eagerness to expose the errors of those reports. *The Next 200 Years* offered a brash alternative vision calculated to help restore badly shaken confidence in capitalism, the market system, and the promise of technology. After surveying the range of futurible remedies, Kahn and his fellow Hudsonites concluded that on the subject of growth, "No obvious limits are apparent. . . . Problems always exist, but solutions always emerge—often as a result of the dynamism of growth."[36]

More specifically, they foresaw a long-term transition to population stability springing from the worldwide abolition of poverty, inexhaustible energy from alternative energy sources, the discovery of immense fresh reserves of minerals, food production ample for all, a whistle-clean environment thanks to technological progress, and a world standard of living higher than the North American standard of today. By 2176, the year of the U.S. quadricentennial, the world population would stand at 15 billion, "with a $300 trillion GWP [gross world product], yielding $20,000 per capita," measured in 1976 dollars. The richest countries would have a per capita annual product of nearly $50,000 and the poorest just under $10,000.[37]

In the 1980s, the battle continued with another set of contradictory reports, *The Global 2000 Report to the President* and Simon and Kahn's *The Resourceful Earth: A Response to Global 2000*. *Global 2000* did not attempt to foresee the far future, but in general it followed the trajectory of thought already laid out by the reports to the Club of Rome. During the last twenty years of the twentieth century, growth rates would fall in all parts of the world, the gap between the developed and less developed nations would widen, and the environment would deteriorate further. The authors looked forward to a new century filled with disease, hunger, and death unless nations acted now. "The time for action to prevent this outcome is running out."[38]

Simon and Kahn with the assistance of more than two dozen contributors planned *The Resourceful Earth* as a detailed refutation of *Global 2000*. In effect they turned *Global 2000* upside down. "The world in 2000," they proclaimed, "will be less crowded, less polluted (though more populated), more stable ecologically, and less vulnerable to resource-supply disruption than the world we live in now."[39] Economic growth would continue at roughly the same rates as in the decades immediately following World War II. The only possible fly in their future ointment would be a continuation of "the constraints currently imposed upon material progress by political and institutional forces." Ill-advised government efforts to restrain prices, own and manage resource production, phase out nuclear power, and otherwise meddle in the marketplace could hamper growth and reverse all the favorable trends in the world system: policies precisely like those recommended in dangerous reports like *Global 2000!*[40]

The great debate on growth and its limits has continued on down to the present, as evidenced in such recent books as Feather's *G-Forces*, where growth is extolled, and Mary E. Clark's *Ariadne's Thread* (1989), a counterculturalist survey of world futures. Clark explicitly accepts the warnings of the authors of *The Limits to Growth* and *Global 2000*. She looks forward to an economic future where the watchwords are local self-sufficiency and respect for the planet, not growth and competition.[41]

Clark's views are typical of the counterculturalist response to the controversy about growth. Counterculturalists do not oppose growth as such, only the values that make growth an end in itself. Similarly, they do not oppose technology as such, only technology that dehumanizes and enslaves. As noted above, when the technologies chosen to help humankind are "appropriate," scaled to real human needs, non-violent to nature, subject to community control, and, wherever possible, not capital-intensive, then technologies can contribute positively to the enrichment of human life.

For those subscribing to the radical paradigm, by contrast, growth is usually seen as intrinsically good, because only through achieving high levels of productivity can enough wealth be created to eliminate poverty. The trouble is that under capitalism such productivity always winds up benefitting the rich and keeping low- and middle-income families well below them on the social pyramid. In a worker-controlled society, growth would mean wealth for everyone, if we redefine "wealth" to mean goods and services that people actually want and need, not what they are brainwashed to think they want and need by high-pressure corporate marketing.

Meanwhile, radicals contend, the newly perceived scarcity of land, minerals, energy, food, and the like helps the rich to tighten their grip on economies and states through what Richard J. Barnet has called "the politics of scarcity." Despite environmental setbacks and spot shortages, enough resources exist to give everyone on earth a reasonably good life. Yet by manipulating prophecies of doom and visions of scarcity, a scarcity the power-mongers of bourgeois society have created by their own policies, they prosper more than ever. As Barnet warns, "The pessimism of the Malthusians has a good deal of dreary evidence to support it, but ideologies of abandonment should evoke the deepest suspicion. They are myths for the rich wrapped in the intimidating mantle of science. . . . Indeed, the fatalism of the Cassandras is another form of '*Après moi le déluge*.' "[42]

The radical position may be summed up with a metaphor. We can liken modern civilization to a great passenger liner at sea.[43] Far from having sunk, the liner is doing just fine. But its passengers are not all treated the same. Some live in lavish suites, partake of the finest delicacies, monopolize the choicest deck space, and dance the night away in ballrooms hung with crystal chandeliers. Others sleep on bunk beds in cramped little cabins, eat hamburgers, and watch movies. Still others—the greatest number—live in squalor in the ship's hold, fight for their scraps of bread with the rats, and never even glimpse the ocean's broad expanse. To the second-class passengers in their tiny cabins and the third-class passengers in steerage, the ship's captain proclaims over the intercom that because of ship-wide scarcities, everyone must tighten his or her belt, or the ship will one day run out of supplies, and all aboard will starve.

If you actually believe the captain, as any radical futurist would be happy to point out, then you too are part of the problem.

In any event, it is time to turn to another set of questions, suggested by Barnet's analysis of the politics of scarcity. His thesis is that society, not nature, imposes the most significant barriers to human growth and progress. We are hampered not so much by Mother Nature or Father Time as by our own societal arrangements, which determine how resources are used, and by whom, and for what ends. The question then arises: what is the future of human society?

NOTES

1. Lester R. Brown, et al., *State of the World 1990* (New York: Norton, 1990), p. xv.

2. See James Lovelock, *Gaia: A New Look at Life on Earth* (New York: Oxford University Press, 1979). Lovelock is a contributor to Norman Myers, ed., *Gaia: An Atlas of Planet Management* (Garden City, N.Y.: Doubleday, 1984), and more recently the author of *The Ages of Gaia: A Biography of Our Living Earth* (New York: Norton, 1988). The "Gaia" series also includes Myers, *The Gaia Atlas of Future Worlds: Challenge and Opportunity in an Age of Change* (New York: Doubleday, 1991).

3. For a sample of geological thinking influenced by the Gaia hypothesis, see Tyler Volk and David W. Schwartzman, "Biotic Enhancement of Weathering and the Habitability of Earth," *Nature*, 340:6233 (August 10, 1989): 457–460. Volk and Schwartzman suggest that without the creation of soil from rock by microbes, insufficient carbon would be discharged into the sea to cool the earth, and the earth's temperature would have always remained too hot to support anything but the most primitive microbial life. If they are right, life (in the form of microbes) made possible the evolution of all higher life forms. See also William K. Stevens, "Evolving Theory Views Earth as a Living Organism," *New York Times* (August 19, 1989), C1 and C4.

4. George Handley Knibbs, *The Shadow of the World's Future: or, The Earth's Population Possibilities and the Consequences of the Present Rate of Increase of the Earth's Inhabitants* (London: Ernest Benn, 1928), 12.

5. Harrison Brown, *The Challenge of Man's Future* (New York: Viking Press, 1954), 99.

6. Gordon Rattray Taylor, *The Doomsday Book: Can the World Survive?* (New York: World, 1970), 216–217. For a panoramic view of the debate on population futures circa 1970, see Edward Pohlman, ed., *Population: A Clash of Prophets* (New York: New American Library, 1973).

7. See, for example, Robert Repetto, "Population, Resource Pressures, and Poverty," in Repetto, ed., *The Global Possible: Resources, Development, and the New Century* (New Haven: Yale University Press, 1986), especially Table 6.1 on p. 132.

8. Compare the 1988 and 1990 editions of *World Population Data Sheet* (Washington: Population Reference Bureau). The *Data Sheet* is published annually.

9. Colin Clark, "World Population," *Nature*, 181:4618 (May 3, 1958): 1235–1236. This article is also reprinted in Pohlman, ed., *Population: A Clash of Prophets*, 161–164. Clark enlarged on his ideas in *Population Growth and Land Use* (New York: St. Martin's Press, 1967) and *Starvation or Plenty?* (New York: Taplinger, 1970).

10. Herman Kahn, William Brown, and Leon Martel, *The Next 200 Years: A Scenario for America and the World* (New York: William Morrow, 1976), 6–7, 34, and 106–138.

11. Frank Feather, *G-Forces: Reinventing the World: The 35 Global Forces Restructuring Our Future* (Toronto: Summerhill Press, 1989), 41.

12. Lester R. Brown and John E. Young in Brown, ed., *State of the World 1990*, 59.

13. Myers, ed., *Gaia: An Atlas of Planet Management*, 67. The full discussion appears on pp. 60–67. For an almost identical argument, consult W. Jackson Davis, *The Seventh Year: Industrial Civilization in Transition* (New York: Norton, 1979), ch. 9.

14. Kahn, Brown, and Martel, *The Next 200 Years*, 83.

15. Brown, *The Challenge of Man's Future*, ch. 5.

16. Davis, *The Seventh Year*, pp. 51 and 73. It is interesting to note that virtually all the scenarios presented in Hawken, Ogilvy, and Schwartz, *Seven Tomorrows*, anticipated soaring energy prices as an engine of change. Each scenario was quite different, but in each, the rising costs of energy played a significant role. Had *Seven Tomorrows* been written ten years earlier or five years later, instead of in 1982, oil prices might have been ignored entirely.

17. L. S. Stavrianos, *The Promise of the Coming Dark Age* (San Francisco: W. H. Freeman, 1976), 196. For "eco-logic," see Davis, *The Seventh Year*, ch. 13, especially 280–281.

18. World Commission on Environment and Development, *Our Common Future* (New York: Oxford University Press, 1987), 181–189.

19. Kahn, Brown, and Martel, *The Next 200 Years*, Table 6, p. 82.

20. *Ibid.*, 63–64 and 67.

21. Petr Beckmann, "Solar Energy and Other 'Alternative' Energy Sources" and "Coal," in Simon and Kahn, ed., *The Resourceful Earth*, 426 and 437; and William M. Brown, "The Outlook for Future Petroleum Supplies," in *ibid.*, 385.

22. See Philip Shabecoff, "Major 'Greenhouse' Impact Is Unavoidable, Experts Say," *New York Times* (July 19, 1988): C1 and C6.

23. Stephen H. Schneider, *Global Warming: Are We Entering the Greenhouse Century?* (San Francisco: Sierra Club Books, 1989), 89 and 103.

24. Bill McKibben, *The End of Nature* (New York: Random House, 1989). For another, equally dire forecast, see Michael Oppenheimer and Robert H. Boyle, *Dead Heat: The Race Against the Greenhouse Effect* (New York: Basic Books, 1990).

25. See Peter Passell, "Staggering Cost Is Foreseen to Curb Warming of Earth," *New York Times* (November 19, 1989): 1 and 18.

26. A good introduction to theories of global cooling is available in Reid A. Bryson and Thomas J. Murray, *Climates of Hunger: Mankind and the World's Changing Weather* (Madison: University of Wisconsin Press, 1977).

27. Many of the objections to global warming forecasts are surveyed in William

K. Stevens, "Skeptics Are Challenging Dire 'Greenhouse' Views," *New York Times* (December 13, 1989): A1 and B12.

28. See Schneider, *Global Warming*, 84–88.

29. Associated Press, "No Global Warming Signs Spotted," *New York Times* (March 30, 1990): A–11. See also William K. Stevens, "Separate Studies Rank '90 as World's Warmest Year," *New York Times* (January 10, 1991), A1 and D21.

30. Christopher Flavin, "Slowing Global Warming," in Brown, et al., *State of the World 1990*, 17–18.

31. A convenient summary of the ozone problem is available in Cynthia Pollock Shea, "Protecting the Ozone Layer," in Lester R. Brown, et al., *State of the World 1989* (New York: Norton, 1989), 77–96. For the Worrest reference, see p. 83 and n. 32.

32. Feather, *G-Forces*, 393–394 and 399.

33. *Ibid.*, 180 and 183.

34. Meadows, et al., *The Limits to Growth*, 142–143.

35. H.S.D. Cole, et al., *Models of Doom: A Critique of the Limits to Growth* (New York: Universe Books, 1973). 8–9.

36. Kahn, Brown, and Martel, *The Next 200 Years*, 13.

37. *Ibid.*, 55–56.

38. Council on Environmental Quality and the Department of State, Gerald O. Barney, study director, *The Global 2000 Report to the President: Entering the Twenty-First Century*, volume one (Washington: U.S. Government Printing Office, no date [1981]), 42.

39. Simon and Kahn, eds. *The Resourceful Earth*, 1 (italics omitted). This sentence deliberately reverses the sense of a similar sentence in *Global 2000*, 1.

40. Simon and Kahn, eds., *The Resourceful Earth*, 3–4; see also "Editors' Note on Economic Growth to the Year 2000 and Beyond," 46–48.

41. Mary E. Clark, *Ariadne's Thread: The Search for New Modes of Thinking* (New York: St. Martin's Press, 1989), especially 7–14 on global models and ch. 12, "Rethinking Economics."

42. Richard J. Barnet, *The Lean Years: Politics in the Age of Scarcity* (New York: Simon and Schuster, 1980), 309–310, and cf. 17, where Barnet indicates that one of his reasons for writing *The Lean Years* was to analyze and test "the gloomy predictions of the Club of Rome computer."

43. Compare with Richard J. Barnet's image of the luxury liner in *The Lean Years*, 303.

5 _____

The Future of Wealth and Power

THE DISTRIBUTION OF WEALTH

To judge from performance on standardized tests of intelligence and achievement, natural scientists are appreciably brighter than social scientists. Students of nature explain the mysterious. Students of society (it is said) belabor the obvious.

Such epigrams may be unfair, and perhaps not even true. But one thing is quite clear. The phenomena of society are not easier to explain than the phenomena of nature. On the contrary, the workings of human society are vastly more complex than those of nature, and correspondingly more difficult to decipher and forecast.

At the heart of the matter lies the almost inconceivable complexity of our species, the only intelligent species in the universe known to us, and the only species capable of building voluntary societies. Any man or woman is already far more complicated than any "lower" animal or any plant. When millions of men and women gather in societies, cultures, states, and economies, they multiply their creaturely complexity many times over. Moving from non-human to human systems produces an exponential increase in the number of factors and variables that investigators must identify, measure, and foresee. Unless we accept the late B. F. Skinner's thesis that all human behavior is determined by conditioning, one of those factors—the free will of individuals—is unforeseeable almost by definition.

Futurists subscribing to the radical paradigm would maintain that the most basic, and coincidentally the most measurable, activity of *Homo sapiens* as a social animal is economic activity. Since the beginnings of human life on earth, we have always spent most of our lives producing, distributing, and consuming wealth, defined as goods and services for which we are willing to work. Radicals believe that the system by which human beings organize work and wealth determines all "higher" activities, from the political to the cultural. Knowing the dynamics of that system, were such a thing possible, we would also know the future of society.

Futurists in the technoliberal and counterculturalist traditions recognize the importance of economic activity. But they object to what they would style the simple-minded economic determinism of the radical paradigm. As Bernard Cazes writes, with reference to my *Short History of the Future*, the "intellectual vices" of leftist thought include "the mania of explaining everything as an outcome of capitalism" and "the underestimation of politics, regarded as a mere reflection of the capitalist economy."[1] In opposition to the radical agenda, many technoliberals view economic activity as an outcome of political systems; and for counterculturalists, economic activity is an expression of underlying cultural values.

Even if economic activity were not the principal engine of social change, it is incontrovertibly fundamental to our physical existence and well-being. It also makes as good a starting point as any to survey the range of societal futures.

Two questions are of special urgency to economic futurists: how wealth will be distributed in the next century, both within and among nations; and what kind of economic system will dominate the global economy. As is usual in futures inquiry, both questions are two-sided. On the one side, they concern what is likely to happen. On the other, they raise normative issues. What should happen? What would be best for humankind?

Those who take a generally approving stand on the transformations of modernity would argue that "modern" means not only "secular" and "capitalist" or "socialist," but also "democratic." That is, a leading characteristic of the modernization process is the way in which it has promoted an inexorable narrowing of the gap between the high and the low, the powerful and the powerless, the rich and the poor. As the centuries wear on, the plebeian rises slowly from serfdom and poverty toward a position of civil, political, and economic equality with everyone else in the society.

Not that literal equality has been attained, in any country in the modern world. Democratization is far from complete. But exponents of modernity would contend that by and large, through the centuries, it has pressed forward. Its logical end-point is universal equality, if not of wealth and power, then at least of opportunity to acquire either or both. As a radical futurist, the late Michael Harrington, wrote of capitalism just before his death, "Capitalism was a radical new innovation, the greatest achievement of humankind in history, a culture and a civilization as well as an economy." Capitalism "opened up possibilities of freedom and justice" never known before.[2]

The chief evidence for this reading of history consists of a long chain of world-shaking events that can be traced all the way back to the sixteenth century. Advocates of modernity point, in particular, to the emergence of capitalism, the English and French Revolutions, the Industrial Revolution and the rise of trade unions, the revolutionary cycles in Europe in 1830 and 1848–1849, the arrival of universal manhood and womanhood suffrage early in the twentieth century, and, through it all, the virtually uninterrupted growth of the modern industrial world economy, which has doubled and redoubled the productivity of labor. In the process, many once poor and in some instances collapsing countries in the so-called Third World have received at least a taste of modern affluence. More to the point, they have begun to acquire the means and know-how to emulate the advanced economies of Europe, North America, and Japan.

These are statements that would meet with the approval of most technoliberals and not a few radicals, although each camp would explain the process and assess its costs quite differently. Having little use for modernity, nearly all counterculturalists would dissent. They would argue that the "developed" countries are in fact overdeveloped. The overdeveloped countries have piled up riches, but their people do not live well in spite of their relative affluence. Their vaunted democracy is a sham.

Be this as it may, the long-term trend in the history of Western civilization has been toward economic and political democracy. Contrasted with the peasants and artisans of the Middle Ages, ordinary men and women today have higher incomes and more influence over the conduct of their rulers. Such incomes may still be too low, and such influence may still be too weak, but in comparative terms, progress has occurred.

What, then, of the future? Can we expect these democratizing trends, if real, to continue? Are they irresistible, or can they be derailed? And have they been worth all the trouble?

From the radical perspective the material gains recorded over the past few centuries, although quite tangible and real, have been largely negated by the systematic undercompensation of labor, the still more ruthless exploitation and distortion of Third World economies, and the structural violence of the marketplace, which grinds the weak under foot and culminates in an oligopoly of immense multinational corporations obsessed with profit-taking at any cost. Only the steadfast resistance of the working masses, through their unions and political parties, has made possible any progress at all for ordinary folk.

In the future seen by radicals, if the capitalist system continues to thrive, its machinations may cause a further widening of the chasm between classes and between nations, leading to an economic doomsday and bloody revolution. The only rational alternative is the peaceful transition to a new socioeconomic order through the reinvigoration of democracy. The revolution of our times, as Harrington added, "is creating a social and political environment that, if not subjected to democratic control from below, will subvert the possibilities of freedom and justice that capitalism did so much—if reluctantly—to foster."[3]

Evidence of a widening chasm is close at hand. During World War II and for two decades thereafter, working people in the advanced countries probably gained ground on the plutocrats at the top of the socioeconomic pyramid. In a time of headlong economic growth and technological innovation, aided by various left-leaning regimes with the fervent support of electorates, enough wealth was created and enough political pressure exerted to make possible a general increase in material standards of life throughout much of the world.

But the good times were followed by a long period of worldwide economic malaise, starting around 1970. More conservative governments came to power, with policies favoring the affluent. Bureau of the Census figures show that in the United States, for example, the share of income going to the top 20 percent of the population increased between 1967 and 1987 from 40.4 percent to 43.7 percent, while the share of the bottom 20 percent declined from 5.5 percent to 4.6 percent.[4] Similar patterns of income redistribution can be seen in other advanced capitalist countries, such as Canada, Great Britain, and France.[5]

In fact, since the 1960s, the more a family in America earns, the faster its earnings rise, and the larger its share of the national pie becomes. If one calculates net loss or gain of family income rather than share of total national income, the impact on living standards is still more obvious. Just for the period between 1979 and 1987 U.S. Budget Office research indicates that the poorest 20 percent of the American population lost 9 percent of its adjusted family income and the next poorest 20 percent lost .5 percent. The middle 20 percent gained 5.2 percent, the next-to-wealthiest quintile gained 9.3 percent, and the wealthiest enjoyed a gain of 15.6 percent.[6] There were also major differences within the top 20 percent: the richest 5 percent increased their earnings more than twice as much as the richest 20 percent, and the richest 1 percent more than twice as much as the richest 5 percent.

As the Center on Budget and Policy Priorities in Washington reported in the summer of 1990, the wealthiest 1 percent of all Americans now earn a total income after taxes almost as high as the incomes of everyone in the poorest 40 percent put together.[7] "No parallel upsurge of riches," Kevin P. Phillips writes, "[has] been seen since the late 19th century, the era of the Vanderbilts, Morgans and Rockefellers."[8]

Most of these staggering increases in the wealth of the wealthy are due, of course, not to higher salaries earned for actual work performed, but rather to increases in income derived from the sale, ownership, borrowing, or lending of property and securities, operations summed up in Phillips's apt phrase, "paper entrepreneurialism." Income from capital gains has risen three times as fast as income from salaries and wages since 1979.

All this is exactly what radicals have long been predicting. In their view, as the capitalist system matures, it runs into walls of its own making, limits to growth that bring depressed incomes to all but the wealthy. Long-term historic trends are reversed. In time large segments of the middle class will be pauperized and the newly poor, or their children, will eventually sink into the working class, lending added support to the forces that must one day smash the system.

But do twenty years of moderately worsening conditions for the bottom half of the population in selected countries foretell pauperization? Or are we seeing a momentary dip in a curve that has moved generally upward for at least two centuries and will probably soon resume its rise?

A comparable debate has been in progress for many years on the subject of the widening (or closing?) gap between the rich and poor nations. At first glance, the international class system looks something like the class system within nations. Measured by annual product or income per capita, there are at least three readily distinguishable groups of nations: thirty-five that have an average per capita income (in 1990) of $14,000, comprising one-fifth of the world's people; another group of thirty-five with per capita incomes averaging $3,000, comprising one-tenth of the world's people; and one hundred countries at the bottom of the global class system with per capita incomes averaging $375, where the remaining 70 percent of earth's population lives. In terms of shares of the world pie, the poorest 70 percent of humankind earn only 7 percent of its income, while the richest 20 percent earn 82 percent.

These extremes of wealth and poverty in the world economy have persisted throughout the century. In a purely material sense, all segments of the human community have grown richer. But have the gaps between the rich, middling, and poor nations widened or narrowed and what will they do in the future?

There is no easy answer, in part because methods of evaluating wealth vary from country to country, and from researcher to researcher. Economists agree, however, that the world economy fared well in the 1950s and 1960s. The world economic growth rate during this period was about 5 percent, with many poor countries experiencing even higher growth, counterbalanced by their rocketing rates of population increase.

Acknowledging that population growth would have to slow dramatically in the developing nations before they could hope to catch up, technoliberals were confident this would happen in good time. The authors of *The Next 200 Years* pointed to ten forces, from marketing of natural resources and export of labor to technology transfers and foreign aid, that would ensure the eventual transition of the developing nations to affluence. Projecting trends into the twenty-second century, they found that "the current [1976] 100–1 ratio of per capita product between the wealthiest 10 percent and the poorest 20 percent of the world population could shrink to about 5–1 after

200 years, give or take a factor of two or three."[9] In short, the gap would probably not close, but it would shrink significantly, and all nations would enjoy at least a lower middle-class status in the global system.

Radicals contested these rosy expectations. Left to its own devices, the system now in place would drain the poor countries of all their riches, and leave them more impoverished than ever, a feeling shared (for not quite the same reasons) by counterculturalists. Even quite a few technoliberals were doubtful. Welfarers emphasized the urgent need of the poor nations for massive infusions of capital and technical assistance (preferably from the governments of wealthy countries acting through international bodies), lest too much reliance on market forces produce exactly the scenario depicted by radicals.

In the late 1960s and early 1970s, gloomy mavericks like the ecologist Garrett Hardin took the opposite view. Hardin compared the rich countries to a flotilla of lifeboats at sea. The rest of humankind consisted of survivors desperately treading water and begging for admission into the lifeboats. Take them all aboard, said Hardin, and the boats are swamped. "Everyone drowns. Complete justice, complete catastrophe." Take just the few aboard that you may have room for, and you eliminate the safety factor. Besides, how can you choose which to save and which to let die?

Only the third option, for which Hardin plumped, made any sense, although it flatly contradicted both Christian and Marxist ethics. Every rich country must look after itself. "Admit no more to the boat and preserve the small safety factor. Survival of the people in the lifeboat is then possible (though we shall have to be on our guard against boarding parties)." To be sure, a world government might be able to act more humanely. But there is no such animal. "For the foreseeable future, survival demands that we govern our actions by the ethics of a lifeboat."[10] As the radical futurist Richard J. Barnet commented sarcastically, "A gentle shove, and those who were doomed to die anyway because of their history of reckless reproduction, will make it possible for the rest to survive in comfort."[11]

For obvious reasons, lifeboat ethics have never really caught on, although radicals would insist that the policies of the rich countries and their multinational corporations are almost as bad. But Hardin's apocalypticism may be more relevant today than it was when he first began writing about lifeboats. After 1970, as in the domestic economy of the United States, so in the world economy. Growth rates slowed. Instead of 5 percent, countries were lucky to post an annual economic growth rate of 3 percent through the 1970s and 2 percent through the 1980s. Unemployment rose to intolerable heights in the developing nations. Their indebtedness now exceeds one trillion dollars.

With economic growth much slower worldwide and population growth rates declining, but only slightly, in the developing countries, the net result has been a widening of the infamous gap between the world's rich and poor.

Exceptions are plentiful. Several marginally rich countries like the Soviet Union have lost ground in recent years, while some of the poor ones like Thailand have gained. But the net result has almost certainly been a widening of the gap, especially in Latin America and Africa, where nine countries reported negative growth between 1973 and 1986, and seventeen reported growth at rates lower than 2 percent.[12] Dividing the world's countries into four classes (rich, middle, poor, and poorest), Alan B. Durning sees the differential in per capita incomes between each class increasing slowly between 1950 and 1970, increasing more rapidly in the 1970s and more rapidly still in the 1980s. With reference to income distribution, he concludes that the world "as a whole is probably less equitable than any nation."[13]

What do futurists expect for the international class system in the 1990s and thereafter? Many technoliberals, as we have seen, think that in the long run it will grow more egalitarian. But they are in a minority. If present-day trends continue, with no fundamental structural changes in the world-system, we may assume that by the middle of the next century, the gap between the rich and the poor nations will have grown much wider. The nations in the top 10 percent will enjoy not a 100–1 lead, as they do now, but a 200–1 lead in per capita income over the nations in the bottom quintile.

There may be exceptions. A few aspiring countries in East Asia may join the club of the rich, copying the progress already recorded by Japan and Hong Kong. As the structures of state socialism are dismantled and replaced, several Eastern European nations may achieve income levels comparable to those of Western Europe. Some countries in the Third World now rated as poor or peripheral may swarm up the ladder of success to a middling position. Nevertheless, given a continuation of current trends, extremes of wealth and poverty in the world as a whole will probably increase, rather than decrease, in coming decades.

CAPITALISM

But the "given trends" just discussed need not continue. More important to futurists than trends are strategies to reduce the gap between rich and poor and ensure balanced growth worldwide. What they recommend is almost wholly a function of the paradigm with which they most closely identify (technoliberal, radical, counterculturalist), which in turn dictates how they view the dynamics of capitalism.

Hence, the paramount question in the realm of economic futures is the question not of income distribution, or rates of growth, or any other statistical indicator, but the future of capitalism itself. How does capitalism work, and how does its modus operandi shape its future, and ours?

From the technoliberal perspective, the future of capitalism is bright, not only for capitalists, but for everyone. Capitalism has proved its immeasurable superiority to socialism by outproducing the flabby economies of the Soviet

Union and other socialist states, most of which are now scrambling to enter the capitalist world market as full partners. But the superiority of capitalism was apparent to technoliberals long before the débâcle of European socialism in 1989. It works, they contend, because it motivates people. The relentless pursuit of profit, higher wages, and affluence benefits every segment of the population. Managers and workers put forth their best efforts. Production and consumption are maximized. Efficiency is rewarded.

Technoliberals note that the class structure of society has also undergone a fundamental transformation under the aegis of capitalism. Instead of the universal proletarianization foreseen by Marx, we have universal *embour-geoisement*. That is to say, instead of most people in society sinking toward the bottom and becoming propertyless manual workers at the mercy of the labor market, most people in advanced capitalist societies are rising into the middle class. As bourgeois in their own right, they are the class allies of the great capitalists, who encourage and enable them to develop skills, build careers, and acquire capital. In the course of time, one of Marx's visions will materialize in a way he never imagined. Society will become classless, as virtually everyone joins the bourgeoisie.[14]

In futures inquiry, a prominent spokesperson for embourgeoisement theory is the Harvard sociologist Daniel Bell, in *The Coming of Post-Industrial Society* and various later works. Just as Marx divided the history of the human race into three ages (before, during, and after capitalism), so Bell divides it into the eras of pre-industrialism, industrialism, and post-industrialism.[15] Pre-industrial men and women made their living by hunting, fishing, herding, and farming. During the industrial age, people in the economically advanced sectors of the world have derived most of their income from manufacturing. In the post-industrial era, which has already arrived in the United States, the majority of workers will be engaged not in the raising of food or the manufacturing of goods but in the services and professions. Instead of tillers and toilers, well over half the population is likely to consist of doctors, engineers, scientists, teachers, secretaries, sales persons, and the like. The principal resource of the post-industrial economy will be neither land nor machinery, but knowledge; and its possessors, men and women of expertise, will replace businessmen as the "dominant" human type. "In the post-industrial society, technical skill becomes the base of and education the mode of access to power."[16]

Bell offered no timetable for world post-industrialization in 1973, when he published *The Coming of Post-Industrial Society*. He explicitly denied that his theory bore a "deterministic trajectory," as did Marx's. All the same, he expected that the post-industrializing process, now most visible and most advanced in the United States, would become "a major feature of the twenty-first century." Post-industrialism would play a large part in restructuring the societies of Western Europe, the Soviet Union, and Japan in the next thirty to fifty years.[17]

More recently Bell has added the vision of a four-tiered America in the year 2013, with 85 percent of its population enrolled in one or another segment of the middle class. Of these, 25 percent would consist of professional and managerial workers [the upper middle class], 35 percent of skilled and technical workers and persons furnishing administrative support [the middle middle class], and 25 percent of service workers [the "service" or lower middle class]. The remaining 15 percent of the American population would comprise an "underclass" of unemployed or casual laborers who drift in and out of the work force.[18]

Bell's future America is not a literally classless society, nor in any sense a utopia. Hierarchies would persist, along with sharp distinctions based on gender, race, and age cohort. The underclass, however small, might pose embarrassing problems for the system. Cultural contradictions would persist between the ethic of enterprise and the ethic of personal freedom and self-actualization. But from the point of view of class analysis, the America of Bell's 2013 would be a fairly homogeneous society, with no need or place for semi-skilled labor. Almost everyone would be a trained, skilled worker of one kind or another. Thanks to computers, robotics, and all the technological paraphernalia of automation, the day of the grease-smeared industrial proletarian would be gone forever.

Herman Kahn and his associates at the Hudson Institute ventured a similar but even more sweeping forecast of the future all-bourgeois society in *The Next 200 Years*. Citing Bell's work, but altering his terminology and identifying much more consciously with the technoliberal paradigm, they argued that the most advanced countries were now entering the "superindustrial" period, a watershed in history as great as the invention of agriculture and the Industrial Revolution. Superindustrial economies feature high technology and extraordinarily large enterprises. Most workers are engaged in service industries. Wealth multiplies. Knowledge replaces experience as the chief qualification for gainful employment.

But a truly "postindustrial" age would not be achieved anywhere until some point in the twenty-first century. Postindustrialism, in Kahn's vocabulary, constitutes a fourth stage in history, beyond agriculturalism, industrialism, and the service economy, when so-called productive labor in any sector of the economy "will constitute only a small part of human endeavors." People will be able to spend most of their time developing and enjoying themselves and each other, rather than working.[19]

Such forecasts were fairly common in the early to middle 1970s, as futurists examined the trends of the time. Until about 1970, economic growth had been more or less continuous for a quarter-century, not only in the advanced capitalist countries, but throughout the world. Technological progress seemed to promise unlimited wealth in the future, as well as the unshackling of workers from the inhuman logic and rhythm of the machine. As the British sociologist Anthony Giddens noted in the early 1970s, the United States led the world in its progress toward a middle-class society, with roughly half the work force holding white-collar occupations, as opposed to one-third or less of the work force of other leading capitalist countries.[20] Why not, therefore, a future in which nearly everyone joins the middle class, and not only in the "advanced" societies, but, ultimately, in Asia, Africa, and Latin America as well?

Although such a conclusion was anathema to Giddens, it reflects fairly well the brightest hopes of technoliberal futurists, whether marketeers or welfarers. These hopes have dimmed a little in the more austere economic climate of the 1980s and early 1990s, and in light of the growing inequality within and among nations. Addressing another point, Lester Thurow has challenged the assumption that employment in the services and professions will continue to grow at its currently high rates. He contends that the expansion of the service industries in the U.S. has all but reached its natural limits, and foresees a marked increase in manufacturing jobs. "The sun is about to set on the post-industrial era."[21]

But Thurow anticipates that neo-industrialism will prove as lucrative to all concerned as Bell's post-industrialism. Moreover, the apparent collapse of the exhaustive experiments in planned economic development conducted by the Soviet Union and its erstwhile allies in Eastern Europe and elsewhere has served to reinforce the conviction of technoliberals that only the capitalist road to the future is worth taking. Even some radical economists, such as Robert Heilbroner, have conceded, with many reservations and grumblings, that "less than 75 years after the contest between capitalism and socialism officially began, it is over: capitalism has won." Socialist activism may serve as a source of humanizing progress within capitalism, but socialism "is not yet a plausible alternative."[22]

The vision of an all-bourgeois society also reflects a sense of class especially widespread in late twentieth-century America. Polls regularly indicate that up to 85 percent of Americans think of themselves as members of the middle class already. Many are probably deluding themselves. Their views are less widely shared by ordinary folk in other advanced capitalist societies. But consciousness is a powerful force. If people strongly identify with a given class, it may make no difference at all, in their political and economic behavior, whether they actually belong to that class or not.

The radical retort to the technoliberal forecast of a prosperous, classless global capitalism in the twenty-first century has taken many forms over the past few decades. The radical mood as we enter the 1990s is somewhat chastened and downbeat, typified by the utterances of a Robert Heilbroner. But radicals cling to many elements of their traditional critique of capitalism, and suspect that in the long run, perhaps the very long run, capitalism will destroy itself after all.

The classical theory, developed by Marx and Engels in the middle of the previous century, holds that capitalism will indeed destroy itself through its own internal contradictions. To make profits, entrepreneurs must sweat surplus value from their work force. In other words, labor must be underpaid, which sharply curtails the buying power of working people and leads to systematic underconsumption of the products of industry. Capitalism supplies incentives to maximize production, but its Achilles' heel is the inability of workers to consume everything they produce.

As the system evolves, it is shaken by declining profits as capitalists seek to reduce labor costs by purchasing labor-saving technologies from fellow capitalists, and also by periodic economic crises brought on by overproduction and underconsumption. There is a tendency for many capitalist enterprises (especially smaller or ill-managed enterprises) to go under. Their corpses are devoured by larger, better endowed, or more skillfully managed firms. This process continues until only a few producers are left, vast monopolistic enterprises insulated by their capital reserves from economic shocks. But eventually even these behemoths will be brought face to face with reality. When society consists of a tiny band of monopoly capitalists and an angry multitude of proletarians slaving at their pleasure, the end of capitalism will be near at hand.

In the early 1990s, this scenario does not have the ring of plausibility. Heilbroner insists that in a purely economic sense capitalism has managed to avoid its doom by creating and sharing enough wealth to keep most people in the advanced capitalist societies comfortable. It has also shrewdly provided for the small remaining underclass by rigging a welfare "safety net."

Hence, relief must be sought in another quarter altogether. "While capitalism's internal economic contradictions are not what will destroy it," says Heilbroner, "its internal cultural contradiction may. Capitalism does wonders for economic growth, but little for moral growth or cultural enrichment. Capitalism is a system full of self-debasement." More specifically, it shrinks human life to the dimensions of a TV commercial, where all that matters is the sale and consumption of products. It withers political participation, fosters anomie, discourages international cooperation, and blights the environment. "Business civilization lacks any capacity for long-term consideration about society as a whole."[23]

Heilbroner's indictment may be difficult to translate into a scenario for the actual overthrow or demise of capitalism, but it resonates with other radical critiques of the capitalist world economy, in which a good many counterculturalist futurists also join. Whatever may be said in defense of capitalism as a system for the production and sale of goods and services, it imposes high costs that may, in one way or another, and sooner or later, cause its downfall.

For example, Marx's anticipation of monopolistic tendencies within capitalism looks better and better as we approach the next millennium. In the 1980s, the top five hundred American corporations, only one-tenth of one percent of all the companies in the United States, owned two-thirds of all the business resources, employed two-thirds of all the workers, and collected 70 percent of all the profits. To look at just one major industry, the number of leading corporations in the newspaper, magazine, and radio and television business fell between 1980 and 1986 from forty-six to twenty-nine. The United States has thousands of book publishers, but ten giant corporations account for more than half the revenues from book sales.[24]

In the short run, all this may benefit both capitalism and the consumer, by weeding out inefficiency and cutting costs. In the much longer run, it may prove deadening. Large monopolistic enterprises tend to acquire elaborate corporate hierarchies that stifle innovation and devour profits without giving much in return.

Another example of the long-term costs of capitalism noted by radicals is the exorbitant price of government. Capitalism needs government to regulate competition, furnish necessary but unprofitable services such as rail transport, provide military and police protection, bribe the underclass with welfare payments, and co-opt the middle class with health insurance and pensions. All this carries a high price tag, and agencies of government tend to grow and proliferate uncontrollably. The very strategies that enable capitalism to curry the loyalty of its victims may, in the radical analysis, help to bring it down.

There are also the indirect social costs of capitalism, difficult to measure, but arguably much higher than the costs of government. If the radicals are right, capitalism plays havoc with people's lives in the name of profit. It creates an impoverished underclass, many of whose members are driven to careers of crime and vice, which in turn diminishes the quality of life for everyone in the society. When profit dictates, it whisks industrial installations from one part of the world to another, leaving a stranded proletariat that cannot find work. It pillages the environment, as in the Reagan era, by systematically evading the very regulations that its own governments have instituted. In the years when the business cycle produces low or negative growth, it generates massive unemployment throughout the economy, frustrating and embittering millions of middle-class folk, as well as the poor.

A further indirect social cost may arise from the cultural contradictions in capitalism noted by Heilbroner and developed at greater length by several counterculturalist critics. Capitalism grows out of what Mary E. Clark calls "the quantoid worldview," the view that nothing matters except quantities. By urging people to use up more and more goods as fast as possible, capitalism is fundamentally irrational and self-destructive. The quantoid worldview underlying capitalism creates a culture of waste, alienation, nihilism, and violence. In the best counterculturalist tradition, Clark follows E. F. Schumacher and Hazel Henderson in pleading for a new decentralized, people-centered economics, "economics with a human face," in which entrepreneurs would manage businesses, but capital would be publicly or cooperatively owned.[25]

There is yet another fundamental problem of capitalism that may cause it to stumble and fail in the far future. As Immanuel Wallerstein and his fellow world-system theorists have long maintained, capitalism has given rise to a single world-economy characterized by a universal division of labor.[26] Each sector of the system is dependent on economic exchanges with other sectors for its continued well-being. Every country is linked to every other by investment, trade, migration, and networks of transport and communications. In a very real sense, the economic system operative in every country is the capitalist system, even when, as in Eastern Europe before 1989, socialist states own the capital. Such states may own the capital, but they have to use it in accordance with the rules of the all-encompassing capitalist global market.

The result is exploitation on a world scale, the kind of exploitation that leads to the division of the world into rich and poor nations, as discussed above. The economies of what Wallerstein terms the "peripheral" and "semiperipheral" [very roughly, "poor" and "middle-income"] countries are manipulated by the governments and giant multinational corporations of the industrialized core to the best advantage of core capitalists and their dependents. Some of these multinational concerns have sales worldwide many times greater than the gross national products of whole countries in the periphery or semiperiphery.

Exploring the future, Wallerstein accepts the finding of the Russian economist Nikolai Kondratieff that business under capitalism goes through cycles with a periodicity of about fifty years. During the "A-phase" of a Kondratieff long wave, growth is rapid and profits rise; during a "B-phase," the economy stagnates and profits decline. The capitalist world-economy passed through an A-period from the middle 1940s to 1967 or perhaps 1973, and since then has been languishing and will continue to languish in a B-period, which should last until about the year 2000.[27]

Thereafter, writes Wallerstein, innovations in such technologies as microprocessing and genetic engineering may be "sufficiently perfected to sustain major worldwide leading industrial sectors."[28] A new spate of profiteering from these innovative technologies will expand the economies of the core countries, as the relocation of the less profitable industries (such as steel, chemicals, and electronics) from the core to the semiperiphery is finally completed. The likeliest countries to benefit from this A-phase of the next Kondratieff long wave are the United States and Japan, working together as a consortium, along with such other Pacific Rim nations as Australia and Canada. If they succeed in seizing and holding the technological edge, which Wallerstein thinks probable, they may dominate the global market for thirty years or more, bringing us down to the middle decades of the twenty-first century, when the world-economy will slide into a new crisis.

During the years of U.S.-Japanese hegemony, say, from 2000 to 2030, how will other parts of the world respond? Western Europe, left behind, will scramble to improve its position by allying economically and politically with the Soviet Union and other areas not engulfed by the U.S.-Japanese consortium. The peripheral nations, such as China, India, and Nigeria, will meanwhile find themselves more involved than ever "in the commodity chains of the world-economy. And the price of this increased involvement would almost surely be, as it has been in the past, a seriously expanded exploitation of the periphery."[29] The economies of the peripheral nations will be distorted to suit the needs of core-country capitalists, their resources and environments will be ravaged, and their people will be pauperized. In all likelihood, their misery will be severe enough to prompt formidable anti-systemic movements of resistance to domination by the core countries, movements that can issue in great wars and revolutionary upheavals for which the masters of capital will have to pay dearly.

Wallerstein also foresees that during the next A-phase, "the capitalist world-economy will use up its last margin of rectification." Having squeezed working people dry, raped the earth, conquered every market, and provoked widespread resistance, "it will have exhausted its ability to maintain the cyclical rhythms that are its heartbeat. It will give out."[30] The only question is how its demise will come, whether through a world war featuring the U.S.-Japanese consortium against the Euro-Soviet consortium, through a reconstruction of the system undertaken by a dictatorship of the privileged, or through collapse and chaos followed by the emergence of an egalitarian democratic world order.

Wallerstein clearly favors the third alternative, but he has never expected the transition to socialism to occur soon. As he wrote in 1980, "We are living in the historic world transition from capitalism to socialism. It will undoubtedly take a good 100–150 years yet to complete it, and of course the outcome is not inevitable." All we can say with some assurance is that we are now in a "late phase" of the capitalist world-economy, and that "with the end of this peculiar moral aberration that capitalism has represented . . . the slow construction of a relatively free and relatively egalitarian world may at last begin."[31]

DEMOCRACY

Thinkers drawn to the radical paradigm, like Wallerstein, generally hold capitalism largely responsible for the failure of democratization in the modern world. They would agree that capitalism is an "aberration," a force that has caused modern society, one might say, to deviate from its path. By contrast, Daniel Bell in *The Coming of Post-Industrial Society* maintains that "the control of society is no longer primarily economic but political."[32] In the post-industrial era, political struggle has taken the place of class struggle.

Wallerstein and Bell are not as far apart as they might at first seem. In one instance, political action may help end the grip of an economic system (capitalism) on modern society, and usher in a truly democratic era. In the other, politics is liberated from ideological constraints by post-industrialization and takes center stage. Either way, the political process is assured a promising future. Either way, economics is destined to lose its high position—eventually—in the scale of human priorities.

But Bell is less sanguine than most radicals (or, for that matter, most technoliberals) regarding the future of democracy. "In the post-industrial society," he writes, "the clash of individual interests, each following its own whim, leads necessarily to a greater need for collective regulation and a greater degree of coercion . . . in order to have effective communal action."[33] Contests for power between individuals and groups, and between politicians and technocrats, require society to impose limits on both democratic decision-making and personal freedom. The simple "participatory democracy" for which so many naive radicals and counterculturalists clamor, Bell warns, cannot resolve all our differences.

Debates among futurists on the prospects for political democracy take much the same form as debates on the future of the economy and the distribution of wealth, but they are by no means as common. Most futurists who have pondered the issue would agree that representative democracy has made astonishing progress since the late eighteenth century. By the close of the third decade of the twentieth century, nearly all advanced capitalist countries were governed by the freely elected representatives of the people, defined as every adult in the society, male or female, rich or poor.

The next two decades witnessed serious setbacks for the democratic process, as fascism spread like the Black Death throughout Europe and the dictatorship of the proletariat in Soviet Russia was ruthlessly transformed into the dictatorship of one man and his political satraps. Anyone writing from the perspective of the late 1930s or early 1940s, such as James Burnham in his seminal work, *The Managerial Revolution* (1941), could be excused for harboring doubts about the inevitable triumph of Western-style democracy.

Even after the defeat of Hitler in 1945 and the democratization of the former Axis powers, the future of world democracy appeared uncertain. Stalin continued his reign of terror in the Soviet Union, burlesqued with cold fury by George Orwell in *Nineteen Eighty-Four* (1949). Stalinist regimes blossomed in Eastern Europe and China. Aldous Huxley in *Brave New World* (1932) and *Brave New World Revisited* (1958), and Bertram Gross in *Friendly Fascism* (1980), made the subtler point that even in the nominally democratic societies of Europe and North America, the growing power of corporate oligarchs and seemingly benevolent behavioral engineers might someday remove all choice from human life, converting men and women into social insects. Meanwhile, representative democracy was also faring poorly in Latin America, the new nations of Africa, the Middle East, and Southeast Asia.

Still more recently, in the 1980s and beyond, representative democracy appears to have resumed its march, tallying substantial gains throughout Latin America and Eastern Europe, including the Soviet Union itself. Its progress inspired Francis Fukuyama to proclaim the "end of history" in 1989. The titanic ideological battles of the past, writes Fukuyama, battles such as those between monarchism and republicanism or between fascism and communism, have become unthinkable for all "post-historic" peoples. Here and there, backward countries mired in the old dialectic of "history" might resist the democratic tide. But in all others, just as capitalism has won its long struggle with socialism, so democracy now stands unchallenged on the field of combat. We have reached "the end point of mankind's ideological evolution and the universalization of Western liberal democracy as the final form of human government."[34]

Technoliberals generally share this view of the future of politics, but seldom as sweepingly as Fukuyama. The Hudson Institute's official position, in *The Next 200 Years*, was that even with increasing affluence and *embourgeoisement* worldwide, democracy would not prevail everywhere in the twenty-second century. "Many countries will be relatively or at least nominally democratic, though some democracies will probably be more authoritarian than truly parliamentary."[35] The only reason given by the Institute for its uncharacteristic pessimism was the observation that democracy (in 1976) remained "relatively fragile" in most parts of the non-Western world. How political processes could change so little over the next two centuries, despite all the social and economic progress foreseen, the authors did not trouble to explain.

The radical retort to technoliberalism is that Western-style bourgeois democracy should not be confused with government by the people. Its future triumphs, if any, might even represent a setback for democratization. When so much wealth is concentrated in the hands of the few, who control the media, the schools, the bureaucracy, and the workplace, ordinary citizens can wield little influence. Their political parties and trade unions are routinely co-opted, their brains are washed, and their choice at the ballot box is usually between a capitalist Tweedledum and a capitalist Tweedledee. Although most radicals acknowledge that the growth of representative democracy offers working people a *chance* to organize and make their voices heard, all too often it is a chance they cannot effectively exploit. As Rosa Luxemburg wrote many years ago, the social reality of bourgeois democracy undermined its political form. Socialists had a duty to "unmask the harsh core of social inequality and unfreedom which exists under the sweet husk of formal freedom and equality."[36]

In the coming years of late capitalism, even the marginal benefits conferred by formal freedom and equality in capitalist democracy may be lost. Radicals point to a variety of likely changes in the socioeconomic order that might have disastrous political implications. In the 1960s, in *One-Dimensional Man*, Herbert Marcuse observed that the mode of domination in capitalist societies had already begun to shift from the crude but instantly recognizable tactics of the old robber barons to the realm of administration. The bosses were changing, little by little, into faceless corporate bureaucrats, who quietly take control of laboratories, research institutes, and the national government, with the result that "the tangible source of exploitation disappears behind the façade of objective rationality."[37] In the name of orderly administration, democracy is more thoroughly subverted than ever before.

Subversion will grow still more thorough if the new breed of private and public administrators take full advantage of the technologies of information processing and behavioral surveillance and control now becoming available to them. David Burnham has sounded some of the relevant alarms in his book *The Rise of the Computer State* (1983). He concludes with a grim scenario of life in America in the year 2020, where, thanks to systematic abuse of computer and telecommunications technologies, freedom does not ring, and justice is not blind.

A further threat to democratization, in the radical analysis, lurks in what radicals see as the ever-expanding gulf between the rich and poor, within capitalist societies and between nations in the world community. If that gulf continues to widen, especially if it is accompanied by severe business recessions, mass unemployment, destitution in the Third World, and grave harm to the environment, the likely political response of the haves and have-nots is not difficult to foresee. Disadvantaged classes and nations may declare open war on the capitalist world-system. In retaliation, privileged classes and nations may resort to clampdowns on dissent, suspension of civil liberties, perhaps even martial law and neo-fascist seizures of state power. In such times, bourgeois democracy would be a luxury the bourgeoisie could not afford. Even if no rebellions of the poor and no backlashes of the rich occurred, the sheer fact of growing economic inequality would inevitably diminish the political influence of the dispossessed.

But futurists of all ideological persuasions favor measures to make democracy more real and more effective. Technoliberals, both welfarers and marketeers, agree that democracy (as they understand it) is good for capitalism. Welfarers, in particular, want to see democracy strengthened, enlarged, and protected. They often recommend such nostrums as increased use of referenda, limiting office-holding to one or two terms, providing the services of ombudsmen to help citizens in their struggles with impersonal bureaucracies, and electronic polling of voters by legislators via two-way cable television or home computer systems.[38]

Among radicals and counterculturalists, the cry is usually for "participatory" democracy, as opposed, or in addition, to "representative" democracy.

Radicals have long insisted that electing representatives is not enough. Even if the people's chosen representatives were men and women who could be trusted to represent faithfully the wishes of their constituents in legislatures and chief executive offices, this would still leave most of life—the home, the workplace, the community, the army, the schools, even government itself—dominated by such antidemocratic forces as patriarchy and bureaucratism. The people must therefore struggle for active, daily participation in decision-making at all levels, and not least in the factory or the office or the farm, where most of us spend most of our waking lives.

At the same time radicals do not ignore the need for democratic struggle in the political arena. Condemning the "communism" invented by Lenin, Stalin, and Mao as a lethal parody of socialism on which the world has finally turned its back, most radical futurists view socialism as inherently demo-cratic. Whatever the costs, government of, by, and for the working people is both possible and necessary in the next century. Socialists are of a mind with Michael Harrington, the late chairman of the Democratic Socialists of America, who dedicated *The Twilight of Capitalism* to "the future of an almost forgotten genius: the foe of every dogma, champion of human freedom and democratic socialist—KARL MARX."[39]

Counterculturalists, too, believe in participatory democracy at all levels. But they are equally emphatic in not wishing to see the centralized structures of capitalist power replaced by new centralized structures of power under the control of masses, even enfranchised masses.

The political ideas of Alvin Toffler, a futurist who borrows from every paradigm, are typical of the counterculturalist position. He brings his best-selling book *The Third Wave* (1980) to its resonant conclusion with a chapter on "Twenty-First Century Democracy," in which he appeals for a new kind of democratic governance, appropriate to the next, post-industrial stage in world history. The forms of polity characteristic of agrarian (First Wave) and industrial (Second Wave) societies are now obsolete. In the industrial age, the legitimating principle was majority rule. In the "de-massified" society of the Third Wave, writes Toffler, there is no clear majority on any issue. Its power will be transferred to minorities, representing a plurality of class, ethnic, cultural, and other interests. Temporary "modular parties" will sup-plant the old mass parties. Randomly selected samples of the citizenry will replace, or at least supplement, elected representatives, and cast binding votes on public issues. Some decisions now taken exclusively at the national or federal level will be referred upward, as appropriate, to transnational bodies, and many others will be referred downward to local and regional bodies.

The choice for Toffler is quite clear. Old-style majoritarian democracy is breaking down everywhere. "Today's widespread disillusionment, anger, and bitterness against the world's Second Wave governments can either be whipped into frantic frenzy by demagogues calling for authoritarian lead-

ership or it can be mobilized for the process of democratic reconstruction."
If we wait too long to begin such reconstruction, the further disintegration
of Second Wave polities will send "the forces of tyranny jackbooting through
the streets." But if we begin now, if we launch "an experiment in anticipatory
democracy in many nations at once . . . we can head off the totalitarian
thrust."[40]

Toffler's *The Third Wave* found many enthusiastic readers throughout the
1980s, and (surprisingly) from adherents to all three futurist paradigms. A
good example is the Canadian futurist Frank Feather, who in political matters
fits the counterculturalist mold as well as Toffler. But Feather prefers to
speak of four waves beyond industrialism, rather than just one. If the third
wave is a service economy, as in Bell's schema, then the fourth will be an
information economy, followed by societies based on leisure and travel, and
finally the exploration and settlement of outer space. The advanced capitalist
societies are already deep into the third wave, and the fourth wave, the new
information society, is well on its way.

In this fourth wave, Feather labels the appropriate form of governance
"partocracy," his acronym for participatory democracy. "In an information
society," he writes, "people are increasingly less satisfied with mere material
goods. Their chief desire is for self-realization and personal growth, and for
participation in decision-making and the management of the economic, social
and political system." Citizens will increasingly demand an informed say in
all public affairs. Home computers plugged into national nets will enable
them to learn the issues, take part in polls, vote on vital public measures,
and later elect their representatives, all from their armchairs. Eventually,
representative bodies themselves may disappear, vestigial organs that have
outlived their usefulness. As Fourth Wave society matures, political processes in the Western world will be gradually transformed into "a true
'partocracy' of real-time electronic participation of/for/by the people early in
the 21st century."[41]

Feather's enthusiasm is obviously sincere, although (much like Toffler) he
provides little evidence to support his forecasts. A still more vivid expression
of counterculturalist political values may be found in Ernest Callenbach's
novel *Ecotopia* (1975), which imagines the near-future secession from the
United States of northern California, Oregon, and Washington. In the new
sovereign state of Ecotopia, the big corporations have decamped, replaced
by small co-operatives. A national government exists, run principally by
women, but most of the day-to-day political life of Ecotopia takes place at
the local level, and racial minorities govern themselves in their own mini-
cities.

What stands out as the chief contribution of the political utopography of
counterculturalist futurism, clearly, is its insistence on the decentralization
of power. The future of democracy, counterculturalists foresee, lies in the
transfer of responsibility to the people directly, and to their many and varied

communities. Democracy in the counterculturalist future will be an affair neither of the rising middle class nor of freshly empowered masses, but of individuals, families, and diverse groups. Toffler speculates that the transition to the new politics may even be attended by bloodshed. As futurists always say of their preferred models, it will be well worth any sacrifice.

For radicals, bloodshed may also be the price of future socialist revolutions, especially in countries outside the pale of Western representative democracy. It may even be the price in the West itself, if the bourgeoisie in its time of troubles rids itself of its democratic "façade" and resorts to totalitarian governance.

In any case, talk of bloodshed raises the specter of yet another political problem, not integrally related to the future of democracy. Whatever force may be needed to complete the transition to socialism or Third Wave politics (if such a transition ever happens), there is another and historically more significant mode of violence in human societies that we have thus far managed to ignore almost entirely: international and intertribal war. Will there be wars in the twenty-first century, and beyond? Will they be system-wide? Can they be prevented and if so, how? To such questions, we turn in our next chapter.

NOTES

1. Bernard Cazes, "Une utopie en trois actes," *Analyses de la société d'études et de documentation économiques, industrielles et sociales*, 75 (May 1990): 76–77.

2. Michael Harrington, *Socialism: Past and Future* (New York: Arcade Publishing, 1989), 4–5.

3. *Ibid.*, 7.

4. See Carol J. De Vita, *America in the 21st Century: A Demographic Overview* (Washington: Population Reference Bureau, 1989), 15–15 and Figure 5.

5. See, for example, World Resources Institute and International Institute for Environment and Development, *World Resources 1988–89* (New York: Basic Books, 1988), Table 14.4, pp. 242–243. Extremes of wealth and poverty are somewhat less pronounced in Japan.

6. Reported in Martin Tolchin, "Study Shows Growing Gap Between Rich and Poor," *New York Times* (March 23, 1989), A1 and A24.

7. From wire service reports published in various newspapers on July 24, 1990.

8. Phillips, "Reagan's America: A Capital Offense," 26.

9. Kahn et al., *The Next 200 Years*, 55–57.

10. Garrett Hardin, "Living on a Lifeboat," *Bioscience*, 24:10 (October, 1974): 561–568. The quoted material appears on pp. 562 and 568.

11. Barnet, *The Lean Years*, p. 303.

12. See Table 14.1 in World Resources Institute and International Institute for Environment and Development, *World Resources 1988–1989*, 236–237.

13. Alan B. Durning, "Ending Poverty," in Brown et al., *State of the World 1990*, 137, especially Figure 8–1. Durning bases his observations largely on the work of

Robert Summers and Alan Heston of the University of Pennsylvania, as documented on 228 n. 5.

14. See Kahn et al., *The Next 200 Years*, 202, where the authors assume that in advanced capitalist societies an "open, classless society" already exists.

15. Bell freely acknowledges his indebtedness to Marx. "One can say that the sequence of feudalism, capitalism and socialism, and pre-industrial and post-industrial society both proceed from Marx." *The Coming of Post-Industrial Society: A Venture in Social Forecasting* (New York: Basic Books, 1973), 114. In Coates and Jarratt's *What Futurists Believe*, Bell cites Marx, along with Karl Mannheim, Robert McIver, Max Weber, and Colin Clark, as the chief influences on his thought. *What Futurists Believe*, 101.

16. *The Coming of Post-Industrial Society*, 358.

17. *Ibid.*, x.

18. Daniel Bell, "The World and the United States in 2013," *Daedalus*, 116:3 (Summer 1987): 26–29.

19. Kahn et al., *The Next 200 Years*, 1 and 20–24.

20. Anthony Giddens, *The Class Structure of the Advanced Societies* (New York: Harper and Row, 1975), 178–179.

21. Lester Thurow, "The Post-Industrial Era Is Over," *New York Times*, September 4, 1989, A27. Thurow's references are all to the American economy. As he notes, the service industries grew more slowly in other industrialized countries in the 1980s, helping to explain the relative decline in the productivity of the U.S. economy.

22. Robert Heilbroner, "No Alternative to Capitalism," interview in *New Perspectives Quarterly*, 6:3 (Fall 1989): 4 and 10. See also Heilbroner, "The Triumph of Capitalism," *The New Yorker*, 64 (January 23, 1989): 98–109. An enthusiastic technoliberal vision of a more democratic capitalism growing from the initiatives of "progressive" corporations is available in William E. Halal, *The New Capitalism* (New York: Wiley, 1986).

23. *Ibid.*, 7–8.

24. See Michael Schwartz, ed., *The Structure of Power in America: The Corporate Elite as a Ruling Class* (New York: Holmes and Meier, 1987), and Ben H. Bagdikian, *The Media Monopoly*, 2nd ed. (Boston: Beacon Press, 1987).

25. Clark, *Ariadne's Thread*, especially 293–295 and 357–363.

26. Immanuel Wallerstein sums up his thesis on the world-economy in "The Rise and Future Demise of the World Capitalist System: Concepts for Comparative Analysis," in Wallerstein, *The Capitalist World-Economy*, 1–36.

27. Wallerstein, "The Capitalist World-Economy: Middle-Run Prospects," 279–280. The discussion that follows is largely based on this article. In an earlier work, "Crisis as Transition," in Amin et al., *Dynamics of Global Crisis*, 11–54, Wallerstein expected the beginning of the next A-period by 1990 or thereabouts. See especially p. 40.

28. Wallerstein, "The Capitalist World-Economy: Middle-Run Prospects," 284.

29. *Ibid.*, 285.

30. *Ibid.*, 287.

31. Immanuel Wallerstein, "The Future of the World-Economy," [1980] in Wallerstein, *The Politics of the World-Economy: The States, the Movements, and the Civilizations* (New York: Cambridge University Press, 1984), 111.

32. Bell, *The Coming of Post-Industrial Society*, 373.

33. *Ibid.*, 475.

34. Francis Fukuyama, "The End of History?," *The National Interest*, 16 (Summer 1989): 4.

35. Kahn et al., *The Next 200 Years*, 205.

36. Rosa Luxemburg, *Gesammelte Werke*, IV:359, quoted in Michael Harrington, *Socialism: Past and Future*, 68.

37. Herbert Marcuse, *One-Dimensional Man: Studies in the Ideology of Advanced Industrial Society* (Boston: Beacon Press, 1964), 32. As Michael Harrington commented, "This is the left-wing version of the theory of postindustrial society; it describes an essentially postcapitalist, managed system." Harrington, *The Twilight of Capitalism* (New York: Simon and Schuster, 1976), 217.

38. See, for example, Norman H. Nie, "Future Developments in Mass Communications and Citizen Participation," in Albert Somit, ed., *Political Science and the Study of the Future* (Hinsdale, Ill.: Dryden Press, 1974), 132–154.

39. Harrington, *The Twilight of Capitalism*, 5.

40. Alvin Toffler, *The Third Wave* [1980] (New York: Bantam Books, 1981), 442–443.

41. Feather, *G-Forces*, 365 and 374.

6 _____

The Future of War and Peace

WAR IN HISTORY

In the postindustrial world, according to the authors of *The Next 200 Years*, "Wars no longer 'pay' and the recourse to large-scale organized violence becomes restricted generally to defensive situations or attempts to preserve some aspect of the status quo." Because "the best path to wealth, safety and power is through internal development and not through war, . . . a postindustrial society may be relatively free from violence and war."[1]

Popular in the mid–1970s when the Superpowers were enjoying a brief détente, this view of the future is likely to thrive again as the East-West Cold War fades from recollection. It also conceals a rare irony. In the 241 pages of *The Next 200 Years*, speculations about future warfare occupy only eight paragraphs. Yet its senior author, Herman Kahn, was for most of his life a leading American student of the future of warfare, especially nuclear war. His years of research on military strategies and weapons systems at the RAND Corporation and later at his own Hudson Institute helped shape U.S. defense policy. His books *On Thermonuclear War* (1960), *Thinking about the Unthinkable* (1962), and *On Escalation: Metaphors and Scenarios* (1965) may have done more to alert the public to the perils of a third world war than all the writings of all the nuclear pacifists put together. At the end of his life, he reviewed and updated his earlier writings on global war in yet another study, *Thinking about the Unthinkable in the 1980s* (1984).

Futurists tend to ignore (or apologize for) Kahn's books on military futures, just as he himself largely ignored it in *The Next 200 Years* and in many of his other writings.[2] General works on the future such as Arthur C. Clarke's *Profiles of the Future*, Willis W. Harman's *An Incomplete Guide to the*

Future, Alvin Toffler's *The Third Wave*, and Barry Hughes's *World Futures* allude only briefly to warfare. Scholars who devote much of their energy to the future of peace and war, such as Richard Falk and Frank Barnaby, often escape identification as futurists altogether.

Why the indifference? Not all futurists neglect military futures, but those who do presumably believe either that major war under modern conditions would bring the future to a dead stop or is unlikely to occur for the reasons cited by Kahn and his colleagues in *The Next 200 Years*. In either case, they might contend, the only futures worth exploring are those that exclude the possibility of global war.

But to ignore the future of war is a distinctly ostrichlike maneuver. Leaving aside for the moment the question of whether conflicts on the scale of World Wars One and Two will occur in the future, it is clear that wars exert an immense influence on systems of governance, economies, societies, cultures, and the environment. If there is a significant chance that warfare, global or regional, will occur in the next few centuries, no futurist can afford to leave military futures out of consideration. Even if one assumes that the warfare system will sooner or later disappear, the question remains of how the trick will be done. How may a lasting world peace be achieved and preserved, and what effect will it have on the rest of human life?

The history of humankind thus far offers little comfort or encouragement to futurists who side with the authors of *The Next 200 Years*. The six thousand years that have elapsed since the founding of the first civilizations in the Middle East have been six thousand years of bloody hell. The political scientist Francis Beer estimates that 2,400–3,500 "world major wars" were fought between 3600 B.C. and 1980 A.D., with 1.1 billion battle deaths. Only 597 years during this long period, barely one year in ten, were free of such wars.[3] If one includes regional and local wars, the figures rise much higher still. Beer's estimates are rough, but the picture they paint, in its essentials, is no doubt correct.

Beer also considers long-term trends, as do many other students of warfare. His findings are inconclusive. The consensus of scholars who have written on the subject is that over the centuries wars have tended to diminish in frequency and duration but increase in intensity and cost. Modern rapid transport and communications often produce swifter outcomes than in the "good old days" of slowly lumbering armies, but modern technologies of mass destruction ensure that whoever goes to war will pay a much higher price. In terms of futurist paradigms, it is typical for thinkers infected with counterculturalist assumptions to look nostalgically at such good old days, and de-emphasize their warlikeness, while regarding modern warfare as genocidal. Technoliberals, contrariwise, usually see militarism as an unfortunate legacy from past traditional societies that will soon become extinct (or at least manageable) in the capitalist millennium.

The evidence, such as it is, would seem to support neither side. Wars of unspeakable ferocity were fought in medieval and ancient times. There continue to be wars, well over a hundred civil and international wars since 1945 alone, causing the deaths of more than 21 million people, more than twice the number of soldiers and civilians who died in the mindless slaughter of World War One.[4] All nations and all races have fought major wars. Men everywhere, with the active support of women everywhere, have fought and died in wars. If battle deaths were not as high in premodern centuries, the likeliest explanation is the relatively more "primitive" state of the military arts in premodern centuries. Who can doubt that if the Caesars, the Khans, and the Sultans had possessed bombers, tanks, and nuclear and chemical weapons, they would have used them?

Clearly, the gravest threat to the human future is posed by the deployment of such super-weapons in wars involving all or most of the world-system. Until at least the seventeenth century, what Beer and others call "world major wars" were simply conflicts between sizeable countries that belonged to different political neighborhoods or conflicts not confined to a particular locale. The many wars waged between various European countries and the Ottoman Empire are apt examples. But these were seldom, if ever, "world wars" in any literal sense. Even the Thirty Years War of 1618–1648, which consisted of at least a dozen smaller wars with changing sets of combatants, was not a global conflict, since virtually all the fighting occurred in Central Europe. It was a major convulsion of the then-nascent "world-system," in Wallerstein's use of the phrase, but it remained a European affair.

Toward the close of the seventeenth century, as the importance of Europe's overseas trade and colonies steadily grew, other parts of the world became entangled in the wars of the capitalist world-system. The first that might deserve to be called a "world" war was the War of the Grand Alliance (1689–1697), known as "King William's War" in North America. Essentially a struggle between the England of William III, with his Spanish, Dutch, and Habsburg allies, and the France of Louis XIV, most of it was fought on the European mainland. But it soon became a two-hemisphere conflict, as hostilities spread to the English and French colonies in North America and the West Indies. From 1701 to 1815, the European powers waged a series of six more world wars, beginning with the War of the Spanish Succession (1701–1714). In all six, France was opposed by Great Britain. Habsburg Austria at first sided with Britain, later with France, and in the climactic wars of 1792–1815 once again with Britain. Major battles were fought not only in Europe but also in North America, the Caribbean, and India.

Up to this point, although armed conflict in the capitalist world-system had passed well beyond the boundaries of Europe, most of the blood shed was European or of European origin. In the still more elaborate world wars of the first half of the twentieth century, no race was spared. The so-called First World War of 1914–1918 pitted German-led Africans against British-led Indians in East Africa, Turks against Arabs and Britons in the Middle

East, Russians against Turks in the Caucasus, Japanese against Germans in China, and French-led African and British-led Indian troops against Germans in northern France. Forces from countries all over the world, including the United States, Canada, Australia, New Zealand, and Brazil, took part in the fighting in Europe.

Still worse was in store during the Second World War of 1939–1945, which cost twice as many lives as its predecessor. This time around, almost one-third of the military and civilian casualties were sustained by countries with nonwhite populations (chiefly, China and Japan), and military and naval engagements beyond Europe (in North Africa, East and Southeast Asia, and the Pacific) were almost as decisive as the battles in Europe itself.

It is little wonder that ever since the end of the Second World War, many novelists and futurists have been obsessed with visions of a Third. The number of novels and films imagining such a horror cannot be counted.[5] Memories of the Second World War are still too fresh, and the wounds it inflicted still not sufficiently healed, to inspire the brimming confidence about the future so common in the nineteenth century. When one also considers that global warfare is a disease of the world-system that really began in the seventeenth (not in the twentieth) century, the hope of eventual world peace may seem still more forlorn.

Fortunately, despite all the dire imaginings, there have been no authentic world wars in the second half of the twentieth century thus far. But, as mentioned earlier, wars have continued in various local and regional theaters since the end of the Second World War in 1945, with horrendous loss of life and property.

Nearly all of them, as foreseen by George Orwell in *Nineteen Eighty-Four*, have been wars in the Third World. Some have matched Third World nations or peoples against one another, with relatively little interference by the industrialized nations. Some, the greater number, have been wars of revolution against Western domination or wars either instigated by rich countries or transformed into larger struggles when rich countries entered the fray. Of the fifty bloodiest civil and international wars fought since 1945, at least thirty were wars in which the industrialized nations took a leading role. Several of these, such as the Korean conflict of 1950–1953, were in fact localized "world" wars, waged by one Superpower in the East-West Cold War against the proxy or proxies of another Superpower.

It does not take a world-class mind to explain the warlikeness of the international system. Tribes, nations, and empires have always resorted to warfare, when they thought they could gain significant advantages by so doing. Wars have been fought for thousands of years to annex land and other valued resources, help allies, command trade routes, repel invaders, secure defensible borders, win liberation from foreign rule, achieve hegemony in a given region, and much more.

The world wars of the capitalist-world system after 1689 did little more than play variations on an old tune. All of them were clearly attempts by one major power or powers to dominate the system economically and politically, or prevent such domination by others. Early on, the chief threat to a relatively stable world order of multiple sovereignties was posed by the Spanish and Austrian Habsburgs and then for a century and a half by France. In the twentieth century, bids for world hegemony were mounted by Germany and Japan; and during the Cold War by the United States (from the Soviet point of view) or by the Soviet Union (from the U.S. point of view).

It is difficult to imagine how the capitalist world-system could have functioned or survived without such wars. Had world wars to preserve or restore the balance of power not been fought and won, history would have taken an entirely different course. A planet ruled by Charles V, Louis XIV, Napoleon Bonaparte, or Adolf Hitler (and their successors) would most likely not have been a planet safe for democracy, capitalism, civil liberty, the secular state, or most of the other political and economic hallmarks of modernity.

The many smaller local and regional wars waged in the world-system both before and after 1945 have also been indispensable to its evolution. For better or worse, they have greatly accelerated the Westernization and modernization of the Third World. They have created dozens of new national states in Europe, Asia, and Africa. Like the system-wide world wars, they have been nurseries of technological and economic progress. In some instances they have even helped to bring about a more equitable distribution of wealth within national societies, by disposing of feudal ruling classes, abolishing slavery, raising the wages of workers, or enhancing the status of women.

It follows that warfare, far from being an exotic or exceptional phenomenon, has been, thus far, an intrinsic feature of the capitalist world-system, as in all previous civilizations. We described it a few pages ago as a "disease." From the point of view of its victims, the millions of casualties, both civilian and military, the lives disrupted or ruined, the cities devastated, the world turned upside down, warfare is indeed pathological. The behavior of the warriors themselves is in many ways subhuman, and necessarily so. But can there be a world without recurrent bouts of such a disease? Can there be a world without war? If not, what price will history exact from warlike nations in years and centuries to come?

WAR AND THE FUTURE

Futurists and others who have pondered the future of warfare in the modern world-system since the Soviet acquisition of the atomic bomb in 1949 have dwelled largely on the prospect of a third world war fought with nuclear weapons between the Soviet Union and the United States, with or without the support of their various allies. Even after Great Britain, France, and China successfully tested nuclear weapons (in 1952, 1960, and 1964, respectively), the only two "superpowers" on earth were still the Soviet Union and the United States. As time passed, the lesser nuclear powers gained greater freedom of maneuver. But they were in no position to initiate a world war. It was difficult to imagine the outbreak of any world war that did not pit the Soviet Union against the United States. Starting in 1983, I offered for seven years at SUNY Binghamton an annual lecture course entitled "World War III," a course devoted almost entirely to the chances of a U.S.-Soviet nuclear conflict.

Then came the World Revolution of 1989—as, some day, it may be called. One by one, the nominally socialist countries of Eastern Europe disposed of their one-party regimes. Democracy also spread to the Soviet Union itself, as various republics announced their intentions to secede or seek autonomy, and opposition political parties were at last permitted to challenge the authority of the ruling party. Troops crushed a peaceful student and worker uprising in Beijing in the spring, but the Chinese people had served fair warning on the party of Mao and Deng that its days were numbered. The climactic events of the World Revolution of 1989 were the breaching of the Berlin Wall in November and the execution in late December of Nicolae Ceausescu, the communist dictator of Romania.

The net effect of this cycle of revolutionary action in the formerly communist world, coupled with the virtual collapse of the economies of the Soviet Union and its erstwhile satellites in Eastern Europe, was to bring the Cold War not only to a halt, but to an end. Although it may revive some day in a new form, the threat of global nuclear war between the Superpowers that clouded our future from the late 1940s to the late 1980s has suddenly passed from the realm of the quite possible into the realm of the almost unimaginable. The Warsaw Pact, with its once formidable armies poised to attack Western Europe through its forward positions in East Germany and Czechoslovakia, is no more. For their part, the countries of the NATO military alliance would nowadays much rather invade the former Warsaw Pact countries with goods and capital than with troops and missiles.[6]

Nevertheless, nuclear weapons, together with a mighty array of non-nuclear or "conventional" weapons, still exist. Knowledge of how to build them would continue to exist even if all nations agreed to renounce their use and destroy their arsenals. As we have seen, warfare is also endemic in the modern world-system, as it was in all previous eras. Just because a global war between the Soviet Union and the United States has become (at least for the time being) unlikely, does not mean that warfare itself is obsolete. The capabilities of nuclear weapons, in particular, should never be underestimated or forgotten.

Much of the research done by futurists and others on the consequences of a global nuclear war is, therefore, still relevant. Such a war could begin as a non-nuclear conflict and escalate to the use of nuclear weapons when one side or the other found itself in danger of defeat. Or it could start as a devastating pre-emptive nuclear strike against all available military targets (sometimes known as "counterforce" strategy) if one side decided that its best chance of prevailing lay in disabling its enemy's capacity to retaliate. Such a strike could be accompanied by nuclear explosions in outer space over the enemy's territory to generate a massive electromagnetic pulse capable of disrupting communications and transport on the ground, and by attacks on enemy governance and command centers ("decapitation" strategy). These supplementary actions might leave the enemy unable to mount an effective or concerted counterstrike even if some of its nuclear weapons survived. Most strategists in recent decades have given little consideration to direct attacks on population centers ("countervalue" strategy), which they see as a desperate last resort.[7]

In all likelihood the escalation of conflict until it reaches the nuclear level poses a greater danger to humankind in the future than the premeditated first strike. Nuclear weapons can be deployed in so many ways, in missile silos, in artillery, on aircraft, on surface vessels, on submarines, in space vehicles, or even in suitcases, that no country can ever be quite sure of its immunity from a paralyzing counterattack. Yet once a war escalates to the use of nuclear weapons, even to relatively low-yield "tactical" or "battlefield" nuclear weapons, limiting its further escalation up the ladder to thermonuclear doomsday may prove virtually impossible . In the epigrammatic words of the American defense expert Morton Halperin, "The NATO doctrine is that we will fight with conventional forces until we are losing, then we will fight with tactical [nuclear] weapons until we are losing, and then we will blow up the world."[8]

At almost any level, nuclear war involves the additional danger of being literally uncontrollable. The bombs that demolished Hiroshima and Nagasaki in 1945 were monstrous contraptions of staggering explosive force. The many years that have passed since their detonation have done little to diminish our awe of them. Yet the strategic nuclear warheads currently available are typically from five to fifty times more powerful, equivalent to 100,000 or more tons of TNT. In multiple independently-targeted reentry vehicles such as the American MX or D5, ten or more warheads of this size can be delivered with a high degree of precision to various targets by a single missile.

What such weapons can do to the armed forces and to the command, control, communications, and intelligence facilities of an enemy, no matter how well shielded or hardened against attack, is not easy to imagine. In time of all-out nuclear war, the result will almost certainly be the collapse of political control and the shattering of the military chain of command. Headless armies will discharge their weapons as they see fit, hoping for the best. As a former Hudson Institute associate, Paul Bracken, foresees, "The breakup of communications after attack leads to decentralized assessment and to joint decision making among the isolated islands of forces, with pathological strategy implications."[9]

What would be left, after a substantial exchange of nuclear weapons, or a totally disabling nuclear first strike? Everything depends on how many countries were involved, how many nuclear warheads were detonated, their megatonnage, the targets selected, and the proportion of ground bursts to air bursts. But students of nuclear war generally agree that the long-term aftermath of such a conflict would be at least as catastrophic as the immediate effects of the nuclear weapons themselves. Initial radiation, heat and blast waves, fires and firestorms, greater than hurricane-force winds, whirling debris, early fallout, and choking dust and smoke would claim millions of lives in the first few minutes or days after a nuclear strike. Such losses would occur even if no civilian targets were selected for attack, since the offices of heads of government, military command posts, air and submarine bases, and many other strategic assets are usually located in or near population centers.

But in the months and years thereafter, at least in worst-case scenarios, far more people would die. The fabric of society might well unravel, if enough damage had occurred. A country with lines of transport and communications severed, power plants bombed or deprived of fuel, governments and armed forces incinerated in the war, medical supplies no longer available, and farms no longer growing food or inaccessible to population centers, would be a country threatened with famine, pestilence, and civil disorder on a scale not experienced in the Western world since the Middle Ages.

Magnus Clarke, for example, in a careful study of what might befall Great Britain in a major [167-megaton] strike, estimates that somewhere between 30 percent and 50 percent of the population would die within a month of the attack; ten years later, the British population would have fallen to about 20 percent of its current level. A similar study by Stan Openshaw, Philip Steadman, and Owen Greene reaches more or less the some conclusion.[10]

Losses in a country as densely populated as Britain would, of course, run somewhat higher than in countries such as Canada, the United States, or the Soviet Union. But urbanized societies anywhere are exceptionally vulnerable to nuclear assault. In a study based on research commissioned by the U.S. Congress, Arthur Katz reports that a counterforce attack on American military targets would cause up to 16 million fatalities and injure up to 32 million people. He finds that in a countervalue war, an efficient nuclear strike of just over 500 megatons could reduce America's industrial capacity to 3 percent of its prewar level in eight basic sectors of the economy and kill one-third of its population. Katz questions whether the country could survive such an ordeal, and warns that "world political and economic life may degenerate into factionalism and chaos" in the aftermath of nuclear world war.[11]

There is also the possibility of serious, even lethal degradation of the world's atmosphere and climate in the months and years after a major nuclear conflict. In 1975 the National Academy of Sciences issued a report estimating that nuclear weapons would inject enough oxides of nitrogen into the upper atmosphere to reduce the ozone layer that shields the earth from ultraviolet radiation by as much as 70 percent.[12] Such a sudden and drastic loss of ozone protection would expose surviving plant, animal, and human life to toxic levels of radiation, with the same consequences to health that might follow from a massive attack on the ozone layer by chlorofluorocarbon emissions.

Worse still is the chance of a "nuclear winter," first called to our attention late in 1983 by teams of climatologists and ecologists in the pages of *Science*.[13] These scientists argued that the huge volume of smoke and dust propelled into the atmosphere in a major nuclear war would plunge the Northern Hemisphere, the tropical latitudes, and even much of the Southern Hemisphere into an artificial winter lasting anywhere from three months to two years.

Running eighteen possible scenarios of nuclear exchange through their computers, the scientists concluded that temperatures in the Northern Hemisphere would drop to at least $-10°$ F. and to as much as $-50°$ F. in a matter of weeks. Temperatures would almost immediately start rising again, but it would take up to two years in the most extreme scenarios to restore normal ranges. Early in the nuclear winter, for days, weeks, or longer, skies would be almost black even at high noon. The consequence of such a climatic disaster would be the probable loss of a whole growing season, leading to worldwide starvation. Millions of deaths would also occur from exposure to extreme cold, the tropics would be defoliated, and the oceanic food chain would be disrupted, if not destroyed, as a result of the death of the phytoplankton, which need sunlight to live. One of the ecologists writing in *Science*, Paul R. Ehrlich, cannot "exclude the possibility of a full-scale nuclear war entraining the extinction of *Homo sapiens*."[14]

In recent years, the nuclear winter hypothesis has come under attack from respected members of the scientific community. At the annual meeting of the American Association for the Advancement of Science in 1987, a panel of climatologists produced new research evidence indicating that a major nuclear war would have a much less drastic impact on the earth's atmosphere than the impact foreseen in the articles published in *Science*. The moderating influence on postwar weather of the oceans, the ability of prevailing winds to dissipate smoke, and the washing-out of soot particles by rainfall were all cited as mitigating factors.[15] The authors of the *Science* articles have modified their expectations somewhat, in the light of further research, but they remain fundamentally unrepentant.[16] Everyone agrees, however, that a fairly large number of high-yield nuclear ground bursts or air bursts over cities could send enough dust and smoke into the atmosphere to reduce the earth's ambient temperatures sharply. At the very least such a reduction could have grave effects on crop yields, and make life in an already postwar world still more perilous.

THE END OF WAR?

The magnitude of the losses likely in any major war involving nuclear weapons raises the question, once again, of whether nations will ever wage wars on such a scale in the future. Even a major war utilizing only conventional weapons seems more or less unthinkable, in light of the cost of World Wars I and II. What heads of state in their right minds would order armies into battle knowing it would mean the almost certain destruction of their own country and the suicide of modern civilization? Is major war now only a fantasy? Has the failure of the nuclear powers to engage in direct hostilities against one another since 1945, despite many provocations, proved that major war is obsolete?

Several answers are possible. Even if we assume that rational heads of state would no longer intentionally start a major war, who can guarantee that they will always be rational? As Yehezkel Dror noted many years ago, states sometimes behave psychotically.[17] Even states that behave "normally" may have leaders at the top of the command structure who crack under the stress and strain of the moment. In a crisis, writes Daniel Frei, such factors as fatigue, poor health, information overload, and the sheer length of the crisis may lead to "cognitive and behavioral maladaptations," such as misperceptions of data, refusal to process new evidence that appears to contradict earlier evidence, and premature or overconfident decision-making. Those in charge "may launch a nuclear holocaust without being aware of what they are doing."[18] There is also the danger, admittedly slight, of a nuclear war that begins by accident, for example when a missile is launched in error, prompting retaliation and then counter-retaliation.[19] Nor can any commander-in-chief be absolutely sure that a war starting as a localized, low-risk conflict will not degenerate, against the wishes of the chief combatants, into a much larger affair involving the whole world-system.

But accidents and mistakes aside, it may well be true that the initiation of major wars, nuclear or non-nuclear, is no longer an option seriously considered by the leaders of any nation big enough to wage such a conflict. The obsolescence of military options was foreseen during the last anxious phase of the Cold War by Werner Levi in his book *The Coming End of War* (1981). Levi argued that the destructiveness of modern weapons and the growing economic interdependence of nations made world warfare in the future increasingly unlikely.[20] His views seemed almost hopelessly naive in the context of the fierce East-West rivalry of the early 1980s. But they were only a restatement of the position taken by many scholars a hundred years ago, and more.

In the classic formulation of the nineteenth-century French sociologist

Auguste Comte, humankind was already entering the "positive" age, the age of science, industry, and commerce. In earlier times, the nations had fought one another in the name of various gods and metaphysical abstractions. Warriors and lawyers dominated public affairs. But in the scientific age now dawning, warfare would have no place. World peace and prosperity would be assured by the rule of bankers and businessmen, under the ethical guidance of sociologists. Eventually all of humankind would unite in a single global republic.[21] Various fellow social scientists, including political economists, shared Comte's expectations of the disappearance of war. In a commercial age, sword-waving aristocrats on horseback were seen as anachronisms. Their place would be taken by peaceable men of affairs, intent on trade and profit and progress, not slaughter.

Growing tensions in the world-system between 1890 and 1914, the world wars of the first half of the twentieth century, and the horrors of the Cold War brought such visions into disrepute. But since the late 1980s, scholars chiefly of the technoliberal persuasion have dusted them off and restored them to their previous luster.

A case in point is Francis Fukuyama, in his celebrated essay, "The End of History." Earlier, we cited Fukuyama's views on the closure of ideological debate. In the same essay he also foresees the end of war between nations that have left "history" behind. In history, as defined by Fukuyama, countries compete for land and glory, impelled by ideologies and religions. In the developed nations, human consciousness has evolved beyond such concerns. The end of the Cold War signifies not a return to the pre–1945 world of rival Great Powers, but rather the "growing 'Common Marketization' of international relations, and the diminution of the likelihood of large-scale conflict between states." Nations that have reached the end of history are "far more preoccupied with economics than with politics or strategy." Although wars may continue among less developed countries, or even between more developed and less developed, the posthistoric lands will no longer waste their time fighting one another.[22]

A comparable argument for the end of war, without benefit of Fukuyama's neo-Hegelian window dressing, appears in the American political scientist John Mueller's *Retreat from Doomsday: The Obsolescence of Major War.* War, according to Mueller, is merely an idea, "an institution, like dueling or slavery, that has been grafted onto human experience." It can just as easily shrivel up and disappear, without any fundamental reorganization of human political or economic life. In fact major war, meaning armed conflict between developed countries, has been slowly turning into an embarrassing anachronism since the eighteenth century "because of its perceived repulsiveness and futility."[23]

Mueller admits that major warfare in the developed world did continue all through the nineteenth and early twentieth centuries in spite of such perceptions. But increasingly, it has engaged only states at different stages

in their political evolution. In particular, liberal democratic states have scru-
pulously avoided armed conflict with other liberal democracies. As more
rich countries convert to liberal democracy, the chances of war recede correspondingly. Other factors that seem to diminish warlikeness are prosperity
and the age of states. Whether industrially developed or not, relatively
affluent countries and countries that have been independent for a long time
nowadays rarely resort to war. In the so-called Third World, Mueller ob-
serves, war is actually largely confined to a "Fourth World" of very new and
very poor states. In time, the entire non-Western world may "follow Japan's
example by avoiding war and questing after prosperity."[24]

Are Levi, Fukuyama, and Mueller right, or are they merely victims of
wishful thinking? The East-West Cold War ended so recently and so abruptly
that we have had little opportunity to put its demise into any sort of historical
perspective. But the future of war in the world-system is too important a
subject to ignore, no matter how difficult it may be to fathom at this particular
point in time.

Various alternatives suggest themselves. The strongest point in the "end
of war" thesis is the assumption that liberal capitalist democracies will probably avoid war with one another. Their track record suggests that this may
be true. Nevertheless, will they always remain liberal capitalist democracies
on the present-day model? If they do, will they never be tempted to commit
aggression against countries outside the pale of the liberal democratic community, aggression that may in due course involve them willy-nilly in conflicts with sister democracies?

Also, can we count on the maturation of countries that are neither rich
nor poor, and therefore not yet fully liberal or democratic or affluent, such
as Romania or Thailand or South Africa or Ireland, countries often plagued
by major religious or ethnic schisms? Is their arrival in the capitalist millennium guaranteed? Will nuclear weapons, meanwhile, spread from the
eight or nine countries that already possess them, to a dozen more, including
perhaps several unstable and unpredictable dictatorships far less reluctant
to use them in battle than the older nuclear powers?[25] Such questions are
difficult to answer in any definitive way.

Even the axiom that liberal capitalist societies do not fight one another is
not unassailable. Radicals and some counterculturalists maintain that one of
the chief causes of war in the modern world is competition for hegemonic
control of markets. Some of the most liberal societies—for example, France
and Great Britain in Africa in the late 1890s—have come close to blows over
conflicting claims. When (and if) all developed countries adopt the liberal
democratic model, they may discover that the united front they once
mounted against despotic late-comers in the world political arena has dissolved, and that they have no choice but to compete, sometimes violently,
with one another. Immanuel Wallerstein's scenario of the United States and

Japan arrayed against a united Europe linked to the Soviet Union, jousting for markets and eventually resorting to global war, is only one of several imaginable outcomes of such a competition.

Another plausible scenario is offered in my *Short History of the Future*. The major powers (including the Soviet Union) may, indeed, agree to set aside their differences. But they may also pool their resources to create a new world order in which the developed countries "police" the rest of the planet, perhaps in the name of a reorganized United Nations. In such a world, the exploitation of the poor countries (during the Cold War, mitigated by the rivalry of the Superpowers) will become much more thoroughgoing. Poor countries will no longer be able to play the Superpowers off against one another. Any poor country that steps out of line will be subject to swift discipline by a multinational force (as in the Persian Gulf War of 1991), or by the major power or powers in whose zone of influence the offending country is located.

More specifically, in *A Short History of the Future*, the Soviet Union is awarded hegemony in the Middle East and the Indian subcontinent, Japan and China take charge of Southeast Asia, a unified Europe dominates Africa, and the whole Western Hemisphere is the preserve of the United States. Within its sphere of influence, each major power is in effect sovereign, acting as it pleases without interference by the others.[26] Such a new world order would be free of major war, and—if the dominating powers were sufficiently ruthless—free also of protracted warfare in the Third World. But the peoples of the poor countries would pay a high price, both politically and economically. Deprived of independence and a fair chance to join the club of the rich nations, they would become little more than serfs and vassals of the mighty.

Or take this scenario one step further. Assume that the various developed countries make an attempt to impose their new world order, but most of the poor countries do not prove amenable to the "discipline" of the hegemonic powers. They resist, by sabotage and terrorism, by guerrilla warfare, by nonviolent methods where feasible, by joining forces against their would-be masters, by selective use of homemade nuclear or chemical weapons, whatever may be required to break the will of the hegemonic powers and drain their treasuries. The common front of the developed countries disintegrates after repeated costly embarrassments. The world economy reels. Some developed countries ally with poorer ones, in an effort to save at least their own skins, which leads to a renewal of armed conflict within the club of the wealthy. The end product is global chaos, a war of all against all.

Clearly, there is no way to anticipate just how the wind will blow in a world no longer hostage to the East-West Cold War. The point of these alternative scenarios is not to predict what will happen but to suggest that the end of the Cold War and the coming of the liberal democratic bourgeois state do not necessarily spell the end of major war, or the building of a just world peace. Perhaps, as Mueller insists, war is only a perishable idea, and not intrinsic to the human condition. But he offers no proof.

In effect end-of-war theory is just another variant on the now venerable notion that history follows an evolutionary course: in this case, a more or less inexorable world-historical progress from tyranny to democracy, from slavery to freedom, from warlikeness to the ways of peace. End-of-war theory is also a theory of modernization. Like all such theories, it relies on long-term trend extrapolation. But are the trends truly long-term? Will they continue? Are they irreversible? If they do continue, will they apply everywhere? If they do apply everywhere, is the utopian end point of world peace and prosperity a literal end, or only a station along the way, to be followed by still further transformations that may make possible the eventual return of warfare, on a new and "higher" plane?

NEW WORLD ORDERS

John Mueller's thesis in *Retreat from Doomsday* is seductive not only because he foresees the end of major war, but also because he thinks we need do nothing to accomplish its downfall. The end of war is a free gift of world history. It will happen "without creating an effective world government or system of international law; without modifying the nature of the state or the nation-state."[27]

For all the reasons cited above, such foreviews must be approached with great caution, and a generous dash of skepticism. They are the counterpart of the technoliberal marketeer's belief that market forces will lead everywhere to freedom, democracy, and prosperity without significant political intervention. Both sets of expectations may be proven right in the next century. The marketeers and end-of-war theorists may, after all, be vindicated. But most futurists who think about war anticipate just the opposite: more wars, fought with ever more lethal weapons, nuclear, radiological, biological, and worse, deployed on earth and in space, unless states and citizens alike make deliberate efforts to build a new world order system.

The schemes for a peaceful world offered by futurists depend on the paradigms that orient their thinking. If at least some technoliberal marketeers predictably subscribe to end-of-war theory, most technoliberal welfarers insist that wars, especially major wars, will not be eliminated without intergovernmental action, initiated at various levels. Radicals and counterculturalists favor more drastic remedies. They hold the present-day world-system largely responsible for wars, which, in their judgment, it breeds by its very nature. But technoliberals, both moderate and left-leaning, are responsible for most of the vast literature on system-wide reform in the cause of global peace and security.

The more moderate welfarers generally put their faith in diplomatic efforts by governments, such as strengthening the peacekeeping functions of the United Nations, bilateral and multilateral agreements to limit or reduce armaments, and greater reliance on the international legal system by all nations. The aim of such endeavors would be the curtailment of national sovereignty and the creation of a global climate of opinion in which the international community would condemn and punish the actions of "outlaw" regimes, thereby deterring similar actions in the future and minimizing the likelihood of war.

In defense of their position, middle-of-the-road welfarers contend that these measures, when tried, have already started to bear fruit. They note that the United Nations, for all its many shortcomings, has been somewhat more effective than its predecessor, the League of Nations, in containing and discouraging armed conflict. The many arms limitation treaties negotiated since World War II have made more difference than the largely futile attempts of the powers represented at the international disarmament conferences in the 1920s and early 1930s. In addition, the spread of nuclear weaponry has been slowed by the Non-Proliferation Treaty of 1968, and the testing of nuclear weapons has been sharply reduced by the Partial Test Ban Treaty of 1963 and the Threshold Test Ban Treaty of 1974. Can much more be achieved, working along substantially the same lines?

Moderate welfarers would say yes. A typical formula is offered by the peace scholar Seyom Brown in *The Causes and Prevention of War* (1987). After reviewing the various available and futurible options, Brown draws up an "integrated strategy of war prevention and control" that will, he hopes, secure the greatest number of benefits with "the least overall sacrifice in social value" by tending to "the security and survival needs of existing communities." His formula includes a moral campaign against what he calls "impermissible" acts of war (such as destruction of the environment by triggering a nuclear winter or the deliberate killing of unarmed civilians), structural change (such as the expansion of national accountability to international law), fuller resort to diplomacy, further reductions in armaments, and the adoption of military strategies that will allow nations to contain rather than expand wars if and when they do erupt.[28]

Brown recognizes that special allowances must be made for those who are disadvantaged by the present-day international order, such as the Palestinians.[29] But essentially his integrated strategy, like those of other technoliberals, is a prescription for protecting the existing national and class system. It assumes that although more progress must be made, the present-day international order can save itself from major war in the future without a fundamental overhaul.

Some less moderate technoliberals would maintain that "more progress" is not enough. In the late 1940s and 1950s, for example, thousands of internationally-minded liberals in several countries appealed for the creation of a federal world government.[30] A few continue to favor such a solution, although their numbers have now dwindled significantly. World federalism remains a technoliberal (rather than radical or countercultural) solution because it does not envisage any change in the economic or social systems of nations, no interference in their internal affairs, and no rearrangements of national frontiers except by mutual consent of the affected parties. In most plans a world parliament, usually elected by the voters of all countries, is created to oversee international relations. Under its authority, national armies are replaced or supplemented by a permanent world police force, charged with maintaining peace on every continent.

From the beginning, advocates of world government have divided into two principal camps, the so-called maximalists and minimalists. Maximalists would extend the powers of the world parliament to include a number of other major activities, such as protection of the global environment, coordinated economic and technical assistance to developing countries, the exploration of outer space, and various other good works. Minimalists would stop at measures to safeguard world peace. The best-known minimalist plan for world federation, first published in 1958, is *World Peace through World Law*, by Grenville Clark and Louis B. Sohn. Clark and Sohn show how the Charter of the United Nations can be transformed, step by step, into the constitution of a world federal government. *World Peace through World Law* is a minimalist text, even though it does incorporate a proposed agency for assistance to the developing nations, which the authors view as essential only because it would help remove a principal cause of global instability and conflict. The federal government, they caution, must wield no powers except those deemed absolutely necessary for the maintenance of world peace. "All other powers should be reserved to the nations and their peoples."[31]

Despite the enthusiasm generated by world federalist activists in the fifteen years immediately following the Second World War, the failure of national governments to show much genuine interest in their ideas soon took its toll. Clearly the weakest feature of world federalism is that, like the mice in Aesop's fable, no one knows how to bell the cat. In short, there is no mechanism, except appeal to reason, to induce governments to strip themselves of what many would consider the essence of their sovereignty.

Nowadays, few liberal internationalists resort to the scorned phrase "world government." Most see world government as hopelessly impracticable and have settled for a variety of eclectic proposals that usually turn out to be almost as far-reaching, but may seem less difficult to implement. Their views are illustrated by Robert C. Johansen's suggestion of a "global security policy" requiring a complex array of unilateral, bilateral, and worldwide initiatives by states, as well as direct action by citizens' groups. Under his plan, the United Nations would be considerably strengthened, volunteers from many countries would form a global police force, and an international agency would undertake to monitor all military deployments by satellite. Sovereignty would be curtailed, but only to enable states to exercise their sovereignty more effectively in "other" areas.[32] A similar proposal, for a "common security system," is broached at the end of *The Conquest of War*, by Harry B. Hollins, Averill L. Powers, and Mark Sommer.[33]

The most elaborate of these eclectic schemes, perhaps, is the contribution of Richard A. Falk to the World Order Models Project, an international scholarly experiment launched in 1968 in New Delhi. Falk advocates many of the same initiatives proposed by Johansen, adding further major roles for corporate interests and for existing or not-yet-existing regional political and economic authorities, such as the European Economic Community. In what he calls his "preference model of world order," national states would retain their sovereignty. But states would be persuaded or constrained to reduce their present capabilities by one-half or more, while the powers of regional, transnational, and global actors would double or quadruple. The preference model would also feature a system of "central guidance," headed by a tricameral World Assembly, presiding over four subordinate agencies dedicated to world security, world economic development, human development, and ecological balance. Falk notes that "a central guidance system need not amount to 'a world government' solution," although he fails to make entirely clear how they would differ.[34]

Radical futurists have shown less interest than technoliberals in the future of war and peace, in keeping with their traditional aversion to utopianizing. Most of their attention centers on the ills of the present-day system, which they argue thrives on warfare and cannot be salvaged by the kinds of intergovernmental initiatives favored by technoliberal welfarers. But once capitalism is jettisoned, presumably the bourgeois state would disappear as well. Some radicals have suggested that it would be replaced, at least in the short run, by a workers' world republic or perhaps a fraternal union of autonomous socialist polities.

In years past, radicals opposed the idea of an immediate world federation of bourgeois and socialist states, on the plausible grounds that such a federation would become an instrument for the furtherance of the goals of global capital.[35] More recently, these criticisms have been muted. Many radicals might now agree with the Romanian (and Marxist) political scientist Silviu Brucan that new institutions are needed to keep the earth's people alive while they pursue their diverse goals. What would be the good of socialism, he asks, in a world devastated by nuclear weapons?

His own formula is to replace the United Nations with a World Authority, charged with the building of a world police force and world tribunal to maintain peace. The World Authority would also work to restructure the global economy, in order to close the gap between the developed and developing nations. In essence, his plan is the same as Clark and Sohn's design for a minimalist world federation. But Brucan insists, not very convincingly, that his World Authority would not be a "world government," since it would not abridge the sovereignty of nations, except in its two areas of specifically delegated responsibility.[36]

For the longer haul, when capitalism has met its foreordained fate, a full-fledged world government might arise to put the affairs of the human race in order. Immanuel Wallerstein has often speculated about the emergence, in the relatively far future, of a "socialist world-government," fundamentally unlike the international system of the present day or the repressive world empires of antiquity. He expects, like Friedrich Engels, that "state machinery . . . will over time transform itself into routine administration." But such a new world order would not be a utopia, "and history will not come to an end, even if a particular stage of historical development does."

Much of my own work as a futurist has been devoted to anticipating the shape and structure of a democratic socialist world republic, which I see as the only ultimate guarantor of peace, social justice, and the planetary environment. I doubt that such a republic can come into being except as part of a concerted worldwide revolutionary movement of workers and intellectuals, probably at a time when the existing system is in the throes of a major global crisis. The movement would create not a federation of existing nation-states, but a unitary world republic, perhaps on the constitutional model of the Fifth French Republic. It would monopolize armed force. It would leave the various nations of the earth with no more sovereignty than a British county or a French department enjoys today. A fictional narrative of how such a global commonwealth might grow out of the debris of a worldwide economic collapse and a third world war is available in *A Short History of the Future*.[38]

Critics of the unitary world republic concede that it might be effective in keeping the peace, but cannot be achieved and would tend to be overcentralized and hence repressive, if it were achieved. My reply is that bigness and repressiveness are not correlates; some of the most repressive states in history have been among the smallest. In any case the various schemes of technoliberals are even less achievable and would be far less effective.

Who is right? Obviously, everything hinges on one's assessment of the potential peaceableness of the sovereign nation-state, bourgeois or socialist. If it can be brought to heel by prosperity or by intergovernmental agreements, there may be no pressing need for a world republic. If it cannot, I firmly believe that world political integration is the only long-term solution to the problem of war and peace.

Finally, there are the counterculturalists, who have also contributed to the great debate on the future of the world political system. They concur with their radical cousins that much of the hope for peace in the human future rests with the individual and collective actions of private citizens, as opposed to the doings of states. But they are deeply suspicious of radical or technoliberal plans for world government, in whatever form and under whatever label. The counterculturalist agenda, as we have seen, is profoundly decentralist and anti-statist. A world government, even if constructed along socialist or minimalist lines, might simply perpetuate the value-system of modern civilization, leading to environmental spoliation, suppression of diversity, regimentation of lives, and a hypertrophic materialism no less ruinous, in the end, than global warfare.

The alternative suggested by counterculturalist prophets is the voluntary disengagement of people everywhere from the war system. As consciousness is transformed and values change, the war system will lose its power to intimidate or coerce. Counterculturalists generally favor the "alternative" or "non-traditional" methods of working for peace enumerated by Richard Smoke and Willis W. Harman in their recent book *Paths to Peace*, including the delegitimation of war through revolutions in consciousness, conflict resolution achieved by the intervention of nongovernmental groups, and nonviolent civilian-based defense.[39]

The last mentioned strategy—civilian-based defense—is one stressed by many counterculturalists as a way to break the cycle of violence and counterviolence that repeats itself again and again through all the pages of world history. If adequately motivated and prepared, unarmed civilians may be able to deter aggression or at least deny aggressors the fruits of their "victory" by refusing to collaborate with them, as Gandhi's Indians refused to collaborate with their British masters in the years before the winning of Indian independence. The goal is a new world order in which communities are basically self-reliant and self-governing, although international governmental agencies may still be needed to provide certain essential services.

Central to the counterculturalist argument is the belief that not only wars but also warlikeness will be obsolete in the coming "new age" of transformed consciousness. The maturation of conserving ideologies, from pacifism and anarchism to feminism and reverence for the environment, will reinforce one another to produce a new sense of the sacredness of life. In counterculturalist (and some radical) images of the future, women have a special function as teachers and role models in the creation of the new consciousness, since they have long been the targeted victims of domestic violence. By their nonviolent rejection of the discredited values of patriarchy, sexism, and militarism, women can help bring the human race to the point where resort to violence will seem antediluvian.[40]

Few attempts have been made to imagine the far future of a counterculturalist world, in which warfare has long disappeared, and small, diverse, self-reliant communities live in a rich and complex harmony with one another. Such a world may consist of thousands of "Ecotopias," in the vision of Ernest Callenbach, or it may resemble "The House of Earth," the global neighborhood of autarchic nations that replaces the socialist World Commonwealth in the last chapters of *A Short History of the Future*.[41]

Such distant prospects are perhaps more useful as inspirations than as forecasts. In any event, the outcome of counterculturalist speculation about war and peace is not unlike the outcome in technoliberal and radical images. In virtually all futurist thinking, the foreseeable future ends in peace, not war. Wars may be slated for the near and medium-run future, but in the long run, everyone anticipates, for a bewildering array of conflicting reasons, the end of war.

NOTES

1. Kahn, Brown, and Martel, *The Next 200 Years*, 22 and 221.

2. See, for example, Jerome C. Glenn, "The Most Misunderstood Futurist," *The Futurist*, 17:5 (October 1983): 61–62. The sketch of Kahn's contribution to futures studies in Edward Cornish et al., *The Study of the Future*, notes his career as a military expert, but lists none of his books on war in its review of his major writings as a "futurist," pp. 176–180.

3. Francis A. Beer, *Peace Against War: The Ecology of International Violence* (San Francisco: W. H. Freeman, 1981), 37–40; especially Tables 2–12 and 2–13.

4. See William Eckhardt's compilation, "Wars and War-Related Deaths, 1945–1989," in Ruth Leger Sivard, *World Military and Social Expenditures 1989* (Washington: World Priorities, 1989), 22.

5. But see the valiant attempt by Paul Brians to inventory all the fictions of a nuclear world war in *Nuclear Holocausts: Atomic War in Fiction, 1896–1984* (Kent, Ohio: The Kent State University Press, 1987).

6. Recent books on the new complexion of world politics include Bogdan Denitch, *The End of the Cold War: European Unity, Socialism, and the Shift in Global Power* (Minneapolis: University of Minnesota Press, 1990); and William G. Hyland, *The Cold War Is Over* (New York: Times Books, 1990).

7. For an unsparing introduction to counterforce strategy, see Robert C. Aldridge, *First Strike!: The Pentagon's Strategy for Nuclear War* (Boston: South End Press, 1983). Decapitation strategy is well summarized in Barry R. Schneider, "Invitation to a Nuclear Beheading," in Charles W. Kegley, Jr., and Eugene R. Wittkopf, ed., *The Nuclear Reader*, 2nd ed., (New York: St. Martin's Press, 1989), 291–301.

8. Quoted in David Langford, *War in 2080: The Future of Military Technology* (New York: William Morrow, 1979), 56.

9. Paul Bracken, *The Command and Control of Nuclear Forces* (New Haven: Yale University Press, 1983), 232.

10. Magnus Clarke, *The Nuclear Destruction of Britain* (London: Croom Helm, 1982); and Stan Openshaw, Philip Steadman, and Owen Greene, *Doomsday: Britain after Nuclear Attack* (Oxford: Blackwell, 1983). In *Doomsday*, see especially Table 7.1 and Figure 7.1 on 140–141. After writing *The Nuclear Destruction of Britain*, Clarke moved to Tasmania.

11. Arthur Katz, *Life after Nuclear War: The Economics and Social Impacts of Nuclear Attacks on the United States* (Cambridge, Mass.: Ballinger, 1982), 347. For Katz's figures, see especially chs. 3 and 5, and, on the vulnerability of the Soviet Union to nuclear attack, ch. 10.

12. National Research Council, *Long Term Worldwide Effects of Multiple Nuclear-Weapons Detonations* (Washington: National Academy of Sciences, 1975), 6. The

report anticipated up to 70 percent loss of ozone over the Northern Hemisphere and up to 40 percent over the Southern.

13. See R. P. Turco, O. B. Toon, T. P. Ackerman, J. B. Pollack, and Carl Sagan, "Global Atmospheric Consequences of Nuclear War," *Science* 222:4630 (December 23, 1983): 1283–1292; and Paul R. Ehrlich, Mark A. Harwell, Peter H. Raven, Carl Sagan, G. M. Woodwell, et al., "The Long-Term Biological Consequences of Nuclear War," *ibid.*: 1293–1300. Important follow-ups to these articles include Sagan, "Nuclear War and Climatic Catastrophe: Some Policy Implications," *Foreign Affairs*, 62:2 (Winter 1983–1984): 257–292; and Harwell, *Nuclear Winter: The Human and Environmental Consequences of Nuclear War* (New York: Springer-Verlag, 1984).

14. Paul R. Ehrlich, "The Biological Consequences of Nuclear War," in Ehrlich, Sagan, et al., ed., *The Cold and the Dark: The World after Nuclear War* (New York: Norton, 1984), 59.

15. See Starley L. Thompson and Stephen H. Schneider, "Nuclear Winter Reappraised," *Foreign Affairs*, 64:5 (Summer 1986): 981–1005. See also James Gleick, "Less Drastic Theory Emerges on Freezing after a Nuclear War," *New York Times* (June 22, 1986): 1–1 and 1–20; Gleick, "Science and Politics: 'Nuclear Winter' Clash," *ibid.* (February 17, 1987): C6; and Malcolm W. Browne, "Nuclear Winter Theorists Pull Back," *ibid.* (January 23, 1990): C1 and C8.

16. See the letter from Carl Sagan and Richard Turco in *New York Times* (March 5, 1990), A14; and Sagan and Turco, *A Path Where No Man Thought: Nuclear Winter and the End of the Arms Race* (New York: Random House, 1990).

17. See Yehezkel Dror, *Crazy States: A Counterconventional Strategic Problem* (Lexington, Mass.: D. C. Heath, 1971), especially ch. 2. Dror identifies as a crazy state any polity or organized group that exhibits such characteristics of political psychopathology as intense commitment to unrealistic goals, willingness to take unreasonably high risks (including martyrdom), and adoption of unorthodox methods of pursuing goals (such as hostage taking or genocide), methods that may often be clearly "counterinstrumental." Nazi Germany is Dror's prime example of a recent crazy state, but in his introduction to a later edition of the book, he adds to the list the Uganda of Idi Amin, the Libya of Muammar Qaddafi, and the Iran of the Ayatollah Khomeini. See "Introduction to Kraus Reprint Edition," in Dror, *Crazy States* (Millwood, N.Y.: Kraus Reprint, 1980), xiii. Presumably he would now include the Iraq of Saddam Hussein.

18. Daniel Frei, with Christian Catrina, *Risks of Unintentional Nuclear War* (Totowa, N.J.: Rowman and Allanheld, 1983), 119.

19. See Arthur Macy Cox, *Russian Roulette: The Superpower Game* (New York: Times Books, 1982), ch. 1. Frei concludes that the safeguards deployed by the nuclear powers make "the risk of nuclear war by accident . . . minute and negligible." Frei, *Risks of Unintentional Nuclear War*, 165.

20. Werner Levi, *The Coming End of War* (Beverly Hills: Sage, 1981).

21. Auguste Comte, *Système de politique positive*, 4 volumes (Paris: L. Mathais, 1851–1854), available in an English translation by H. J. Bridges et al., as *System of Positive Polity*, 4 volumes (London: Longmans, Green, 1875–1877; reprinted, New York: Burt Franklin, 1967 [?]). This is one of the most important and influential studies of the future ever written, nowadays almost entirely forgotten and unread. For brief introductions to Comte's world view, see Frank E. and Fritzie P. Manuel, *Utopian Thought in the Western World* (Cambridge: Harvard University Press, 1979),

ch. 30; and John Bowle, *Politics and Opinion in the Nineteenth Century: An Historical Introduction* (London: Jonathan Cape, 1954), ch. 5.

22. Fukuyama, "The End of History?" 16 and 18.

23. John Mueller, *Retreat from Doomsday: The Obsolescence of Major War* (New York: Basic Books, 1989), ix and 4.

24. *Ibid.*, 23–24 and 252–253.

25. See Leonard S. Spector, *The Undeclared Bomb: The Spread of Nuclear Weapons, 1987–1988* (Cambridge, Mass.: Ballinger, 1988), and *Nuclear Ambitions: The Spread of Nuclear Weapons, 1989–1990* (Boulder: Westview Press, 1990).

26. W. Warren Wagar, *A Short History of the Future* (Chicago: University of Chicago Press, 1989), 39–41.

27. Mueller, *Retreat from Doomsday*, ix.

28. Seyom Brown, *The Causes and Prevention of War* (New York: St. Martin's Press, 1987), ch. 10, especially p. 215.

29. See his plan for the "legitimation of nonstate communities," *ibid.*, 228–230, which shows a greater concern for preventing nonstate communities from triggering major wars than for helping the nonstate communities achieve their goals.

30. For overviews of the world government movement and the many thinkers who developed detailed plans for a democratic federation of nations, see Frederick L. Schuman, *The Commonwealth of Man: An Inquiry into Power Politics and World Government* (New York: Knopf, 1952), and W. Warren Wagar, *The City of Man*, ch. 4.

31. Grenville Clark and Louis B. Sohn, *World Peace through World Law* (Cambridge: Harvard University Press, 1958), xiii. Later editions of their book were published by Harvard University Press in 1960 and 1966. A representative recent proposal for world political integration on the basis of a strengthened regime of international law and law enforcement is Benjamin B. Ferencz, *A Common Sense Guide to World Peace* (Dobbs Ferry, NY: Oceana, 1985).

32. Robert C. Johansen, *Toward an Alternative Security System: Moving Beyond the Balance of Power in the Search for World Security* (New York: World Policy Institute, 1983).

33. Harry B. Hollins, Averill L. Powers, and Mark Sommer, *The Conquest of War: Alternative Strategies for Global Scrutiny* (Boulder: Westview Press, 1989), ch. 13.

34. Richard A. Falk, *A Study of Future Worlds* (New York: The Free Press, 1975), 51. Falk's preference model is described in great detail in ch. 4, and on the distinction between world government and central guidance, see 178–184, especially the footnote on 184.

35. See Elliot R. Goodman, *The Soviet Design for a World State* (New York: Columbia University Press, 1960). Goodman discusses Soviet criticism of Western schemes for world federation and Soviet hopes for the eventual building of a socialist world state. His book reflects the paranoid mentality of the early Cold War, but it raises issues often neglected by world order scholars.

36. Silviu Brucan, "The Establishment of a World Authority: Working Hypotheses," *Alternatives: A Journal of World Policy*, 8:2 (Fall 1982), 209–223.

37. Wallerstein, *The Politics of the World-Economy*, 157–158. See also Wallerstein, *The Capitalist World-Economy*, 35.

38. See Wagar, *A Short History of the Future*, chs. 6–9. For earlier (and non-

fictional) versions of the same concept, see W. Warren Wagar, *Building the City of Man: Outlines of a World Civilization* (New York: Richard Grossman, 1971); and "Peace by Revolution: Civilian-Based Offense," in Howard F. Didsbury, Jr., ed., *Challenges and Opportunities: From Now to 2001* (Bethesda, Md.: World Future Society, 1986), 125–140.

39. Richard Smoke with Willis Harman, *Paths to Peace: Exploring the Feasibility of Sustainable Peace* (Boulder: Westview Press, 1987), especially chs. 3–5; and see Table 2 on p. 96, for the comparison of "medieval," "industrial," and "emerging" [counterculturalist] paradigms.

40. See, for example, Leslie Cagan, "Feminism and Militarism," in Michael Albert and David Dellinger, ed., *Beyond Survival: New Directions for the Disarmament Movement* (Boston: South End Press, 1983), 81–118; Birgit Brock-Utne, *Educating for Peace: A Feminist Perspective* (New York: Pergamon, 1985); and Christine Sylvester, "Patriarchy, Peace, and Women Warriors," in Linda Rennie Forcey, ed., *Peace: Meanings, Politics, Strategies* (New York: Praeger, 1989), 97–112.

41. Callenbach, *Ecotopia: The Notebooks and Reports of William Weston* [1975] (New York: Bantam Books, 1977); and Wagar, *A Short History of the Future*, chs. 10–12.

7

The Future of Living

WORK, LEISURE, AND FAMILY

In studying the future of society, we have explored first, the economic and political foundations of human life in coming times, and, second, the prospects for armed conflict in the emergent global order. What remains is everything that the organization of wealth and power makes possible: in short, the living of human lives.

For some people, the acquisition of wealth or the wielding of power are ends in themselves. But for others wealth and power are means to higher ends. Experiencing the pleasures—and pains—of work, leisure, love, family, learning, art, thought, and faith may be, or may someday become, the whole point of human existence.

The literature of futures inquiry on each of these topics is extensive, but there are few comprehensive studies that cover them all. Also, most general works on alternative futures slight or even ignore the future of living, as if such matters were too subjective or too difficult to forecast (which may in fact be true). The result is that a great deal of the best speculative work has been produced by narrowly specialized researchers who may be naive or ill-informed about other relevant parameters.

But not all of it. Futurists adhering to the counterculturalist paradigm, who are often not narrowly specialized at all, have shown much more interest in the future of life-styles and values than their technoliberal and radical rivals. They contend that what is most needed to rescue humankind from its present discontents are changes at the level of consciousness. In psychocultural transformation, they believe, lies our best hope of saving the environment, building a just economic and political order, and preventing war.

Nevertheless, futurists of all persuasions have devoted at least some of their energies to the future of living, and it would be misleading to dwell exclusively on the speculations of counterculturalist prophets. Technoliberals have an implicit vision of how life should be lived in a capitalist and technologically advanced future society. Radicals have an implicit vision of how life should be lived in an egalitarian socialist future. In both cases, the implicit vision may also become quite explicit, now and again, in the writings of this or that technoliberal or radical futurist.

Explorations of the future of work illustrate some of the crucial differences between technoliberal, radical, and counterculturalist futurism. In the technoliberal paradigm, writers expect that as technology increases in sophistication and power, it will liberate men and women from the necessity of spending most of their waking hours at work. Manual and mental labor, alike, will be performed more and more by self-maintaining robots and computers. Workers will still be needed to oversee operations, make managerial decisions, and provide creative and technical services. But the work day and work week will shrink and vacation periods will grow longer. More and more tasks will be carried out at home work stations rather than in distant offices and factories, saving millions the trouble of commuting to the workplace every day.

Technoliberals foresee a dramatic change in the composition of the labor force to keep pace with technological progress. In a representative survey of future life styles, Marvin Cetron and Thomas O'Toole anticipate that as jobs are lost to automation, as steel workers or secretaries or stock clerks disappear from the labor force thanks to technological progress, their places will be taken by robot technicians, computer programmers, gene-splicers, paramedics, holographic specialists, and the like. The entertainment, travel, and other leisure-time industries will boom. A more productive economy will find ample work for everyone willing to acquire the skills needed from year to year as technology rolls inexorably forward, eliminating old jobs and introducing new ones. Cetron and O'Toole see no shortage of jobs in the new age of high technology. "Only a shortage of creative, imaginative people to fill them."[1]

Radicals agree that many of these developments will probably come to pass, but at what cost? As the Australian Labor minister and futurist Barry Jones asks, what will happen to the underskilled, the middle-aged and elderly, the part-timers excluded from benefits packages, the unemployed who may need months or years to retrain? Will high technology also mean increasing specialization of labor, with increasing alienation of workers from the work process? Will there be a continuing proliferation of low-paying service jobs designed primarily to exploit women and teen-agers? How will employees react to the erosion of job security in a fast-changing work environment?[2]

For the immediate future, radicals generally favor policies that would protect workers as much as possible from the hazards of progress. But contemporary radicals seldom object to the progress of labor-saving technology in and of itself. On the contrary. Many remain loyal to Herbert Marcuse's dream in *Eros and Civilization* (1955) of a society without repression, a free society in which the machine, properly used, would abolish nearly all toil. In Marcuse's post-capitalist future, life would be lived not for profit or gain, but for the sheer joy of living. Any work that still needed doing would be made pleasurable, as in the utopian vision of Charles Fourier.

Marcuse's influence is rife in my own utopia, *Building the City of Man* (1971). The socialist world commonwealth of the next century, I foresee, "will sever the economic nexus between work and production."[3] As automation reaches its climax, only a few technicians will be needed to keep the world industrial complex functioning smoothly. Work can then be redefined as personal and interpersonal growth, with at least half a citizen's "work" consisting of life-long education.

Counterculturalists share some of the concerns and hopes of radicals, but with a somewhat different vision of the desirable future. The counterculturalist approach figures heavily, for example, in *The Future of Work* (1984), by the British management scholar Charles Handy. The old notion of a full employment society is now, writes Handy, passé. In his preferred future, work will be valued above jobs. Everyone will work as much as they like, but jobs (meaning, work for pay) will be distributed equitably, with everyone assured a decent livelihood through a national income scheme or its equivalent. Incomes will drop, more people will opt for part-time employment, many others will choose self-employment, and early retirement will be common.

But all this turns out for the best in Handy's thinking, because it will be accompanied by the arrival of a new cultural paradigm that alters values and expectations. Although we may have less money to spend, we will have better lives to live. The extended family may return, with its blessings of conviviality, as more and more people choose to work and learn at home, and as retired people trim expenses by living with their children. The transvaluation of work will bestow new honor and dignity on all those who work, no matter what their incomes. In place of the now obsolescent "employment society" will arise the "work society," a leaner, more relaxed, less competitive, and more fulfilling way of life for all.[4]

Still more deeply entrenched in the counterculturalist world view are the writings on the future of work of another British futurist, James Robertson. As a leader of the "new economics movement," an international coalition of economists and environmentalists influenced by E. F. Schumacher, Robertson argues that the present economic system is well on its way to global catastrophe. The continuing blind worship of growth fosters dependency, destroys the environment, and widens the "wealth gap" between rich and poor worldwide. The agenda of the economic counterculture must include not only conserving all the precious natural resources menaced by reckless growth, but enabling individuals and localities to become economically self-reliant, so they can tend to their own needs cooperatively instead of living at the mercy of distant state and corporate structures over which they have no control.

As part of this agenda, Robertson urges the transformation of work from employment dictated by others to "ownwork," work that is chosen purposefully and organized by the workers themselves. "For the individual and the household, ownwork may mean self-employment, essential household and family activities, productive leisure activities, and participation in voluntary work. For groups of people ownwork may mean working in a community enterprise, a co-operative, or some other kind of organization in which they have a share of control, or simply working together as partners in social, environmental, scientific or other activities which they value."[5] As ownwork displaces employment, and as communities learn the joys of self-reliance, the grip of the corporate profiteers and national bureaucrats will be loosened, and, it may be, cast off altogether. Robertson wonders if all this may not happen much sooner than we now expect, given the snowballing pace of social change in revolutionary times.[6]

The reality, as we plunge into the 1990s, is that most of these utopian expectations, technoliberal, radical, and counterculturalist alike, are not being fulfilled. Certainly not yet. Despite the heady advances of high technology, the employed continue to work all day, five or six days a week, the numbers of the unemployed remain high, wages in most jobs remain low, and many of the newer jobs are designed to take merciless advantage of women and young people. The loudly proclaimed "breakthrough" technologies themselves are doing relatively little breaking through at this point in time, from biotechnology and robotics to holography, alternative energy technologies, and artificial intelligence. As of 1990, for example, the American population of industrial robots, according to the Robotic Industries Association, "is not the hundreds of thousands once predicted but 37,000, or about 1 for every 500 factory workers." Robots have proved costly, not only because of their high price tags, but also because products must often be redesigned to make them easier for robots to assemble. Even by comparison with the mid–1980s, sales of robots to industry in America have actually declined, and several major corporations have stopped using them altogether.[7]

It is much too early to write off the newer technologies. It would be folly to jump to the conclusion that, just because earlier predictions misfired, technology will no longer produce dramatic changes in the work environment. But it remains true that utopian revolutions in the workplace, if they are to happen at all, are not happening now, even in the industrially advanced countries. Old values and old ways have proved extraordinarily resistant to change.

The same may be said of the places where people live. Futurists in the past have speculated that the world might one day become a single sprawling city, with everyone living in high-rise and underground flats and flying or riding to work on elevated and subterranean roadways. Alternatively, they have foreseen the suburbanization of all available living space, or the emergence of planned garden cities everywhere, or the return to the kind of pastoral existence celebrated in William Morris's *News from Nowhere*. In recent years counterculturalists have led the way with cries for the breakup of all large cities into much smaller cities, towns, and villages, as in the concept of the "Neighborhood City"—one of seven urban scenarios of future urban change discussed by the sociologist Arthur Shostak.[8]

In the real world, the trend remains what it has been for decades: a steady increase in urban populations, rising crime rates, the flight of the affluent to fast-growing satellite towns and suburbs, the concentration of the poor in inner-city ghettos often subdivided by race or ethnicity, and, especially in the United States and the Third World, a swelling sense of helplessness and hopelessness about the whole urban process. The process lurches out of control, more each year, to the point where it might be wiser to predict that large cities in the next century, failing fundamental social reconstruction, will be hells of poverty and violence, shunned by most "decent" folk.

Of course, as Christopher Lasch would tell us, in the heartless modern world our one safe haven is home and family.[9] The future of the family, of sexual relations, of women, and of children and their schooling, is another set of vital concerns to many futurist writers and scholars. Those touched by counterculturalist influences, like Lasch, look back with moist eyes to premodern relationships, or, with Ernest Callenbach, forward to sexual freedom and gentle matriarchy. Radicals anticipate a family life unspoiled by the machinations of capital. Technoliberals foresee a world of gender equality in which all people will produce and consume to the limits of their ability, taking full advantage of the rich variety of life-options made possible by technology and the free play of market forces.

Certainly the family has not proved to be an entirely safe haven in recent decades. From the close of the nineteenth century onward, an increasing number of marriages have foundered. In the United States, for example, the divorce rate rose between 1900 and 1980 from 0.7 to 5.2 per thousand of population, falling slightly through the 1980s to 4.8 per thousand. About one American marriage in two ends in divorce. Many of these divorces have occurred because women, including mothers, have gradually wrested from a male-dominated world the possibility of legal and financial independence. The gains of women, in this sense, are often losses for men, who have traditionally relied on dependent wives to supply them with a lifetime of poorly paid domestic and sexual services. Women remain almost wholly subservient to men in the greater number of Third World societies, but even there male dominance has begun, however slowly, to erode.

In the next century, technoliberal futurists project a continuation of current trends in the advanced capitalist societies. Women will continue to
record advances in the labor force, until almost all of them play a role in
the workplace comparable to men, and earn incomes only a little lower, on
the average, than their male counterparts. The bourgeois nuclear family,
consisting of parents and children, will persist, in spite of a high divorce
rate, which will be countered by the frequency of successful second marriages
in mid-career. Increasing numbers of couples may choose to remain childless
or forego legal marriage, as they are doing now in record numbers even in
the middle class.

In the technoliberal future, the relationship between couples living together, in and out of wedlock, will approximate, more and more, the sociologist Jessie Bernard's formula of the "shared-role marriage," as delineated
in her book *The Future of Marriage*.[10] Husbands and wives will treat one
another as equals, sharing equally the responsibilities of breadwinning, house
work, and parenting.

At the same time, husbands and wives (and society at large) will also face
the burden of caring for elderly parents, especially women, who, thanks to
modern medicine, will increasingly live beyond the traditional three score
and ten years, and will require both familial and institutional support if they
are to spend their last years in relative comfort and dignity. In 1960, 9
percent of the U.S. population was 65 years of age or older; in 1990, 12
percent; and by 2030, a staggering 21 percent will be over 65. The costs of
their care will multiply and multiply, not only in dollars and cents, but also
in time spent and love demanded, a cost that may be steep when the aged
relative is senile, gravely ill, disabled, or in great mental pain and distress.

The technoliberal vision of the future of women, in particular, is well
captured in *Woman of Tomorrow*, by the cofounder of the glossy futurist
magazine *Omni*, Kathy Keeton. Relying heavily on survey data, Keeton
expects that tomorrow's woman will be energetic, fit, fulfilled by exciting
careers in science and technology, and free to choose from a variety of
reproductive strategies that expand the horizons of mothering into middle
age. She profiles three imaginary women of tomorrow, an art historian and
businesswoman, a realtor who entices clients with holographic images of her
properties, and a space scientist whose daughter is the captain of the first
starship to explore another solar system. "I grow impatient with nostalgia,"
writes Keeton, "the romanticizing of a past that in reality was nothing we'd
care to relive. The future is where we have to be, and it's the only part of
our lives that we have the power to change."[11]

Another speculative work based on questionnaires sent out to representative American women is Elizabeth Nickles's *The Coming Matriarchy*, which
maintains that aggressive, goal-oriented women are likely to become the
leading force in society in the next century. Their characteristic leadership
style, most often the "beta" mode of leadership identified by SRI Interna-

tional researchers, focuses on acquiring and wielding power for the good of
the organization, rather than for purely personal gain. It will give pacesetting
women the edge they need to displace men as the dominant force in the
economy and in government. "In the coming matriarchy," writes Nickles,
"women will have the power advantage, but will not brandish it like a big
stick with cleats. Most likely, in fact, men as well as women will have a
wider range of sanctioned opportunities than they do today, for this will be
a society of nearly limitless options." Instead of setting in motion "a sex-
based role reversal," the empowerment of women will lead to "role diversification."[12]

Counterculturalists, and many radicals, may find the "optimism" of Keeton
and Nickles depressing. Their horizons are limited to successful young bourgeois career women striking it rich and, at least in Keeton's sample, apparently behaving much like their male counterparts. Most of the world's female
population is ignored. At the opposite end of the feminist spectrum stands
Annie Cheatham and Mary Clare Powell's counterculturalist report on their
two-year project, "The Future Is Female," in which they interviewed one
thousand women throughout the United States and Canada. They conclude
that the priorities and behaviors of women are strikingly different from those
of men. Women are more nurturing, more intuitive and spiritually aware,
more attuned to other people's needs and feelings, more protective of life
and the environment. The best hope for a safe, harmonious future for all
humankind lies in the capacity of women to create a new society grounded,
unlike today's society, in women's values.[13]

Futurists with a counterculturalist or radical perspective—the two perspectives overlap significantly in this area—also look forward to a time when
the structure of the family may be quite different from what it is today. As
we have seen earlier, Charles Handy anticipates the return of the cohabiting
extended family, partly as the result of reduced family incomes. Others
speculate that in a less materialistic post-industrial society, men and women
will be free from the constraints of the cash nexus and free, therefore, to
develop relationships based on love and mutual respect, rather than on
money and power. A variety of new familial and sexual styles will evolve,
permitting the family to grow into something richer, more complex, and
more interdependent than the fragile, stripped-down nuclear family of today.
Many different marriage contracts may become available, creating many
different kinds of families, all equal under the law: same-sex marriages, plural
marriages, five-year renewable marriages, non-exclusive relationships, and
more.[14]

Counterculturalist attitudes are neatly encapsuled in the chapters on sex,
women, family life, and schooling in Ernest Callenbach's *Ecotopia*. His
future utopian society in the American Northwest features two major political
parties, the dominant Survivalist party, led chiefly by women, and the Pro-
gressives, a more business-minded party, led chiefly by men. Women are

the equals of men in all respects. The nuclear family has disappeared, replaced by group families consisting of five to twenty people, related or married to one another or not, as the members choose. Couples in the families are largely monogamous, but promiscuity is traditional at four annual festivals, and at no time is the absolute sexual fidelity of a spouse guaranteed or expected. Women retain the right to choose at all times who will be the fathers of their children. Males discharge their natural aggressions in ritual war games, which take a few male lives each year, a modest price to pay for the peace and tranquility of Ecotopia.

The world of Callenbach's genial counterculturalist fantasy is also a world in which the lives of children have changed drastically. Children are raised not only by mothers but by fathers and various other members of the group family, including the elderly. The small schools they attend are privately owned by cooperatives of teachers, with sliding grants to families below a certain income level. The state no longer regulates schooling, except for national examinations given at ages 12 and 18. Schools are free to teach whatever they want and in any way they choose. Broken up into various small colleges in keeping with the Ecotopian principle of decentralization, universities are also privately owned and administered by their own faculties. Callenbach's scenario of the separation of school and state recalls Ivan Illich's eminently counterculturalist proposals for the "deschooling" of society, much debated in the 1970s.[15]

Radicals generally prefer to imagine a future in which state-supported education becomes the chief national industry, imparting to working people everywhere the knowledge they will need to function productively and happily in the post-industrial social-democratic society. The French socialist André Gorz, for example, prescribes a compulsory core curriculum for all children, and 20 hours of paid schooling a week in adult life.[16] Counterculturalists might object (and do) that most radical ideas of schooling, such as those of Gorz, are only mirror images of the values of the dominant technoliberal culture.

Drawing conclusions from all this is not easy. Various alternatives present themselves, depending on the value-system of the inquirer. Technoliberals project into the future whatever they think is best in current trends; radicals and counterculturalists foresee fundamental changes in relationships at work and at home. In no area of futurism, perhaps, does the normative dimension so completely overshadow the empirical.

We should not be surprised. The everyday life of women, men, and children may be far more important in human terms than the dynamics of the world economy or systems of governance. No doubt it is. But its possibilities are always enclosed within the limits set by prevailing structures of wealth and power. Everyday life cannot carry on autonomously. What it will actually be in the future depends less on free human choice than on the future performance of economies and states. Since we know little enough about how they will perform, attempting an "empirical" forecast of the every-day life that they, in turn, will make possible is still more hazardous. It is also more difficult because the values of everyday life are less readily quantifiable. So futurists discuss what they would *like* to see happen, and hope against hope that it does.

HEALTH AND HUMAN ENGINEERING

One of the great pleasures of everyday life is good health. All other things being equal, the person who is strong, fit, and free of disease and infirmity, both physical and mental, is likely to enjoy her or his existence and wish for it to continue as long as possible. Good health is not necessarily a goal of life, but without it, life may not be worth living.

In the next century and beyond, many specialists in the future of health foresee continued progress in keeping people healthy, together with a considerable extension of the normal human life span and vast improvements in the quality of life through biotechnology. Technoliberal health futurists assume that all these advances will be generally beneficial, but radicals and counterculturalists, and not a few left-leaning liberals, fear that some of them may be misused. Advances in medicine and biotechnology, instead of making life better for everyone, may simply increase state or corporate control of citizens, fatten the profits of the health care industry, and otherwise prop up what, for radicals and counterculturalists, is a pathological social order.

The prospects for the health sciences are certainly, almost everyone agrees, robust. Writing in 1980, the economist and one-time Hudson Institute futurist Felix Kaufmann forecast that by the year 2002 every kind of cancer would be curable in the early stages and treatable throughout. By 2015 all infectious and heritable diseases in human beings and domesticated plants and animals would be entirely eradicated.[17] Kaufmann may have been overly optimistic, especially in light of the vigorous resistance to medical attack of viruses (including HIV, whose existence was not even suspected at the time of Kaufmann's article), and the many and growing health problems of Third World populations. But the idea of the literal conquest of infectious disease is no longer fantastic.[18]

Much progress can surely be expected, as well, in the prevention and cure of degenerative diseases, such as coronary atherosclerosis, stroke, and cancer. In the struggle against heart disease, the number one killer in the developed countries, medical researchers are hard at work on a variety of powerful drugs to decrease cholesterol levels in the bloodstream and dissolve arterial plaques. Modest success has already been achieved in lowering serum cholesterol with medication. Doctors have begun removing plaques in diseased arteries by coronary atherectomy, using catheters tipped with drills or lasers.[19] Dietary reform, exercise programs, abstinence from tobacco, medication, and surgery may make death from coronary atherosclerosis relatively rare in just a few decades. Cancer, already far more treatable than it was in mid-century, may eventually yield to biological drugs that fortify the body's immune system, which ordinarily destroys cancerous cells before they become dangerous. Simpler and cheaper diagnostic methods for the early detection of heart disease and cancer are also eminently futurible.

We can look forward, as well, to the availability of bio-analogues for every body part—limbs and organs grown in laboratories by a combination of computer modelling, genetic engineering, and body scanning. Such parts may be cloned from the donor's own cells, a procedure far superior to the transplantation of parts from donors. Loss of a kidney, a leg, or an eye may someday be no more serious or permanent than loss of a fingernail today.

Meanwhile, our repertoire of drugs, devices, and procedures for preventing or encouraging fertility will no doubt be greatly enlarged in the next century. Control of the sex of offspring, contraceptives for use by men, and the growth of embryos and fetuses in an artificial environment outside the womb (ectogenesis) will all enlarge the options available to sexual partners and mothers, as contraceptive and fertility drugs have already done for hundreds of millions.[20]

More distant still is the possibility of the reshaping of the human genome (genetic endowment) through genetic engineering. Already we have learned that certain inherited defects and predispositions to disease are the result of flaws in the DNA of specific genes. Studies indicate that the body cells of a fetus or child can be altered by injecting the patient with retroviruses that carry genes to replace unwanted genes. The next step, clearly, is to treat germ cells, in hopes of eliminating hereditary infirmities and diseases before the child is born.

But take the process one step further still. If we assume, at least for the purposes of argument, that most human abilities and disabilities, and even the essence of individual human personality, spring from characteristics imprinted in the DNA of genes, bioengineering can theoretically give us any sort of human being we choose to create. All we need to know is the nature and function of each strand of DNA in the human genome, whose systematic mapping by scientists all over the world began in 1989. Why stop at the elimination of certain obvious and uncontroversial ills? If we can bioengineer a child who has no hereditary predisposition to schizophrenia or colon cancer, we can also bioengineer a child who has no hereditary predisposition to protruding teeth, thick ankles, or small stature. We may even learn to bioengineer offspring with sunny dispositions, or extraordinary empathy and altruism, or intelligence quotients in the genius range.

The British biologist, sociologist, and science-fiction novelist Brian Stableford has carried such speculation to its limits in his book *Future Man*. Stableford envisions the bioengineering of people with greatly improved spines, hands, skin, digestive systems, eyes, and ears. Beyond this, whole new human species could be bred, modified to live underwater or in space or in the air. He freely admits that contemporary ethical sensibilities would probably put the kibosh on all such projects, but what about the future? "What will eventually happen, in the fullness of time," he notes, "will depend not on how *we* see these matters, but on how our grandchildren and their grandchildren will see them." Since our descendants may have been genetically altered in various less elaborate ways themselves, "they may not be at all inhibited in the matter of multiplying their forms and capabilities *ad infinitum.*"[21] It is hard to quarrel with Stableford's logic.

Another futurible is the prolongation of life beyond (and perhaps far beyond) what we consider the natural life span of our species. Until now, gerontologists have been unable to pinpoint the exact causes of aging, but there are a number of persuasive hypotheses. The root of the problem is apparently the breakdown of the immune system and the inability of DNA to repair itself beyond a certain age, which varies from individual to individual. But why does someone's DNA lose this capacity, and how might it be restored by human intervention?

In Carol Kahn's summation, the solution is likely to pass through four stages: changes in diet and life-style, supplementation of the diet with antioxidants that may prevent DNA damage caused by excess oxidation, the use of hormones and synthetic drugs to improve the function of DNA and vital organs, and, finally, genetic engineering. "Once the techniques have been worked out," says Kahn, "the possibility will exist for not just correcting nature's mistakes, but improving on the blueprint, adding genes for DNA repair, for example, or free-radical scavenging, or a better mix of enzymes for metabolizing carcinogenic compounds." We already have enough information, she quotes one medical researcher, "to add thirty years of useful life to our time on Earth," bringing the upper limit to about 119 years.[22] With genetic engineering, we may be able to do much better still. And if we do, such progress will bear all sorts of implications for the future of world population, the carrying capacity of the environment, and the ratio of older to younger citizens (already destined to rise steeply in the next century).

At least one major category of medical progress remains to be mentioned: in addition to bioengineering, there is what may be called psychoengineering, human intervention to treat, enhance, or modify the human mind. Some of this may be done by simple operant conditioning, as in the work of the late B. F. Skinner, who taught pigeons to play table tennis in exchange for food. Skinner always maintained that all of us are fully conditioned anyway, by our society and culture and upbringing—and would it not be better to be re-programmed by experts so that we can live the lives we want and choose, instead of what society blindly decrees for us?[23]

Alternative methods of psychoengineering include the more directive forms of psychotherapy, the implantation of electrodes into precisely targeted areas of the brain, and the use of psychotropic (psychoactive or mind-affecting) chemicals that take advantage of recent discoveries in what the science journalist Jon Franklin calls "molecular psychology." Of all these methods, clearly the psychotropes are the least cumbersome, and potentially the most effective. Molecular psychologists have discovered that normal and abnormal brain functions alike, from the learning process to emotional states, are regulated by a host of organic chemicals released in minute quantities in the brain itself. Mental "illness" may be almost entirely the result of one or another variety of genetically determined neurochemical imbalance. Mental "good health" may be the result of neurochemical equilibrium.

Two ways of treating or enhancing brain functions, therefore, suggest themselves. One is genetic engineering of the brain, still very much in its infancy. Altering the genes that organize the production of brain cells will, of course, alter cerebral function. A more direct approach is simply to administer drugs (often analogues of natural brain secretions) that rectify imbalances or otherwise intervene in the neurochemical system to produce whatever specific changes are desired. As the research of molecular psychologists expands our understanding of mental health and illness, and tells us exactly what our brains are doing "wrong," the same results may be achieved more often with behavioral modification therapies that do not involve drugs at all. But the temptation to engineer mind-affecting drugs and rely on the quick fixes they can provide, is likely to be quite powerful. Perhaps irresistibly so.

Franklin, whose *Molecules of the Mind* (1987) is the most readable introduction to molecular psychoengineering, provides a long list of good things that may issue from our growing competence to understand and control brain functions. Most forms of severe mental illness, as well as violent and criminal behavior, addiction to drugs, and a broad array of neuroses, may be curable with the knowledge that molecular psychology can furnish. Persons with an inherited predisposition to such disorders will be regularly identified by brain scanners and treated before their symptoms appear, perhaps even in the womb. Scanners and chemical tests will also prove invaluable to educational and marriage counsellors, criminal juries, and employment agencies. There is, further, "the very real promise that current technology will lead to the development of drugs capable of expanding the workings of the normal mind, enhancing memory, heightening creativity, and perhaps, one day, even increasing intelligence. Ahead lies an era of psychic engineering."[24]

In spite of his enthusiasm for the new science of molecular psychology, Franklin is not a fool. He realizes that psychotropic drugs and neurochemical scanning can also be abused. Diagnostic scanning may be used to violate fundamental civil rights and liberties. Drugs tailor-made to produce various mental and emotional states may be taken by thrill-seekers. Drugs that supply the user with wild euphoria, eye-popping hallucinations, intense lust, reckless courage, athletic prowess, or depraved indifference to the suffering of others may be just as easy to manufacture as drugs that overcome manic depression or improve memory. Such psychotropes may be many times more powerful than the crude addictive drugs, steroids, and other illegal substances already in use in our already psychotropic post-industrial culture.

Or what of the dangers of the exploitation of molecular psychology by Yehezkel Dror's "crazy states"? As the revolution in molecular psychology proceeds, and reaches every country, Franklin wonders if "one day we will be rudely awakened to reality by an army that marches across the globe sustained by artificial courage, armed by scientists who invent weapons while under the influence of intelligence enhancers, supplied by automatons who work long hours in munitions factories for the reward of a chemical called something like 'Heaven'."[25]

The same dangers lurk in virtually all the futurible ways of treating disease and enhancing human bodily and mental functions. Genetic engineering can be used, just as readily as psychoengineering, to create a race of criminal psychopaths or docile zombies. Treatments to save or prolong life can be made prohibitively expensive for all but the wealthy, or doled out only to the loyal supporters of the super-state. The stock-in-trade of counterculturalist novelists in our century has been an imaginary nightmare future of dehumanization at the hands of genetic or behavioral engineers, from Yevgeny Zamyatin's *We* (1920) and Aldous Huxley's *Brave New World* (1932) to Ray Bradbury's *Fahrenheit 451* (1953) and Anthony Burgess's *A Clockwork Orange* (1962), and their numberless imitators in contemporary science fiction. For most counterculturalists, the seat of human life is consciousness, our link to the divine ground. To tamper with it is to play God and court the spiritual extinction of our species.

Radicals and technoliberals have no such scruples. The technoliberal reply comes, almost invariably, in two parts. Yes, biotechnological progress may threaten the human future, but there is no way it can be stopped. Therefore all we can do is hope that, as with all technologies, human beings will derive more good from it than bad. "If the benefits of the technology we have so far amassed," writes Brian Stableford, "are great enough to outweigh the increased scope for tyranny which it has created, then the same will probably be true of future technology."[26] Most radicals would deny that under capitalism the benefits of technology have outweighed the losses; but once the direction of society is seized by the people themselves, biotechnology can and will become an invaluable agent of human advancement.

Ideological disputes aside, one thing is more or less certain. Research in the medical and behavioral sciences will carry on, no matter what we might want or think, or what the consequences. We almost surely have the power to prolong life by many decades. Even immortality is not unthinkable. We can learn to eliminate all our diseases and enhance all our functions. We can create new species of human life. And the future is long. The British philosopher Olaf Stapledon's dazzling vision of the billions of years and the myriad human races still to come in his great futurist fantasia *Last and First Men* (1930) has not lost its power to challenge our imaginations.

THE NEXT CULTURE

We turn, at the end of our inquiry, to the future of values. Some futurists would argue that the most urgent task of future man and woman will be the forging of a new and distinctly post-industrial culture capable of bringing all of us into psychospiritual rapport with nature, each other, and ourselves. As William Irwin Thompson writes, the description of cultures other than our own is "also the search for an alternative civilization."[27] For most counterculturalists, human society in all its complexity is the result of its values; empirical reality is the clay of consciousness. Technoliberals and radicals tend to assume that values arise from material circumstances, but they acknowledge that cultures, once in being, help shape the social order and may direct us to the ultimate purpose or meaning of living.

A few working definitions are in order. "Culture," as used here, denotes the totality of beliefs, priorities, and tastes generally shared by a society, and their symbolic expressions in art and thought. "Values"' are the specific beliefs, priorities, and tastes prized by a given culture. Values may be ethical, aesthetic, or metaphysical.

For students of alternative world futures, a major question in confronting the future of values is whether there will be one culture or many in the coming world order. The obvious answer is, "many." There are many today, and in the future there may be even more. The classic argument for a world federal government, for example, is that it could safeguard the integrity of indigenous cultures. Federalists observe that national states like Britain, France, or the Soviet Union promote cultural uniformity, consigning all the separate cultures of their various peoples to the national melting pot. In practice this means the Anglicizing, Gallicizing, or Russifying of a host of minority cultures, Celtic, Arab, Jewish, Turkic, and many others. In spite of a voracious appetite for immigrants (willing or unwilling), even the United States has made vigorous efforts to convert all those who reach its shores—black, yellow, brown, or white "ethnic"—into reasonable facsimiles of eighteenth-century Anglo-Saxons. But a world government could outlaw cultural imperialism, and let every distinct sociocultural entity follow its own star.

Such views are not confined to world federalists. A rough consensus among futurists of all persuasions holds that cultural diversity is a blessing, and a logical corollary of liberal and social democracy alike. Yet many cultures, even those that teach respect for diversity, are missionary cultures. Anyone who adheres to one of their value-systems would like the rest of humankind to believe the same things and live in the same ways. Catholicism, Islam, and Mormonism have generated three such missionary cultures. Marxism has its own evangelical dimension. So does the nominally pluralist liberal democratic culture of twentieth-century America, which seeks to replicate itself in Latin America, Africa, East Asia, and throughout the world. The environmentalist, mystical-magical counterculture of the "New Age" is no less imperialist, despite its gentle mien. The program of counterculturalist prophets is not to create a world that is part bourgeois, part socialist, and part New Age, but to bring in the New Age everywhere.

In some ways the most pervasive missionary culture is one that has no overt or self-aware project for world transformation, but spreads everywhere just the same, and threatens to engulf all its rivals. Call it the "technoculture"—the globalizing culture of modern science, technology, and commerce. Widely scorned by alienated artists and intellectuals, the technoculture of skyscrapers, airports, shopping malls, and computers is nevertheless, for many who have tasted its delights, irresistible. Its values may serve some human beings as well as the loftiest tenets of the world's great religions—or serve them better.

Moreover, it exhibits an insatiable appetite for fresh converts. Through its proliferating networks of worldwide communications and transport, the global technoculture penetrates every nation deeply, leaving no soul untempted. Although it has no missionaries as such, and no explicit faith, its mission is to seduce us all.

If it succeeds, the result, already half visible on the horizon, would be a uniform new world civilization consecrated to comfort and pleasure, in which religious, racial, and national differences would scarcely figure, and all the old gods would have crumbled to dust. In a world community integrated by the globe-shrinking communications and transport networks of the technoculture, what could prevail against it? Better fates for humanity come readily to mind. So do worse.

It may even be true that any future society, like those of past centuries, will need the support of a dominant or majoritarian culture in order to cohere and survive. No findings of social-scientific research can confirm or invalidate such a thesis, given the uniqueness of our present point in the long course of world history. But one eminently plausible scenario for the future is that a majoritarian world culture will eventually crystallize and guide our common lives for many years to come. It may already exist, in the form of the rapidly diffusing present-day global technoculture. Or, conceivably, one of the other missionary cultures, political or religious, could win the race.

The terms *dominant* and *majoritarian* do not, of course, mean monolithic. A variety of minority cultures would probably also be available, clinging to their separate existences as best they could, and in some cases thriving lustily. But holding a globalized humankind together may be well-nigh impossible in the absence of an underlying normative consensus linking the majority of earth's people. Split in many directions by fiercely competing value-systems, civilization could well tear itself apart, and perish. It almost did, in the age of the armed struggle between "democracy" and "fascism" (1936–45) and then again in the long Cold War between "freedom" and "communism" (1946–1989).

What might be the role of ideologies, philosophies, and religions in constructing or helping to sustain the next culture? One possibility, which accords with Fukuyama's thoughts on the end of history, is that the global technoculture will indeed emerge as the next culture, but will clothe itself in the symbols and rhetoric of Western-style liberal democracy. It may also inspire, among philosophers, a neo-materialist or molecularist cosmology that finds all empirical reality, including *Homo sapiens*, predetermined by the particles of the microworld: quanta of energy, atoms and molecules, genes and chromosomes, brain chemicals and hormones, all readily accessible to human control by computer-driven technologies, including biotechnology and molecular engineering.[28] Such a world view would be well suited to a twenty-first century of rampant global capitalism and the next rising phase of the business cycle.

A neo-materialist world view also follows, more or less inexorably, from recent developments in science, as Jon Franklin notes in *Molecules of the Mind*. The old dualisms of body and soul, matter and spirit have been rendered obsolete, he believes, by genetics and molecular biology and psychology. The old dualisms were more comforting, and at some level we shall always hold fast to them, because we are biologically programmed to hold fast to them, but "the denial of unpleasant new paradigms is essentially a sterile process. . . . Materialism is the soul as well as the body of the future, and those who are psychologically flexible enough to see the new patterns, and put them to use, will shape what's to come."[29]

There are, of course, other possibilities for the next culture. No matter what direction the global economy and the natural sciences take, we human beings are quite capable of striking out in the opposite direction, as Daniel Bell maintains we have done for more than a hundred years, by creating a culture of unfettered individualistic "modernism" (actually anti-modernism) at odds with a socioeconomic system characterized by strict hierarchies and specialization of labor.[30] Modernist culture pulls us one way, toward irrationality and chaos; in our social evolution, we go the other way, toward rationality and order. The neo-romantic "aquarian" counterculture celebrated by counterculturalist futurists such as Marilyn Ferguson is one outgrowth of modernist irrationalism, an outgrowth that could imaginably oppose and overtake its materialist rivals in the next century.[31]

But as we near the end of the twentieth century, the chances of postmodernism, the cultural heir apparent of modernism since about 1970, look somewhat better. The culture of the postmodernist avant-garde, at first inspection, seems even more chaotic and irrational than the culture of the older modernism. At once eclectic and hypercritical, postmodernism takes as its goal the deconstruction of all totalities, the unmasking of all claims to objectivity, the demolition of all ideologies, and, according to Roland N. Stromberg, the "abandonment of the whole enterprise of Western intellectual culture."[32]

This is too harsh. But postmodernism is currently everywhere. It animates, for example, the Soviet composer Alfred Schnittke's curious rag-bag of styles from busy baroque polyphony to heartbreaking expressionism. It pervades the patiently mole-like philosophy of the French deconstructionist philosopher Jacques Derrida, the scalding historical relativism of the late Michel Foucault, and the work of many others in all branches of the arts and humanities.[33] In effect postmodernism is only modernism pushed to its logical (or illogical?) conclusions. Its great discovery, which is also implicit in late modernist philosophy and art, is that nothing can be discovered. All our attempts to reconstruct nature, texts, the past, and the future are nothing more than pleas we make in a darkened courtroom, without a jury and without a judge. We wait for a verdict that will—and should—never come.

Will the culture of postmodernism persist into the twenty-first century and, if so, how might it interact with the global technoculture? Cultural critics, eager as always for the fresh copy that only new paradigms can supply, have already begun the search for something post-postmodern. It is surely possible that, in good time, they will succeed. But it is also possible that postmodernism in some form is here to stay. Perhaps the absolute relativism of postmodernist thought is a permanent achievement of the human mind, in the same sense that Gautama Buddha, or Socrates and Plato, or Jesus, or Newton cannot be dislodged from our racial memory, whatever else may happen.

In defense of this position, the British postmodernist theorist Steven Connor regards postmodern cultural analysis as marking "an important, indeed, probably an epochal stage in the development of ethical awareness, in the recognition of the irreducible diversity of voices and interests." But it always runs the risk of "falling into complicity with the increasingly globalized forms which seek to harness, exploit, and administer—and therefore violently to curtail—this diversity." The task of postmodernists of the future, it follows, is to resist the encroachment of the global technoculture by creating a common frame of ethical assent, presumably radical in orientation, that "alone can guarantee the continuation of a global diversity of voices."[34] If postmodernists fail in this task, they will become unwitting allies of the technoculture, abandoning political concerns and retreating into a cloistered world of postmodern thought and art for the sake of thought and art alone.

So these are among our options for at least the first half of the next century: a globalizing technoculture, reinforced by liberal democratic values and perhaps a revival of materialism in an updated "molecular" guise; a counterculturalist New Age culture of amorphous spirituality; the relinquishing of all attempts to form a consensual culture, in the further development and refinement of postmodernist deconstruction, which could play into the hands of the technoculture; or an alliance between postmodernist criticism and whatever survives of the radical impulse.

There is yet another possibility: a world culture shaped by revivals of the positive religions, and in particular Christianity, Islam, Hinduism, and

Buddhism. Will they play a major part in the next culture, or in the formation of a majoritarian world culture? For many years, down through the middle of the twentieth century, social scientists routinely foresaw the inevitable decay and passing of religion as a significant force in human life.[35] They have all, so far, proved quite wrong. One of the many roads traveled by modernism has been a return to the pre-modern religious sources of modern civilization. Thousands of prominent twentieth-century intellectuals have converted from agnosticism or atheism to some form of traditional belief. Powerful religious revivals drawing tens of millions of adherents have swept through parts of the developed world, especially the United States. Others are afoot in Eastern Europe, the Middle East, and the Indian subcontinent as we enter the 1990s. Will secularization, hitherto one of the most irresistible components of the modernizing process, be arrested and reversed in the next century?

Daniel Bell speaks for many contemporary sociologists, and many futurists, in predicting that it will. Modernist culture, he suggests, "has become aware of the limits in exploring the mundane" and will, at some point, make "the effort to recover the sacred."[36] New modes of religious faith will appear on the scene in the Western world, grounded in traditional belief and committed to the recapture of our lost sense of continuity with the past. Such new modes will include "moralizing" religions that appeal to rural and small-town folk appalled by the permissiveness of modern times, "redemptive" religions for anguished intellectuals and professionals, and "mythic and mystical" religions that may put us all in closer touch with the great archetypes of our cultural heritage. "The ground of religion," writes Bell, "is existential: the awareness of men of their finiteness and the inexorable limits to their powers, and the consequent effort to find a coherent answer to reconcile them to that human condition." Having weighed secularism (both in its modernist and communist varieties) and found it wanting, Western men and women will feel impelled to "regain a sense of the sacred."[37]

How these new religious modes may become institutionalized, Bell does not venture to forecast. In essence his argument is that people need religion, suffer when deprived of it, and will in time return to it, whether its truth-claims are valid or not. This instrumental view of religious faith is not uncommon among technoliberals, and the occasional non-Marxist radical. It is generally not shared by counterculturalists, for many of whom the realm of the spiritual is an absolute reality and religion, therefore, much more than a way of satisfying human needs. Nevertheless, futurists of the counterculturalist persuasion, taught by such early twentieth-century seers as Carl Gustav Jung, Arnold J. Toynbee, and Aldous Huxley, would agree with Bell that the coming religiosity will take many forms.

In the counterculturalist vision, the forms taken and their theological content will matter far less than their spiritual essence, their acceptance of nature as mother and fellow human beings as brothers and sisters, and their power to raise the consciousness of our species from the supposedly sordid materialism of the present epoch to a higher cosmic state. Citing the wisdom of Buddha, Lao Tzu, William Blake, and the Christian Gnostic myth of the "apocatastasis" (the restoration of all sinful beings to God), Theodore Roszak anticipates a time when modern society, weary of the spiritual wasteland it has created, makes its way back to religion. "Not the religion of the churches—God help us! not the religion of the churches—but religion of the oldest, most universal sense: which is vision born of transcendent knowledge."[38]

Citing comparable authorities, the counterculturalist lay guru William Irwin Thompson foretells a planetary culture "similar to the nomadic way of life of the old paleolithic hunters and gatherers; the people will carry their cultures in their souls." But we will not simply go backwards in time to our archaic roots: "we will go forward to a remythologizing and resacralization in which science, art, and religion will converge in a new cosmic language for initiates."[39]

There also remains the chance that one or more of the great positive religions may furnish the world view of a still unborn twenty-first-century dominant culture. The major organized religions claim hundreds of millions of followers. Each has gained ground against the forces of secularism in recent years. Religious revivals, however, are often not so much revivals of authentic premodern religiosity as ways chosen by victimized nations or minorities to mobilize their people against exploitation and preserve their historic identity. The strength of such revivals lies in their powerful and immediate appeal to the victims, but the strength is also a weakness. The more eloquently a religion speaks to the needs of specific victims of specific injustices, the less it is likely to attract other segments of humankind.

The Islamic resurgence of recent decades, for example, is more than a religious reawakening: it is also a response in self-defense by less developed nations to the political, economic, and cultural imperialism of the non-Islamic developed world. In the view of one Muslim futurist, Ziauddin Sardar, the much heralded resurgence of the Muslim world is thus far only "an unrest— an unrest that is the product of its acute disillusion with capitalism and Communism, development and modernization, instant answers and political expediency." A true resurgence of epochal proportions has yet to take place. But some day it will, if Muslims can complement resistance (*jihad*) with the hard intellectual labor (*ijtihad*) needed to adapt the dictates of the Qur'an and the Sunnah of the Prophet Muhammad to the exigencies of the foreseeable future. Islam must produce a comprehensive program for its future. "Islamic resurgence," Sardar concludes, "has to be a planned, systematic and coherent endeavor of thought and action that leads to real political and intellectual power and indigenous scientific, technological and economic capability."[40]

Christian, Jewish, Hindu, and Buddhist thinkers have generated similar hopes for the respective futures of their own faiths. The Christian futurist

David B. Barrett in *Cosmos, Chaos, and Gospel* provides a scenario of cosmic evangelization in which the Christian share of the human population rises slowly to 50 percent by the year 2500, and to 99 percent by the year 1,000,000 A.D., when one septillion human beings are scattered throughout the galaxy.[41] Most Christians would not feel comfortable with such detailed prophecies, but they are not out of line with the proclaimed Christian mission of bringing all men and women everywhere to Christ. Islam is also a profoundly evangelistic faith, with more than forty countries in every part of the Eastern Hemisphere predominantly Muslim, and at least forty more countries with substantial Muslim minorities. Even the land of the "Great Satan," the United States of America, is now .5 percent Muslim. The percentage grows each year.

Humanists respond by calling for prolonged intellectual efforts to convert the world's people to belief in science, reason, and human self-sufficiency.[42] No doubt the number of humanists in the world today, although many of them would be reluctant to wear the label, is also numbered in the hundreds of millions. But we must return to the question with which we began. What is the likelihood that any religion or religious philosophy, from Christianity and Islam to humanism, will sharply increase its share of followers in the world as a whole in the next century or serve as the matrix of a majoritarian world culture?

The answer is, very little likelihood. All the religions will undoubtedly persist. Some may grow or decline in relation to others, and all will make some contribution, positive or negative, to whatever majoritarian world culture emerges (if any). But the days of mass conversion are long past. Just as there are no more empty or sparsely settled lands available for colonizing, so there are no more pagans or infidels waiting to receive the Word. The centuries-old seesaw battle between Christianity and Islam has ended, perhaps forever, in a draw. In the twenty-first century, very few Christians will ever become Muslims, and very few Muslims will ever accept Christ. The same is true of the endless struggle in the Indian subcontinent between Muslims, Sikhs, and Hindus. As for humanism, it may well survive and even prosper, but it will not supplant the organized religions.

In the longer run, of course, anything is imaginable. The secular religion of "the service of being" sketched in my *Building the City of Man* and *A Short History of the Future*,[43] is the only faith that makes any sense to me. Something like it may eventually help to undergird a new planetary culture, but I am not enough of an egomaniac to proclaim its inevitability here. As futurists, we are really out of our depth in trying to chart the far future of religion.

The same is doubtless true of any effort to fathom even the near future of the arts: literature, painting, sculpture, dance, music, theater, cinema, photography, and all the many arts still to be born from the marriage of technology and aestheticism. Futurists have rarely tried to project happenings in these fields, and when they have, the results are not inspiring. The most that can be said is that if a neomaterialist culture becomes hegemonic in the next century, it will probably impel artists to revive, in some form or fashion, the graphic realism and naturalism of the middle decades of the nineteenth century. But if postmodernism or a new religious world view or the visions of the counterculturalist New Age prevail, artists are likely to dance to the beat of quite different drums. The arts do, roughly, follow the spiritual and intellectual promptings of the cultures that invoke them. But how they express those promptings, what forms and media and symbols they choose, is a matter for artists, not futurists.

In any event, it is safe to add that the arts are not likely to wither away in the next century. So great is the human need to express the values of reigning cultures in the manifold languages of the arts that no culture, no people, no era has been able to dispense with them. Perhaps, in the very distant future, the arts will displace religion and philosophy altogether, and become the chief labor and delight of humankind. At the very least, we can agree with Ernst Fischer that they are with us forever. As he writes in *The Necessity of Art*, "Man . . . will always stay the great magician, will always be Prometheus bringing fire from heaven to earth, will always be Orpheus enthralling nature with his music. Not until humanity itself dies will art die."[44]

NOTES

1. Marvin Cetron and Thomas O'Toole, *Encounters with the Future: A Forecast of Life into the 21st Century* (New York: McGraw-Hill, 1982), 271.

2. See Barry Jones, *Sleepers, Wake!: Technology and the Future of Work* (Melbourne: Oxford University Press, 1982).

3. Wagar, *Building the City of Man*, 119.

4. Charles Handy, *The Future of Work: A Guide to a Changing Society* (Oxford: Blackwell, 1984). See especially the four scenarios on 179–185.

5. James Robertson, *Future Wealth: A New Economics for the 21st Century* (New York: The Bootstrap Press, 1990), 139.

6. An important source of all counterculturalist thinking on work is the writing of E. F. Schumacher, including *Small is Beautiful: Economics As If People Mattered* (New York: Harper and Row, 1973) and, especially, his last book, *Good Work* (New York: Harper and Row, 1979). See also the lengthier discussion of "ownwork" in Robertson's *Future Work: Jobs, Self-Employment and Leisure after the Industrial Age* (Aldershot, Hants: Gower/Maurice Temple Smith, 1985), chs. 11–12; and the theme of "disintermediation" in Paul Hawken, *The Next Economy* (New York: Holt, Rinehart and Winston, 1983), ch. 8. Disintermediation is Hawken's term for "any direct transaction or exchange of goods or services that bypasses a middleman, professional, specialist, or institution that is normally involved in such a transaction." Hawken, 122. Examples are the purchase of products directly from the makers, raising vegetables in the backyard, and drafting a will or treating an illness without

the aid of a lawyer or doctor. In short, disintermediation means doing one's own work, whenever possible, instead of delegating it to intermediaries.

7. Peter T. Kilborn, "Brave New World Seen for Robots Appears Stalled by Quirks and Costs," *New York Times* (July 1, 1990): 1:16.

8. Arthur Shostak, "Seven Scenarios of Urban Change," in Gary Gappert and Richard V. Knight, ed., *Cities in the 21st Century* (Beverly Hills: Sage, 1982), 69–93, especially 79–81. Shostak's chief source is David Morris and Karl Hess, *Neighborhood Power: The New Localism* (Boston: Beacon Press, 1975). E. F. Schumacher maintained that no city should have more than 500,000 inhabitants. Schumacher, *Small Is Beautiful* [1973] (New York: Harper and Row, 1975), 67.

9. Christopher Lasch, *Haven in a Heartless World* (New York: Basic Books, 1977). See also the caustic critique of Lasch's "populist-fascist romantic politics" in Boris Frankel, *The Post-Industrial Utopians*, 159–161 and 189–191, and notes 24 and 27 on 289–290.

10. Jessie Bernard, *The Future of Marriage* [1972] (Revised Edition, New Haven: Yale University Press, 1982), especially ch. 11.

11. Kathy Keeton, with Yvonne Baskin, *Woman of Tomorrow* (New York: St. Martin's/Marek, 1985), 250.

12. Elizabeth Nickles, with Laura Ashcraft, *The Coming Matriarchy: How Women Will Gain the Balance of Power* (New York: Seaview Books, 1981), 203.

13. Annie Cheatham and Mary Clare Powell, *This Way Daybreak Comes: Women's Values and the Future* (Philadelphia: New Society Publishers, 1986). After conceding that as white, middle-class American lesbians, they cannot literally speak for all women, the authors add, "But we acknowledge the oneness of womankind, not only in our common oppression, but in our yearning for life. . . . We . . . assert our belief that women, as a group, are the planet's best hope for survival." Cheatham and Powell, xxi. A similar point of view is espoused in Elinor Lenz and Barbara Myerhoff, *The Feminization of America: How Women's Values Are Changing Our Public and Private Lives* (Los Angeles: Jeremy P. Tarcher, 1985).

14. See, for example, Roger W. Libby and Robert N. Whitehurst, ed., *Marriage and Alternatives: Exploring Intimate Relationships* (Glenview, Ill.: Scott, Foresman, 1977); and Nick Stinnett and Craig Wayne Birdsong, with Nancy M. Stinnett, *The Family and Alternate Life Styles* (Chicago: Nelson-Hall, 1978).

15. Ivan Illich, *Deschooling Society* (New York: Harper and Row, 1971). Callenbach's ideas on elementary, secondary, and higher education may be found in his *Ecotopia*, 148–154 and 163–169.

16. André Gorz, *Farewell to the Working Class: An Essay on Post-Industrial Socialism* (London: Pluto Press, 1982), 150–151. Cf. Wagar, *Building the City of Man*, ch. 6.

17. Felix Kaufmann, in David Wallechinsky, Amy Wallace, and Irving Wallace, ed., *The Book of Predictions* (New York: William Morrow, 1980), 30.

18. For a layman's introduction to health futures, see Holcomb B. Noble, ed., *Next: The Coming Era in Medicine* (Boston: Little, Brown, 1987).

19. See, for example, Warren E. Leary, "Where Balloons Fail in Clearing Arteries, New Devices May Help," *New York Times* (March 20, 1990): C3.

20. The starting point for exploring the future of reproduction, although somewhat dated now, is Robert T. Francoeur, *Utopian Motherhood: New Trends in Human Reproduction*, 3d edition (Cranbury, N.J.: A. S. Barnes, 1975).

21. Brian Stableford, *Future Man* (New York: Crown Publishers, 1984), 135. For a fuller discussion, see ch. 7, "Engineering People," and also Stableford and David Langford, *The Third Millennium: A History of the World: AD 2000–3000* (New York: Knopf, 1985), ch. 36, "The Diversification of Man."

22. Carol Kahn, *Beyond the Helix: DNA and the Quest for Longevity* (New York: Times Books, 1985), 261.

23. See B. F. Skinner, *Beyond Freedom and Dignity* (New York: Knopf, 1971), and his classic behaviorist utopia, *Walden Two* (New York: Macmillan, 1948).

24. Jon Franklin, *Molecules of the Mind: The Brave New World of Molecular Psychology* (New York: Atheneum, 1987), 38.

25. *Ibid.*, 297.

26. Stableford, *Future Man*, 182.

27. William Irwin Thompson, *At the Edge of History: Speculations on the Transformation of Culture* (New York: Harper and Row, 1971), xi.

28. See my discussion of an emergent neomaterialism in *A Short History of the Future*, 80–83. The future of molecular engineering (or nanotechnology) is projected in K. Eric Drexler, *Engines of Creation* (New York: Doubleday, 1986). For a popular account of nanotechnology and other frontiers of computer science and robotics, see also Grant Fjermedal, *The Tomorrow Makers: A Brave New World of Living-Brain Machines* (New York: Macmillan, 1986).

29. Franklin, *Molecules of the Mind*, 264.

30. Daniel Bell, *The Cultural Contradictions of Capitalism* (2nd edition, London: Heinemann, 1979), especially 15.

31. Marilyn Ferguson, *The Aquarian Conspiracy: Personal and Social Transformation in Our Time* (Los Angeles: J. P. Tarcher, 1987).

32. Roland N. Stromberg, *European Intellectual History since 1789* (5th edition (Englewood Cliffs, N.J.: Prentice Hall, 1990), 320.

33. An excellent introduction to Derrida and Foucault, in the context of their debt to Nietzsche and other forerunners, is available in Allan Megill, *Prophets of Extremity: Nietzsche, Heidegger, Foucault, Derrida* (Berkeley and Los Angeles: University of California Press, 1985). See also Steven Connor, *Postmodernist Culture: An Introduction to Theories of the Contemporary* (New York and Oxford: Blackwell, 1989).

34. Connor, *Postmodernist Culture*, 244.

35. A late example is Michael Harrington, an ex-Catholic "serious atheist," who wrote in a self-consciously Nietzschean vein of the political consequences of the collapse of traditional faith in one of his last books, *The Politics at God's Funeral: The Spiritual Crisis of Western Civilization* (New York: Holt, Reinhart and Winston, 1983). "The God of the Judeo-Christian West is in his death agony and that is one of the most significant political events of this incredible age." *The Politics at God's Funeral*, 11.

36. Bell, *The Cultural Contradictions of Capitalism*, xxix.

37. Daniel Bell, "The Return of the Sacred? The Argument on the Future of Religion," *The British Journal of Sociology*, 28:4 (December 1977): 419–449. The quoted passages appear on 447–448.

38. Theodore Roszak, *Where the Wasteland Ends: Politics and Transcendence in Postindustrial Society* (Garden City, N.Y.: Doubleday Anchor Books, 1973), 421–422. See also Fritjof Capra, *The Turning Point: Science, Society, and the Rising*

Culture (New York: Simon and Schuster, 1982). Capra's and Roszak's backgrounds are quite different, but their views are comparable on most points.

39. William Irwin Thompson, *Darkness and Scattered Light: Four Talks on the Future* (Garden City, N.Y.: Doubleday Anchor Books, 1978), 173 and 176. See my less than sympathetic essay on Thompson's book, "At the Edge of Sanity: William Irwin Thompson and Planetary Culture," *Alternative Futures: The Journal of Utopian Studies*, 1:3 (Fall 1978): 72–80; and his less than sympathetic review of my *Building the City of Man*, "The World State and the Shadow of H. G. Wells," in Thompson, *Passages about Earth: An Exploration of the New Planetary Culture* (New York: Harper and Row, 1974), 56–83.

40. Ziauddin Sardar, *Islamic Futures: The Shape of Ideas to Come* (London and New York: Mansell Publishing, 1985), 53–54 and 57. See also Sardar, *The Future of Muslim Civilization* (London: Croom Helm, 1979).

41. David B. Barrett, *Cosmos, Chaos, and Gospel: A Chronology of World Evangelization from Creation to New Creation* (Birmingham: New Hope, 1987), especially Appendix 1, "A Statistical Overview of World Evangelization, BC 13 Million to AD 4 Billion," 96–97. Shorter-range speculation on the future of Christianity is available in Hiley H. Ward, *Religion 2101 A.D.* (Garden City, N.Y.: Doubleday, 1975), and Rodney Stark and William Sims Bainbridge, *The Future of Religion: Secularization, Revival and Cult Formation* (Berkeley and Los Angeles: University of California Press, 1985).

42. See Paul Kurtz, ed., *Building a World Community: Humanism in the 21st Century* (Buffalo: Prometheus Books, 1989).

43. See Wagar, *Building the City of Man*, 87–90; and *A Short History of the Future*, 193–194.

44. Ernst Fischer, *The Necessity of Art: A Marxist Approach* (Harmondsworth, Middlesex: Penguin Books, 1963), 225.

Epilogue: The Next Three Futures

If you have read this far, you may be asking, "Yes, but what will *really* happen?" The futurist's many-ring circus of alternatives, options, and possibilities may well leave the earnest spectator dizzy and fatigued. Perhaps the study of the future is a better way to experience Alvin Toffler's "future shock" than actually to live through rapidly changing times, when the future—so to speak—arrives ahead of schedule. If carried out with sufficient ruthlessness, the study of the future can even destroy our power to make choices and to plan and follow courses of action.

Because every futurist is a human being, as well as a student of human affairs, it is necessary at some point to weigh all the options and then decide, each of us for ourselves, what we think is most likely to happen to humankind in the next century or more. From the array of most likely possibilities, we should also determine how we can, as individuals or as members of groups, help ensure that the best of the likeliest futures—"best" as we define the good—is the future that in fact materializes. This will inevitably pit futurist against futurist, because our expectations and our ideas of the good vary. But studying the future should never become such an end in itself that it prevents us from functioning effectively as members of civil society in the real world. The object of science and scholarship is always to inform and empower human will, not to paralyze it.

In this brief epilogue, let me sum up my own thoughts about the long-term future of humankind. My working premise is that perhaps the technoliberals, radicals, and counterculturalists are all essentially correct.[1] The human race may be destined to follow all three paths to the future, not simultaneously, but sequentially.

Thus far we have considered technoliberalism, radicalism, and counterculturalism as alternatives. Either capitalism and bourgeois democracy will prove victorious, or democratic socialism, or the Ecotopian New Age. But there is no reason to assume that the whole future of humankind lies down a single path. The future, after all, is a long time. If capitalism, for example, does triumph over its rivals, will its reign last forever? Do the other two futures mutually exclude one another, so that if we choose one, we can never choose the other?

To both questions the answer is clearly no. I find it far more likely that the world system will take each of these paths for long periods of time, and not in a random sequence. The path that most countries in the world are already following in the 1990s, the path of capitalist hegemony and the universalizing of representative democracy, will broaden still further as we enter the next millennium. Much later, capitalism will give way to a hitherto untried form of democratic socialism. Much later still, when humankind is finally ready for it, socialism will be supplanted by a decentralized and ecotopian counterculture.

But first things first. The next future is almost surely the one we are building today, the future of globalized liberal democratic capitalism. By the first or second decade of the twenty-first century, all of humankind will be travelling along that road, although it will mean radically different things for different segments of the world system. For the privileged classes and races of the core countries, and their many loyal hangers-on, it will be a golden or at least a silver age. For small numbers of affluent people in the semi-peripheral and peripheral countries, life will also be sweet. For the rest of humankind, as much as half the population of the core countries and nine-tenths or more in the periphery, life will be toilsome and bare.

Breakthroughs in technology (such as fusion power or the perfection of artificial intelligence), the exploitation of new markets in the former Second and Third Worlds, and the fresh energies released by the diffusion of political democracy will keep the system humming for many years. But eventually, for some or all of the reasons adduced by radical critics of the capitalist world system, it will begin to disintegrate from within. Its failure may become readily apparent by the end of the next bout of worldwide business expansion, say in the 2030s, or it may take one or more additional turns of the wheel, carrying us near the close of the next century or even beyond.

It is hardly possible at this time to anticipate just which of the many shortcomings of technoliberal capitalism, or which combination of shortcomings, will play the greatest part in its collapse. One major factor will be the anger and resentment it engenders in the many nations that never succeed in gaining admission to the heartland of the world system, together with the bitterness of the various ethnic minorities and working classes within the core countries themselves. Capitalism is good for winners. But it also produces losers, whole populations that lose the game of high-stakes, high-tech, high-speed economic growth. At some point this anger may well boil over.

Another likely contributing cause to the disintegration of liberal capitalism will be the mounting costs of keeping the system running smoothly. Servicing deficits, paying for the military adventures required to keep restless poor nations in line, co-opting workers with benefits packages, caring for the increasing number of elderly people, fighting urban crime, safeguarding a deteriorating environment, and all the other expenses of late capitalism will add up to trillions of dollars a year. When the new markets of the twenty-first century (such as post-communist Russia) are saturated with all the goods and capital they can absorb and the financial burdens of maintaining the condominium of the core countries in the new world order become insupportable, the time will approach for yet another cycle of revolution, as great or greater than the World Revolution of 1989.

The technoliberal capitalist world system will still be enormously powerful, but it will also be top-heavy, over-centralized, and insolvent. Lacking the gusto of youth or even middle age, it will be confronted by anti-systemic movements that grow stronger with every passing year. Some of these movements, perhaps most, will represent specific regional or group interests. But international political formations may also emerge sometime in the twenty-first century, vaguely analogous to the loose coalition of Green parties that now flourish in many Western countries and participate in the worldwide struggle to protect the environment from state and capitalist exploitation. One or more of these formations, for example, a militant One World party, espousing democratic socialism and world government, may become leading actors in the international political process.

It is pleasant to think that humankind could make the transition from technoliberal capitalism to social democracy in a peaceful manner, without armed violence and without the kinds of injustice that violence almost always breeds. But such a peaceful transition seems unlikely, or at least unlikely in every country and in every part of the world. The established technoliberal order will not go down everywhere without a fight. Here and there, it will make its stand, as the state capitalist dictatorships of China and Romania made their stands during the World Revolution of 1989, in China successfully (for the time being), in Romania not. It is even possible that the liberal capitalist world system will not collapse until it becomes embroiled, willy-nilly, in a calamitous system-wide war.

In any event, the best chance for moving from oligopoly capitalism to a democratic socialist world order will come in especially difficult times, when the prevailing system has lost much of its credibility. Wars and depressions are the obvious occasions for rapid social change of this magnitude. At such times political change can occur very quickly and spread just as quickly from region to region, as it did after 1789 and again after 1989. The old era ends, and the new begins, with a new reigning world view rooted in the inspirations of radical democracy.

In the early years, we may assume that a worldwide republic of working men and women will do a reasonably good job. It will put an end to the warfare system once and for all by disarming the nation-states and permitting no military force but its own. Liberated from their permanently inferior status in the defunct capitalist world economy, the peoples of the less developed countries will be free to evolve in their own way and at their own speed toward democratic socialism, with the help of modest loans and grants-in-aid from the world commonwealth. Often suspended in the days of late capitalism by a technocracy more and more afraid of its own people, civil liberties will be fully guaranteed throughout the world for the first time in the history of our species. The workers' republic will also undertake a great terrestrial housecleaning project to restore the environment, as much as possible, to pre-twentieth-century conditions.

Yet there is all too good a chance that the republic will in time become superfluous, a fetter on the further development of humankind. It will clearly be needed for many decades to dismantle the machinery of warfare and private capital, and to clean up a looted planet. In a tightly integrated world system, I see no possibility of such things happening piecemeal, as the result of uncoordinated local initiatives.

All the same, in the process of doing its job the workers' republic is bound to inherit many of the technologies, business management practices, and bureaucratic procedures of the capitalist ancien régime. It may well breed its own caste of elitist technocrats who in time will find ingenious ways of evading democratic controls and perpetuating their own power. The ruling caste of the republic may even become hereditary, ensuring that most of its power and privilege passes to its children, and to theirs.

None of this is democratic socialism, of course. Socialism is not compatible with technocracy or technocratic elites. But as long as the world is governed by a central guidance system, in which day-to-day decision-making is vested in a huge bureaucratic apparatus—no matter what its historical origins, official world view, or initially pious intentions—the danger remains that the apparatus will learn how to disempower the people it was created to serve.

Even if the people do manage to retain significant control over the doings of the bureaucracy, what would be the purpose of a world state after its task of renovating the planet had been completed? If inequalities of wealth and opportunity were removed, the environment restored, national armies dissolved, and worker democracy ensconced, what need would there be for a world republic?

At this point, perhaps late in the twenty-first century or well into the twenty-second, humankind will be ready for its third future, the future beyond liberal capitalism and democratic socialism. There are hints of such an age in the Marxian canon, in its view of "communism" as a higher stage of socialism, in the belief that the dictatorship of the proletariat would be replaced in time by a classless society and the dying out of the state, in the assumption that individuals would then be free to choose their own destinies, as individuals, no longer commodified by capitalism and its specialization of labor.

This next and perhaps last revolution may occur without violence and even without concerted political activism. People may decide, first here, then there, then somewhere else, that they no longer need the services of public officials. They will find they can also do nicely without purchasing energy from global grids or imported processed foods in shiny packages. They may start growing their own food. They may switch to locally available, small-scale energy systems, such as wind farms and solar power collectors. They may elect to produce goods and services chiefly for their own use, with self-replicating, self-maintaining advanced technologies that do not require huge outlays of capital or megawatts of energy. Home-grown arts and crafts may further shrink their dependence on the global mass market. They will travel a great deal, and keep in instantaneous electronic touch with the rest of the world, but essentially they will be self-sufficient; and one by one, communities of such individuals will sever their economic and political ties to the global democratic socialist system.

In short, having rescued humankind from war, ecocide, and injustice, the workers' republic will in due time become redundant, and the scaffolding it had erected can be allowed to fall away. Perhaps a few bits and pieces of the old apparatus will have to stay on. For instance, a world agency may be needed to provide traffic control for the planetary and interplanetary transport and communications network. But by and large the republic will simply fade away, its place taken by thousands of self-governing, self-supporting communities of many shapes and sizes scattered all over the face of the earth. Such communities will have learned the hard lessons of power and wealth, of war and peace, taught by modern history. They will survive handily without armies and bureaucracies, without the endless buying and replacing of products, without competition for markets and profits, without poverty or cheap labor, without masters and servants.

Clearly, we are speaking now of an age in which counterculturalist values have triumphed, in which people have managed to fend for themselves, as grownups rather than as wards of omnipotent states or corporations. But the people of this Ecotopian league of communities would not lead primitive lives. Far from it, if they chose. They would be in close contact with people throughout the world, and other worlds. They would have at their disposal sophisticated technologies scaled to their own needs, clean and light technologies that would require a minimal investment of capital and little or no human intervention to keep in running order. If they did need something more elaborate, such as spacecraft, such items would be communally owned and used by an appointment or reservation system, with everyone in the community, or in a group of neighboring communities, sharing their cost.

It goes without saying that all this would be impossible if fundamental advances in miniaturized, low-energy technical systems were not forthcoming in the centuries ahead. But the odds are that they will be forthcoming, in abundance. As information technologies become more and more versatile and powerful, robotics and molecular engineering will liberate our species from nearly all the kinds of labor now performed. It will be easy to manufacture and keep in repair almost any desired product or furnish any desired service in facilities available anywhere. The factory or library ten thousand miles away will no longer be needed. Everything will be possible, in our own backyards.

So far, so good. One may ask how such a various world will avoid a reversion to tribal warfare or a resurrection of capitalism or fascism or Stalinism in new or even more virulent forms. The only possible answer is that once the people are truly empowered, once everyone on earth has fair access to its riches, they will not let themselves be deceived. They will insist on the accountability of their rulers, policies of peace and mutual respect for all men and women, and a full panoply of civil liberties. Am I naive? Very possibly. But if we cannot trust an empowered people, whom can we trust? If the people, the rank and file of our species, is not fit to govern, who is? Frankly, I would rather not know.

In retrospect, hundreds of years from now, historians may even look back on our next three futures as logical and inevitable stages in the evolution of humankind. Just as feudalism made possible the emergence of capitalism, so capitalism established the necessary preconditions for the coming of socialism, and socialism ushered in the neo-romantic counterculture. Each stage in world history is but a prologue to the one that follows it, worlds without end.

If this is true, the counterculture will, in its turn, yield to yet another world view, another paradigm of values, another new civilization, perhaps in the twenty-second century. After the next three futures, comes the fourth.

Yet in one overwhelming respect, whatever follows in the deep end of history will be quite different from anything experienced by our species since its beginning.[2] By then, if not before, human beings will no longer be confined to the sphere on which life in this patch of the universe originated. Our living space will expand spectacularly, and nothing will ever be the same again.

Already human beings have set foot on one extraterrestrial body and sent mechanical probes to others. This is just the beginning. In a matter of a few generations or centuries, large numbers of men and women will almost certainly be living in artificial habitats in space or as colonists on the moon or Mars or some of the satellites of the outer planets. The engineering know-how required for such exploits is all but available today, and can only grow in the years ahead.[3] People will be living in space for any number of reasons: scientific research, zero-gravity industrial production, exploitation of mineral resources, recreation, and—in selected instances—escape from the limitations and frustrations of life on earth.

But there is much more. The universe is infinitely larger than this little solar system we inhabit. Current astrophysical theory, as Robert Jastrow writes in *Journey to the Stars*, suggests that one star in five offers "conditions favorable to the evolution of life and intelligence." By this reckoning, there are forty billion stars in our local galaxy capable of harboring intelligent life.[4] Since ours is also just one of many billions of galaxies, some considerably larger than the Milky Way, the total number of star systems with inhabitable planets may be virtually numberless. It stands to reason that many of these planets will be far more attractive as habitats than arid Mars or the cold moons of Jupiter and Saturn.

In the centuries to come, humankind will turn outward to this starry universe and commence the search, in earnest, for other life, for other civilizations, for other worlds to settle. If we succeed, the time may come when only a small fraction of the human race lives on Terra. The idea of cultural "pluralism" will take on truly cosmic proportions, as *Homo sapiens* and perhaps a host of bioengineered new and better human races colonize the universe.[5]

Crossing the interstellar gulfs to reach these far-flung worlds will not be easy. We will need to develop much more powerful propulsion systems than any now in existence. We may also have to find ways of keeping crewpersons in suspended animation for long periods of time. But in the fullness of time there is every reason to suppose that the technical problems will be solved.

And when they are, the blessings of space exploration and settlement for our scattered progeny will be almost unimaginably rich. The migration to outer space will provide an outlet for expansive energies not available on a pacified earth. It will give people everywhere a sense of participation in a great enterprise that transcends all local divisions and petty terrestrial quarrels. It may also, as Arthur C. Clarke long ago proposed in *Profiles of the Future*, "trigger a new Renaissance and break the pattern into which our society, and our arts, must otherwise freeze."[6]

Still greater dividends can be foreseen. The exploration of interstellar space may eventually bring us into contact with alien cultures, which could have a more profound impact on our civilization than all its earthly renaissances and voyages of exploration combined. If other living intelligent species are distributed too sparsely through the universe to meet one another, we might still learn almost as much from interceptions of their radioed messages, or from excavating the remains of long-extinct alien civilizations.

Even if we never encounter intelligent life anywhere in this galaxy or any other, there is (believe it or not!) intelligent life on earth. It will still be possible for humankind to colonize the galaxy, over a period of hundreds, thousands, or millions of years. Science-fiction writers have often depicted colony ships that go forth to colonize nearby solar systems. Those colonists successful in locating and populating inhabitable planets will eventually reach the point when they, too, can dispatch colonists of their own, to stellar systems hundreds of light-years from Terra and Sol. In good time, the whole galaxy will teem with human life, and we can launch intergalactic expeditions as well.

I say "we." Will those far-future inhabitants of our universe be part of "us"?

Why not? You may see them as ghostly or impossibly remote people, not even quite human in form or faculties. So, perhaps, all parents regard their children, so like themselves, and yet so unlike, bent on living their own lives and following their own stars.

But in reality we are all one family. It matters little whether we live in caves, villages, suburban tracts, or mobile space habitats touring the universe. We are all one, indissolubly tied to a common past and moving together into a common future. Into this future, we send our children, and from it, in humankind's relentless flight through space and time, they will never return.

NOTES

1. For a fuller view, consult my book *A Short History of the Future*, written in 1987. The discussion that follows recapitulates the argument developed there, but in a somewhat different way, and with the changes that living through another three years of world history almost inevitably bring, especially if they happen to include the World Revolution of 1989! *A Short History of the Future*, in turn, is an elaboration in scenario form of my "three futures" thesis, first published as "The Next Three Futures" in the *World Future Society Bulletin*, 18:6 (November-December 1984): 12–19, and, in a revised version, in Marien and Jennings, ed., *What I Have Learned*, 3–21.

2. See "Epilogue: The Deep End," in my *The City of Man: Prophecies of a World Civilization in Twentieth-Century Thought* (Boston: Houghton Mifflin, 1963). The last sentence of the epilogue of *The Next Three Futures* is taken (with a few changes) from the last sentence of *The City of Man*, 272.

3. The key text for space colonies is *The High Frontier: Human Colonies in Space* (New York: William Morrow, 1977), by the Princeton physicist Gerard K. O'Neill. Another useful work is T. A. Heppenheimer, *Colonies in Space* (Harrisburg, Penn.: Stackpole Books, 1977).

4. Robert Jastrow, *Journey to the Stars: Space Exploration—Tomorrow and Beyond* (New York: Bantam Books, 1989), 184.

5. See Ben R. Finney and Eric M. Jones, ed., *Interstellar Migration and Human Experience* (Berkeley and Los Angeles: University of California Press, 1985).

6. Arthur C. Clarke, *Profiles of the Future: An Inquiry into the Limits of the Possible* [1962] Revised ed. (New York: Holt, Rinehart and Winston, 1984), 95.

Suggested Reading

The following suggested titles furnish only a sample of the literature of futures research. They do not cover every topic studied by futurists, or explore any one topic in depth. In the third section, "Overviews of the Future," books are listed under the futurist paradigm that each title best illustrates.

But please note: it is the rare book (and the rare futures scholar) that adheres exclusively to one or another paradigm. Most futurists take their ideas from a variety of disparate sources. A scholar whose work is labelled counterculturalist, for example, may adopt a technoliberal stance on certain issues and a radical stance on certain others. The same is true of technoliberals and radicals. Thus, titles listed under one paradigm may also contain thinking strongly influenced by a second paradigm, or by all three.

In the fourth section, I have suggested a small number of outstanding novels set in plausible future worlds. These are among my personal favorites, but of course there are thousands of others.

1. JOURNALS

Alternatives: Social Transformation and Human Governance. Boulder, CO: Lynne Rienner Publishers, 1975—.

Future Survey: A Monthly Abstract of Books, Articles, and Reports Concerning Forecasts, Trends, and Ideas about the Future. Bethesda, MD: World Future Society, 1979—.

Futures: The Journal of Forecasting, Planning and Policy. Guildford, Surrey: Butterworth Scientific, 1968—.

Futures Research Quarterly. Bethesda, MD: World Future Society, 1985—.

Futuribles. Paris: Association Internationale Futuribles, 1975—.
The Futurist: A Journal of Forecasts, Trends, and Ideas about the Future. Bethesda,
    MD: World Future Society, 1967—.
Technological Forecasting and Social Change. New York: Elsevier, 1969—.

2. AIDS TO RESEARCH

Armstrong, J. Scott. *Long-Range Forecasting: From Crystal Ball to Computer*. 2nd
    ed. New York: John Wiley & Sons, 1985.
Bloomfield, Brian P. *Modelling the World: The Social Constructions of Systems
    Analysts*. New York: Basil Blackwell, 1986.
Bremer, Stuart A., ed. *The GLOBUS Model: Computer Simulation of Worldwide
    Political and Economic Developments*. Boulder, CO: Westview Press, 1987.
Cazes, Bernard. *Histoire des futurs. Les figures de l'avenir de saint Augustin au
    XXIe siècle*. Paris: Seghers, 1986.
Clarke, I. F. *The Pattern of Expectation, 1644–2001*. New York: Basic Books, 1979.
Coates, Joseph F., and Jennifer Jarratt. *What Futurists Believe*. Mt. Airy, MD:
    Lomond Publications; and Bethesda, MD: World Future Society, 1989.
Cornish, Edward, et al., *The Study of the Future*. Washington, DC: World Future
    Society, 1977.
Fowles, Jib, ed. *Handbook of Futures Research*. Westport, CT: Greenwood Press,
    1978.
Frankel, Boris, *The Post-Industrial Utopians*. Madison, WI: University of Wisconsin
    Press, 1987.
Helmer, Olaf. *Looking Forward: A Guide to Futures Research*. Beverly Hills, CA:
    Sage Publications, 1983.
Hughes, Barry B. *World Futures: A Critical Analysis of Alternatives*. Baltimore:
    Johns Hopkins University Press, 1985.
Jouvenel, Bertrand de. *The Art of Conjecture*. New York: Basic Books, 1967.
King, David Burnett. *The Crisis of Our Time: Reflections on the Course of Western
    Civilization, Past, Present, and Future*. Cranbury NJ: Associated University
    Presses, 1988.
Marien, Michael. *Societal Directions and Alternatives: A Critical Guide to the Lit-
    erature*. LaFayette, NY: Information for Policy Design, 1976.
Marien, Michael, and Lane Jennings, ed. *What I Have Learned: Thinking about the
    Future Then and Now*. Westport, CT: Greenwood Press, 1987.
Martino, Joseph P. *Technological Forecasting for Decision Making*. 2d ed. New
    York: Elsevier North-Holland, 1983.
Meadows, Donella, John Richardson, and Gerhart Bruckmann. *Groping in the Dark:
    The First Decade of Global Modelling*. New York: John Wiley & Sons, 1982.
Polak, Fred. *The Image of the Future*. New York: Oceana, 1961.
Sachs, Ignacy. *Development and Planning*. Cambridge: Cambridge University Press,
    1987.
Schwarz, Brita, Uno Svedin, and Björn Wittrock. *Methods in Futures Studies: Prob-
    lems and Applications*. Boulder, CO: Westview Press, 1982.
Shannon, Thomas Richard. *An Introduction to the World System Perspective*. Boul-
    der, CO: Westview Press, 1989.

3. OVERVIEWS OF THE FUTURE

a. Technoliberal

Barney, Gerald O., ed. *The Global 2000 Report to the President*. Washington, D.C.: U.S. Government Printing Office.

Bell, Daniel. *The Coming of Post-Industrial Society: A Venture in Social Forecasting*. New York: Basic Books, 1973.

Cetron, Marvin, and Thomas O'Toole. *Encounters with the Future: A Forecast of Life into the 21st Century*. New York: McGraw-Hill, 1982.

Clarke, Arthur C. *Profiles of the Future*. Rev. ed. New York: Holt, Rinehart & Winston, 1984.

Falk, Richard A. *A Study of Future Worlds*. New York: The Free Press, 1975.

Feather, Frank. *G-Forces: Reinventing the World: The 35 Global Forces Restructuring Our Future*. Toronto: Summerhill Press, 1989.

Kahn, Herman, William Brown, and Leon Martel. *The Next 200 Years: A Scenario for America and the World*. New York: William Morrow, 1976.

Kahn, Herman, and Anthony J. Wiener. *The Year 2000: A Framework for Speculation on the Next Thirty-Three Years*. New York: Macmillan, 1967.

Meadows, Donella H., Dennis L. Meadows, Jørgen Randers, and William W. Behrens III. *The Limits to Growth*. 2d ed. New York: Universe Books, 1974.

Mesarovic, Mihajlo, and Eduard Pestel. *Mankind at the Turning Point*. New York: E. P. Dutton, 1974.

Mueller, John. *Retreat from Doomsday: The Obsolescence of Major War*. New York: Basic Books, 1989.

Naisbitt, John, and Patricia Aburdene. *Megatrends 2000: Ten New Directions for the 1990's*. New York: William Morrow, 1990.

O'Neill, Gerard K. *2081: A Hopeful View of the Human Future*. New York: Simon & Schuster, 1981.

Simon, Julian L., and Herman Kahn, ed. *The Resourceful Earth: A Response to Global 2000*. New York: Basil Blackwell, 1984.

Simon, Julian L. *The Ultimate Resource*. Princeton, NJ: Princeton University Press, 1981.

World Commission on Environment and Development. *Our Common Future*. New York: Oxford University Press, 1987.

b. Radical

Amin, Samir, Giovanni Arrighi, André Gunder Frank, and Immanuel Wallerstein. *Dynamics of Global Crisis*. New York: Monthly Review Press, 1982.

Barnet, Richard J. *The Lean Years: Politics in the Age of Scarcity*. New York: Simon and Schuster, 1980.

Harrington, Michael. *The Next Left: The History of a Future*. New York: Henry Holt, 1987.

Harrington, Michael. *Socialism: Past and Future*. New York: Arcade Publishing, 1989.

Heilbroner, Robert L. *An Inquiry into the Human Prospect*. Rev. ed. New York:
    W. W. Norton, 1980.
Kosolapov, V. V. *Mankind and the Year 2000*. Moscow: Progress Publishers, 1976.
Roussopoulos, Dimitrios I. *The Coming of World War Three*. Montréal: Black Rose
    Books, 1986–1987.
Saifulin, Murad, ed. *The Future of Society: A Critique of Modern Bourgeois Phil-
    osophical and Socio-Political Conceptions*. Moscow: Progress Publishers,
    1973.
Wagar, W. Warren. *Building the City of Man: Outlines of a World Civilization*.
    New York: Richard Grossman, 1971.
Wallerstein, Immanuel. *The Capitalist World-Economy*. Cambridge: Cambridge
    University Press, 1979.
Williams, Raymond. *The Year 2000*. New York: Pantheon Books, 1983.

c. Counterculturalist

Capra, Fritjof. *The Turning Point: Science, Society, and the Rising Culture*. New
    York: Simon & Schuster, 1982.
Clark, Mary E. *Ariadne's Thread: The Search for New Modes of Thinking*. New
    York: St. Martin's Press, 1989.
Davis, W. Jackson. *The Seventh Year: Industrial Civilization in Transition*. New
    York: W. W. Norton, 1979.
Elgin, Duane. *Voluntary Simplicity: Toward a Way of Life That Is Outwardly Simple,
    Inwardly Rich*. New York: William Morrow, 1981.
Ferguson, Marilyn. *The Aquarian Conspiracy: Personal and Social Transformation
    in Our Time*. Rev. ed. Los Angeles: J. P. Tarcher, 1987.
Ferrarotti, Franco. *Five Scenarios for the Year 2000*. Westport, CT: Greenwood
    Press, 1986.
Harman, Willis W. *An Incomplete Guide to the Future*. New York: W. W. Norton,
    1979.
Henderson, Hazel. *The Politics of the Solar Age: Alternatives to Economics*. Rev.
    ed. Indianapolis, IN: Knowledge Systems, 1988.
Kothari, Rajni. *Footsteps into the Future: Diagnosis of the Present World and a
    Design for an Alternative*. New York: Free Press, 1974.
Lorie, Peter, and Sidd Murray-Clark. *History of the Future: A Chronology*. New
    York: Doubleday, 1989.
Myers, Norman, ed. *Gaia: An Atlas of Planet Management*. Garden City, NY: Dou-
    bleday, 1984.
Robertson, James. *Future Wealth: A New Economics for the 21st Century*. New
    York: Bootstrap Press, 1990.
Roszak, Theodore. *Where the Wasteland Ends: Politics and Transcendence in Post-
    industrial Society*. Garden City, NY: Doubleday, 1972.
Schumacher, E. F. *Small Is Beautiful: Economics As If People Mattered*. New York:
    Harper & Row, 1973.
Thompson, William Irwin. *At the Edge of History: Speculations on the Transfor-
    mation of Culture*. New York: Harper & Row, 1971.

Thompson, William Irwin. *Darkness and Scattered Light: Four Talks on the Future*. Garden City, NY: Doubleday, 1978.

Toffler, Alvin. *The Third Wave*. New York: William Morrow, 1980.

4. NOVELS OF THE FUTURE

Amis, Martin. *London Fields*. New York: Harmony Books, 1989.

Atwood, Margaret. *The Handmaid's Tale*. Boston: Houghton Mifflin, 1986.

Bear, Greg. *Blood Music*. New York: Arbor House, 1985.

Benford, Gregory. *Timescape*. New York: Simon and Schuster, 1980.

Bradbury, Ray. *Fahrenheit 451*. New York: Ballantine, 1953.

Brin, David. *Earth*. New York: Bantam Books, 1990.

Brin, David. *The Postman*. New York: Bantam Books, 1985.

Brunner, John. *The Sheep Look Up*. New York: Harper and Row, 1972.

Brunner, John. *The Shockwave Rider*. New York: Harper and Row, 1975.

Brunner, John. *Stand on Zanzibar*. Garden City, NY: Doubleday, 1968.

Burgess, Anthony. *A Clockwork Orange*. New York: Norton, 1963.

Callenbach, Ernest. *Ecotopia*. New York: Bantam Books, 1977.

Clarke, Arthur C. *Imperial Earth*. New York: Harcourt Brace Jovanovich, 1976.

Frank, Pat. *Alas, Babylon*. Philadelphia: Lippincott, 1959.

Gibson, William. *Neuromancer*. New York: Ace Books, 1984.

Harrison, Harry. *Make Room! Make Room!* Garden City, NY: Doubleday, 1966.

Huxley, Aldous. *Brave New World*. Garden City, NY: Doubleday, 1932.

Huxley, Aldous. *Island*. New York: Harper and Row, 1962.

Le Guin, Ursula. *Always Coming Home*. New York: Harper and Row, 1985.

Le Guin, Ursula. *The Dispossessed: An Ambiguous Utopia*. New York: Harper and Row, 1974.

Lem, Stanislaw. *The Futurological Congress*. New York: Seabury, 1974.

Merle, Robert. *Malevil*. New York: Simon and Schuster, 1974.

Miller, Walter M., Jr. *A Canticle for Leibowitz*. Philadelphia: Lippincott, 1960.

Morris, William. *News from Nowhere: An Epoch of Rest*. [1891] New York: Routledge, 1970.

Orwell, George. *Nineteen Eighty-Four*. New York: Harcourt Brace, 1949.

Roshwald, Mordecai. *Level 7*. New York: McGraw-Hill, 1959.

Sargent, Pamela. *The Shore of Women*. New York: Crown, 1986.

Shute, Nevil. *On the Beach*. New York: Morrow, 1957.

Stableford, Brian, and David Langford. *The Third Millennium: A History of the World, A.D. 2000–3000*. New York: Alfred A. Knopf, 1985.

Strieber, Whitley, and James Kunetka. *Warday*. New York: Holt, 1984.

Turner, George. *Drowning Towers*. New York: Arbor House, 1988.

Vonnegut, Kurt, Jr. *Player Piano*. New York: Scribner, 1952.

Wagar, W. Warren. *A Short History of the Future*. Chicago: University of Chicago Press, 1989.

Wells, H. G. *The Shape of Things to Come*. New York: Macmillan, 1933.

Zamiatin, Eugene. *We*. New York: Dutton, 1924.

Zebrowski, George. *Macrolife*. New York: Harper and Row, 1979.

Index

About the Author

W. WARREN WAGAR is Distinguished Teaching Professor of History at the State University of New York at Binghamton. He is the acclaimed author of *A Short History of the Future*; *Terminal Visions: The Literature of Last Things*; and *World Views: A Study in Comparative History*. Dr. Wagar edited *History and the Idea of Mankind* and his articles have appeared in *The World Future Society Bulletin*, *The Futurist*, and *Futures Research Quarterly*.